AF494829

Buffy and Angel Conquer the Internet

Buffy and Angel Conquer the Internet

Essays on Online Fandom

edited by
MARY KIRBY-DIAZ

McFarland & Company, Inc., Publishers
Jefferson, North Carolina, and London

Library of Congress Cataloguing-in-Publication Data

Buffy and Angel conquer the internet : essays on online
  fandom / edited by Mary Kirby-Diaz.
        p.   cm.
      Includes bibliographical references and index.

      ISBN 978-0-7864-4205-8
      softcover : 50# alkaline paper ∞

      1. Buffy, the vampire slayer (Television program)   2. Television
programs — Electronic discussion groups.   3. Television programs —
Social aspects — United States.   4. Television programs —
Psychological aspects — United States.   5. Fans (Persons) — United
States.   I. Kirby-Diaz, Mary, 1945–
PN1992.77.B84B72   2009
791.45'72 — dc22   2008050003

British Library cataloguing data are available

©2009 Mary Kirby-Diaz. All rights reserved

*No part of this book may be reproduced or transmitted in any form
or by any means, electronic or mechanical, including photocopying
or recording, or by any information storage and retrieval system,
without permission in writing from the publisher.*

Cover images ©2009 Shutterstock.

Manufactured in the United States of America

*McFarland & Company, Inc., Publishers
  Box 611, Jefferson, North Carolina 28640
  www.mcfarlandpub.com*

Acknowledgments

Just as it takes a village to raise a child, it takes the support of many people to help an editor put a book together. I must first acknowledge the support of my husband, Gil Diaz, and my daughter, Kelly Diaz, who prodded me about the joys of completing "the project."

Dr. Miriam K. Deitsch, my department chair, at Farmingdale State College, was highly supportive. She encouraged me, nudging me toward completion of this anthology.

Betsy Lusby is my gatekeeper extraordinaire! I could not have distributed three monumentally-sized surveys in less than 3 years without her help. She introduced the surveys to the moderators of fifteen fanboards (including her own, Angel: Carpe Noctem), and kept the surveys actively displayed at the A:CN website for several months after each distribution. With her help, the three surveys were completed in record time.

The late Nancy Dibble (a.k.a. Ansen Dibell), was a dear friend who served as mentor, muse, and a constant source of support. Her passing, on March 6, 2006, left a hole in the world of sci-fi and fan fiction. She was one of my first online friends, funny and sweet and supportive and always, always, true. Nan's pseudonym was Ansen Dibell, and she used it to write best-selling sci-fi novels, all the while teaching creative writing and English literature at the college level. Nan's book on how to write, *Plot*, sold over a million copies. Reading it helped me improve the organization of my lectures, as well as my writings.

Sierra Axelrod, E. Lynn Brobyn, Lori Del Rossi, Dana Evans DPM, Lee Hollins, and Christie McDonald were helpful to me at various stages of my research. They were crucial in introducing me to other online fans who helped my understanding of the fandom, and in sharing perspectives and experiences that helped my understanding of the online fandom. In particular, Lori Del Rossi, E. Lynn Brobyn, and I have spent many hours discussing the online fandoms, fanboards, and 'ships.

I must also acknowledge the many, many, online fans who completed at least one — if not all — of the three huge online surveys of the Buffy and Angel fandoms. My sincere thanks is especially due the folks at the Soulful Spike Society and Angel: Carpe Noctem. The folks at the Soulful Spike Society contributed to my first study on Internet fandom communities. Many of its members have been posting there daily for more than five years, finding it a true home away from home. The folks at Angel: Carpe Noctem not only contributed to, but encouraged me on the separate Internet surveys.

My thanks to David Kociemba, who suggested a working title for the book. Thanks also to Kathryn Hill, Asim Ali, and Viv Burr for input on the bibliography.

Table of Contents

PART 4—PARTICIPATORY COMMUNITIES AND THE PRODUCTION OF CULTURE

Introduction

HEY, PROFESSOR ... YOU
WATCH BUFFY, AND ANGEL?

Actually, I do. I watch Buffy and Angel — which makes me a Buffyite and an Angelite. All this, while also being a professor, a scholar, a woman, a spouse, a mother — and all the other roles in what is sociologically called my role set.

As a sociologist, I know that we each play many parts in life — and that sometimes those "parts" can be ... well ... a bit unusual. At this point in time, membership in one or more fandoms is not unusual in this society. Everyone who watches television on a regular basis is probably in a fandom, whether they realize it or not.

Watch *Law & Order* regularly? Maybe *Grey's Anatomy? Heroes? Lost? American Idol? 24?* Never miss an episode? Maybe even watch *ET* or *Access Hollywood*, or go online to learn the latest about those shows or the actors in them? See ... you're a fan!

Oh, I see: you don't watch TV. You only watch sports. Okay: football, baseball, soccer? Watch every game? Know all the players? Never miss an episode of your favorite sports post-game show? Yep! You're a fan, too!

Now, imagine if there were a place where you could talk about your favorite television shows, your favorite sports teams — all the time, 24/7. Of course there is: it's the Internet. And, if you're a "real fan" — an *intense* fan — the Internet is the place where you can talk about your fandom — *live* your fandom, 24/7. That's what intense fans of *Buffy the Vampire Slayer* and *Angel: The Series*, do: they talk online — 24/7 — about the fandom.

A *fandom* (or *fan culture*) may be defined as the culture that develops around a specific entertainment phenomenon — a television series, a movie, a sports team, a specific entertainer or actor or actress or band. Commitment to a fandom is commitment to a way of life. A fan is not so much a member of a club as a member of a way of life. A fan becomes immersed in the character — watches each episode, dissects each episode, deconstructs each character — especially the character that is the fan's favorite. A fan watches and waits for character development. A fan reads more about the character in fanfic and in character essays. A fan dreams about the character. A fan vicariously lives the character's experience. A "true" fan is highly engaged and committed to the series and characters he or she loves.

Buffyites and Angelites

The "Jossverse" started on television ten years ago with the premiere of *Buffy the Vampire Slayer*. *BtVS* (or just, *Buffy*) first aired on television in 1997. The series was based on a feature movie that only registered so-so at the box office. Later its writer and creator, Joss Whedon, reinvented the movie for weekly television and the rest, as they say, is history. Buffyites (Buffy fans) were born from the fans streaming onto the Internet to discuss the latest episodes. Three years later, in 2000, *Angel: The Series* (or *AtS*, or just *Angel*) spun-off from BtVS, and Angelites were created. Hence: Buffyites and Angelites — each members of separate and united Internet fandoms, all communicating and sharing their experiences online.

What makes these online fandoms especially interesting is their passion and commitment to the fandom. The series are over; no new episodes of television shows are being shot. Comic books and graphic novels about Buffy and Angel and their featured characters satisfied fans for two years as authorized fan fiction. Now, as "alternate new seasons," new comic books and graphic novels are being created to substitute for televised episodes. Fans will be able to continue to enjoy more episodes of *Buffy* and will soon be enjoying new episodes of *Angel*.

The Buffyverse fandom continues apace. Much like the various *Star Trek* fandom(s) of Gene Roddenberry, Joss Whedon's fandoms continue, despite the passage of time and the membership of fans in other, newer fandoms. The articles herein attest to a fandom that is still lively, still actively participating, still producing culture, still interested in two television series that no longer air in prime time.

All of the articles were written by Buffyverse fans who are also academicians. The goals of this book are to expand your knowledge and understanding of fan behavior — sometimes called *fanlove*, through our diverse research and writings on the *Buffyverse*. This is an inter-disciplinary collection of essays, and the writers' works reflect that diversity of disciplines: American studies, anthropology, English, library and information science, media and cultural studies, sociology, music, and visual and media arts. Much has been written about the difficulties presented in simultaneously being a scholar and a fan. Those difficulties multiply exponentially when the scholar is also studying other fans. Interestingly too, each article is generalizable beyond the borders of the Buffy and Angel fandoms. The research and writing of these scholars provides evidence that Internet fandoms can create communities of friends, lasting, profound friendships and new forms of art that reflect our changing society and our changing technologies of communication and art.

The Bronze Age: 1997–2001

Asim Ali has been studying a special community of Buffy fans — *The Bronzers* — for much of the last decade. The Bronze is the after-school/music club/hang-out frequented by the younger crowd living in Sunnydale, California, the town in which *Buffy the Vampire Slayer* is located. In the early days of the series, its official online fan board was called, the Bronze; those who posted there were called, *Bronzers*. The Bronze became the first major online Buffy-verse fandom community, and the only official BtVS fandom community.

Asim has been studying the Bronzers for nearly a decade. I believe it's fair to say that his is one of the longest-running ethnographies of a single Internet fandom community, and the Bronzers are the subject of his doctoral dissertation.

The two articles written by him provide a perspective on fandom that is "up close and personal." The first article offers an introduction to mythos of Buffy and Angel, and to the Bronzers. The second article concentrates on *The Mayberry Bronzers*, a group of Bronzers from the Washington, D.C. area, for whom the Bronze community eventually became a circle of friends. Ali's lengthy study of the Bronzers informs us that online friendships can endure, can be profound, and can evolve into offline friendships through mutual interests in a fandom (or otherwise).

Fandoms as Communities

Elizabeth L. Rambo's essay "I've Got a Little List, or 'You Guys Wanna Team Up and Take Over *SunnydaleU*'?" delineates the many interesting ways an online community can morph from one that communicates about books to one that communicates about a television show. Dr. Rambo's study elucidates that the love that readers — and viewers — have for a character in a book and a character on a television series can be profound. Elizabeth Rambo's research indicates that friendships and communities can evolve from the liking of novelists and the love of fictional characters. Because of that love of a fictional character — or a writer — people can overcome their fears of new technology, in order to communicate their ideas and emotions with others, eventually making friends in a world that uses high-tech communication technology.

My study of online Internet fan boards explores the possibility of the virtual community. I review classical sociological definitions of community and compare the concept to that of the virtual community. The essay includes an exploration of four fan boards, two of which are extant, The Soulful Spike Society and Hellmouth.central, and discusses the role the Internet plays in creating virtual communities of folks interested as much in a fandom as they are in making and keeping online friendships. The study reinforces the importance of shared experiences and willingness to communicate in a new type of community, and reminds us that a community doesn't require geographic boundaries to exist.

Sociological Perspectives on Fandoms

Rebecca Bley takes Erving Goffman's classic sociological theory and applies it to Buffy and Angel fans who communicate via LiveJournal blogs. Many Internet fans who are not inclined to use standard fan board platforms prefer the diary style communication offered by blogs. When we create online blogs, are we "ourselves," or are we someone else? How do we create a facsimile of ourselves — our best selves — online? Rebecca Bley's article uses mainstream sociological theory to answer those questions.

My second essay concentrates on categorizations of fans as story-oriented or series-oriented. Much has heretofore been written about the diffuse nature of online fandoms, but my research indicates that online fandoms may be more focused than previous research has indicated. This essay on story-oriented fans and series-oriented fans illustrates and explains how and why fans are often invested in a series, and why fans become invested in characters and series. The essay helps us to understand online fan behavior across fandoms, and how and why online fan behavior often manifests itself in the production of culture.

Participatory Communities and the Production of Culture

David Kociemba's article focuses on a minor character in *BtVS*— Andrew Wells — as *fan extraordinaire*. Andrew represents the pop culture fan in each of us, and David illustrates how Andrew responds as the stereotypical fan. Kociemba takes a fictional character who is the stereotypical online fan, and explores that character's fan love as addictive behavior, thus providing one hypothesis of "the invested fan."

Online fans often become creatively involved in the production of culture — the transformation of art — for their own self-expression. Once we admit to a fandom, how do we process and use our love of the series? Claudia Rebaza examines women's online fandom reading and writing habits, enhancing our knowledge of online fannish behaviors. She also examines why women — more so than men — write and read fan fiction.

Kathryn Hill's article on fanvidders explores a phenomenon classic to fandoms: the fanvid. For those who have just discovered the glee to be found on YouTube, vidding is an art that is no longer unique to fan cultures. Fanvids are short videos that tell a new story (or sometimes re-tell an old story), using popular songs and VCR/DVD clips from one's favorite television show/movie. Fanvids are controversial — and illegal — since they re-use copyrighted music and copyrighted digital images. They are also profoundly popular among Internet fans and YouTubers. Hill's exploration of fanvidders' culture illustrates how and why some fans produce art heavily influenced by their love of music, a fandom, and digital media.

Contributions and Conclusions

"Contributions" not only introduces you to each writer, but also tells you why they started to study the Jossverse fandom(s). That's important: to know what makes a phenomenon so important, that we would study that which we love. Studying a fandom or fan community always presents a dilemma to researchers. To be truly objective, we should not know anything about the fandom prior to our research. However, to be true to the community of fans we are studying, we do need to be knowledgeable about it. What has emerged in the last decade of fandom studies is an amalgamation of scholar/fan that has provided the various disciplines studying fandoms with a depth of knowledge and insight not otherwise possible.

The writers whose work appears in this book are, in my belief, the best researchers/ writers on the online *Buffyverse* fandom. The scholar-fans whose work is represented here continue to study Buffyites, and Angelites; there's no stopping us. The fandoms are still thriving — and we are still studying them. Remember the Eggman? They are we and we are they and we are all together.

Selected Bibliography

Kathryn Hill, Asim Ali, and I have put together a bibliography that is designed to serve a variety of reading interests. Vivian Burr, who is known for her research on the psychological perspective of the Buffy fandom, suggested that we cluster titles according to subject to better serve your interests, and we've done that.

So, for those of you who are enrolled in courses in popular culture, cultural studies, television studies, mass media, fandoms, collective behavior, media studies, and Internet studies, as well as fans: sit, read, deconstruct, and enjoy the articles in this reader. And, while you're at it, rent some DVD's, sit back, and enjoy what we believe to be some of the best television ever produced: *Buffy the Vampire Slayer*, and *Angel: The Series*.

I've Got a Little List, or, "You Guys Wanna Team Up and Take Over SunnydaleU?"

Elizabeth L. Rambo

In October, 2001, Simon Hedges and I started what may be one of the most obscure *Buffy* e-lists in existence, "SunnydaleU — *Buffy the Vampire Slayer* discussion for Dorothy Dunnett fans." *Buffy the Vampire Slayer* needs no introduction here, but Dorothy Dunnett, unfortunately, probably does. Dunnett, considered one of the best historical novelists of the twentieth century (Anne Malcolm's enthusiastic *New York Times* review is representative), wrote the six-volume Lymond Chronicles (adventures of 16th century Francis Crawford of Lymond), eight-volume House of Niccolò (tracing the rise of 15th century merchant Nicholas vander Poele de Fleury), *King Hereafter* (about Macbeth), and seven mysteries set in the 20th century starring the multi-talented Johnson Johnson, a secret agent wearing bifocals, who lives on a small sailing yacht (the *Dolly)* and paints portraits on the side (Marshall).

A native of Scotland, Dunnett, who died in November 2001, created cosmopolitan Scots heroes and heroines and worked them into the fabric of history with entrancing brio; her novels opened up the entire medieval and early-modern world as her characters traveled throughout Europe, the Middle East, and Africa. She was amazingly erudite (doing most of her own research), widely-traveled, a well-known portrait-painter, a trained singer, and an endlessly charming woman. Everyone who met her, adored her. Dunnett's heroes — Francis Crawford of Lymond, Nicholas de Fleury, Thorfinn Mac-Beth, and the enigmatic Johnson Johnson, as well as the women in their lives, whom I shall not name, for fear of spoiling those who have yet to discover these books — share the solitary agony of the exceptional ones — Buffy, Angel,

Spike, Faith — and her unsentimental plots include much of the same existential angst, surprising twists, tortured romance, and sudden death that distinguish *Buffy* and *Angel*.

Although the first volume of the Lymond Chronicles, *The Game of Kings*, was published in 1961, Dunnett readers have always felt themselves to be few and far between — another common thread with *Buffy* viewers. Many tell stories of pressing the novels on friends and relatives as "the best books I ever read!" only to have said loved ones give up after a few pages or chapters. Like Joss Whedon's television shows, Dorothy Dunnett's novels aim high and reward dedication generously. In 1984, a letterzine founded by Jean Clissold and Karen Brandl, *Marzipan and Kisses* (M&K),[1] brought English-speaking fans together from many different countries. In 2003, the U.S. version of M&K ceased publication, leaving only its sister UK 'zine, *Whispering Gallery*, and its online e-list, now on YahooGroups, *Marzipan*.

But how did all this lead to a *Buffy* list? Dunnett readers tend to be polymaths, if we flatter ourselves, or dilettantes, if we're more honest. We read widely and have many different interests, and many, many "off-topic" posts appear weekly[2] because we are interested in so many things, and because, unfortunately, there are only twenty-one Dunnett novels. Although Dunnett's skillful writing and the complexity of her plots mean that these novels reward re-reading immensely — many fans have read them five, six, or dozens of times — eventually, one does look for other texts. Thus, over the years, *Marzipan* spawned several additional e-lists, some related to Dunnett's work, and others — not so much. For example, in addition to lists devoted to chapter-by-chapter readings/discussions of individual Dunnett novels, there are lists for discussing works by other authors such as J.R.R. Tolkien, Lois McMaster Bujold, or J.K. Rowling (note the common science-fiction/fantasy theme); there are lists for exchanging recipes, or discussing music (a key component of Dunnett's novels), and lists for organizing the various gatherings of the faithful.[3]

In early October, 2001, just as *Marzipan* was putting together a collection of condolences for the widow of a New York Dunnett reader who had been killed in the September 11 terrorist attacks, this post appeared, entitled, "Totally and absolutely O[ff] T[opic]":

> *This question is totally and absolutely off-topic so I apologize up front.*
> *I know there are some members of the list who watch "Buffy the Vampire Slayer" and I have a question regarding the season [six] premier. Since Buffy died in the last episode of last season and was pretty much dead for the majority of the season premier, how come a new Slayer was not activated? I don't know what this says about me that this is an important question, but anyway.... Thanks for your patience* [nethy, "OT: Totally"].

The subject of *Buffy* may have arisen before, but this time, five different list-members responded to "nethy"'s question, some with great passion, like this post from Ann in Scotland, where season five was about one-third through on BBC—our first spoiler-protest, in other words:

> *Waaaeeough [that is a cry of anguish and horror] I have just started watching this artistic and intelligent series. And Buffy dies!!!!! Well maybe it was all a dream, and Buffy is not dead.*
>
> ...
>
> *Please do not apologise, not only important—crucial! What it says, is that you are a woman of taste and discernment. [one of the wittiest scripts that I have seen in a long time]* [McMillan].

The timing of the *Marzipan* group's "discovery" of *BtVS*, less than a month after the World Trade Center and Pentagon attacks, seems not insignificant. Other topics during this time had veered heavily toward "comfort" reading and sources of hope and encouragement. In an early post to *SunnydaleU*, Linda Barlow wrote, "*It's interesting—I've never cared about the show before, but ever since the terrorist attacks, I seem to be obsessed. I think it's the little blond girl kicking the asses of the evil bad guys that really feels good to me right now*" (*"Re: does anyone read...").* Other members responded with similar sentiments.

Each poster contributed a few more details about *Buffy* to the growing off-topic "thread," and when one noted, "*it was a D[orothy]D[unnett] fan I met at Edinburgh 2000*[4] *who made me take a better look at the weird teen fantasy tv series my daughter was watching*" ("Pen"), *it was clear that we had the beginnings of a spin-off or sub-group. Another Marzipan poster revealed that she had discovered Dunnett's novels "through Buffy when a writer for Buffy was interviewed and mentioned that her favorite literary character was Crawford of Lymond*" (Lane, "Re: OT: Buffy").[5] A few of those who responded had only begun watching within the past few months, and were just catching up — conveniently, FX had just begun daily *Buffy* reruns at this time, double episodes Monday–Friday, enabling "newbies" to get up to speed quickly, at least in most cable markets in North America. After two days—*Marzipan* has a 48-hour OT limit—Simon Hedges posted the following: "*Hi Beth, / Do you want to start up a list? I'd be happy to do the admin: the Buffylists out there are all a bit, er, juvenile!*" (Hedges, "Re: Re: OT: Totally").

If there were any justice, Simon Hedges would be co-author of this essay. Brilliant, kind, funny (in a Gilesian sort of way, but better with puns), and almost unflappable, author of many poetic parodies, Simon, who does something mysterious with computers in real life, is about 6' 4" tall and thus easy to spot in a crowd. He is most famous among online Dunnett fans for writing, producing, and directing a Gilbert & Sullivan musical pastiche version of Dorothy Dunnett's eight-volume House of Niccolò series, *The Nikado,* which was performed for Lady Dunnett at the Edinburgh and Philadelphia readers' gatherings in 2000 (Hedges, *Nikado*)[6] and for a very articulate defense of Austin Grey, the much-maligned Riley Finn of the Lymond Chronicles, which he presented at the 2003 Dunnett readers' gathering in New Orleans (Hedges, "Story"). So naturally, I could not refuse his offer. A little later that day (October 5, 2001), I had set up the group and issued an invitation to members of *Marzipan* and its sister lists (Rambo, "OT: Invitation"). It was my first foray into e-list administration; I would not have done it without Simon's offer to do the "administrivia."

I also had a personal agenda. I had discovered "Buffy Studies" earlier in 2001 at my first Popular Culture Association conference (where I had presented a paper on Dorothy Dunnett), and I was eager to pursue it further. I knew that Dunnett readers were some of the sharpest minds in cyberspace, so I was really looking forward to hearing what they had to say about *Buffy* and *Angel*.

Almost immediately, we restricted membership of our unlisted YahooGroup to those who were already Dunnett readers, primarily because online *BtVS* fandom is huge (or was — googling "Buffy" in 2001 netted millions of results) and we had a unique perspective, especially at first. I also hoped that by keeping *SunnydaleU* relatively small, we could have more in-depth discussion and less yadda-yadda. No one has ever categorized Dorothy Dunnett's novels as "chick lit" or "beach reading,"[7] and I knew that these were intelligent people, mostly women (out of 99 current members, five are male), mostly over 30, from the U.S. and Canada, Argentina, the United Kingdom, Ireland, Europe, Asia, Australia and New Zealand — very much representative of a cross section of the Marzipan list (Hedges, "RE: Re: Polls"). Membership has hovered around 100, about 1/10 of the membership of the main *Marzipan* list. Many were new to *Buffy* and *Angel*, and as those who have participated in *Buffy* or *Angel* e-lists or boards might imagine, *SunnydaleU*'s first posts were mainly concerned with getting to know one another, our favorite and least favorite episodes, characters, and so forth.

Unique to *SunnydaleU*, however, was the inevitable question of parallels between Dorothy Dunnett's characters and themes, which first appeared in the eleventh posting of the new list: *"Does anybody else see a resemblance between Spike and Lymond — blond, broody, gruffly discourteous, and protective of young females in a very rough way?"* (Monash, "Call me"). Later, others would argue that Dunnett's Francis Crawford of Lymond was more like Buffy, especially in Season Six and Seven — the tormented leader against his/her will of a band of followers with little comprehension of the struggles their chief must endure (Wright, "Re: Gloominess"). His Spike-likeness is mostly limited to blondness, maleness — oh, and sexiness. In the early weeks of the list, there was considerable diversity of opinion about favorite characters and 'ships (but we didn't call them 'ships — we knew nothing of *Buffyverse* fandom jargon yet). An early post serves as a good example of the kind of variety of perspective the list was getting from viewers who were not yet involved in online *Buffy* fandom in general: *"I really do like Spikey Boy though. He's a hottie. His unrequited love for Buffy makes for some great moments in the series. I can't see them as a couple though. Buffy makes very bad girl friend material. She seems to attract men like Angel and Riley who need more from her than she can give"* (Marydot, "Re: Spike & Drusilla"). However, even before the new list officially began, the topic that we would come to know as "Spuffy" appeared, as the originating *Marzipan* poster commented, *"I kinda hope Spike and Buffy get together. He just 'slays' me, so to speak"* (nethy, "RE: Re: OT: Buffy").

Although I had been watching *Buffy* since the very first episode — in fact, I tuned in because I thought the movie was funny — so sue me! — *SunnydaleU* introduced me, and most of the other members, to many more nuances of the series, and to intricacies of online *Buffy* and *Angel* fandom that I am sure I would never have pursued on my own. In the early weeks and months of *SunnydaleU*, only a few of the of those who joined the list had been watching since season one[8], and even some of the North American members did not have access to cable or FX reruns, so we spent considerable time explaining things to each other. Compelled by the need to discuss each week's episode with the list, but cursed with a Tuesday night teaching schedule, I finally learned to program my VCR — just in time for the musical episode *Once More, with Feeling* (Season 6, Episode 7). Other members acquired VCRs and/or DVD players for the first time, bought new computers, and explored mysteries of the online world that some had never conceived of before. Once we were joined by a Dunnett reader who described herself as also *"lurk[ing] madly on several Buffy lists"* and who introduced *SunnydaleU* not only to Psyche's (now defunct) script and transcript site, but also to the Spike "redemptionistas" of the *Bloody Awful Poet Society (BAPS)*, the floodgates were open (mack29, "REALLY late"). For example, Linda Barlow, a romance novelist, who had not had access to FX reruns, started reading scripts, joined several other *Buffy* lists, and soon became an "executive fan" (MacDonald; Williams pars. 1–6) in her own right, discovering spoiler sources and dispensing spoilers and spoiler speculation on *SunnydaleU* and other lists, particularly the *Stakehouse*. Mara Schiffren joined *SunnydaleU* because she found herself *"thoroughly addicted to Buffy. But ... way too embarrassed to admit it to anyone but the list"* (Schiffren, "Re: Welcome Mara"); evidently she got over it, because in 2004, Mara presented a paper on Angel at the first *Slayage* conference, although it's also interesting to note that her early impression was *"I just don't find Angel anywhere near as compelling as Buffy as a show. The two of them had great chemistry together, but I don't think the chemistry is as good between Angel and anyone else on his show"* (Schiffren, "Re: Angel 3 Spoiler"). It was also Mara who first suggested James Marsters as a candidate for the blond Francis Crawford's role in the "casting game" for an imaginary film based on the Lymond Chronicles (Schiffren, "Buffy/DD").[9]

Soon after *Tabula Rasa* (Season 6, Episode 8) aired, we determined that *SunnydaleU* had enough members named "Nancy"—six—to form our own "Nancy tribe." As I combed through the archives, I realized that I probably should credit one of these, Nancy Wyman, with first mentioning the spiral motif of Season Six, in November 2001, not long after the original broadcast of "Smashed" (Season 6, Episode 9*): "A lot of folks seem to think B[uffy] is going to redeem S[pike]. I think it's more a case of the opposite. In fact, I think the whole theme this year is that the entire cast is going into a downward spiral. That will leave next year for everyone's redemption"* ("Re: Spoiler B6").[10] Nancies have consistently been among the most active posters, particularly "Nancy T.," who not only has such definite opinions that she has her own "Nancy-verse" interpretations for *Buffy* and *Angel*—although she does not write fanfic—but also became the list's most efficient gleaner of news items and spoilers. Nancy Wright, who lives in southern California, had connections that enabled her to attend the Academy of Television Arts and Sciences' *"Buffy* Behind the Scenes" panel in June, 2002[11], along with two other members of the list, and to visit the *Buffy* set for the taping of Season Seven episodes *Beneath You* and *Conversations with Dead People*, which is how we learned that James Marsters had already received at least one copy of Dorothy Dunnett's novel about Macbeth, *King Hereafter*, from a fan (mack29, "Re: My second day") but apparently had not read it (Wright, "My second day").

As new members joined in the first two months of *SunnydaleU* and we informally polled each other about favorite characters, almost every character was named at least once. By December, 2001, as one member noted, *"Spike & J[ames] M[arsters had] been elevated from mere crumpet material to minor deity status"* (beerforsammy, "Spike"), *following the airing of "Smashed"* (Season 6, Episode 9) and *Wrecked* (Season 6, Episode 10), James Marsters's guest appearance on *Andromeda*, and the significant number of list-members who had also joined the *BAPS* list, and later its spinoff, *Tabula Rasa*. The number of posts devoted to lauding the virtues of Spike and/or James Marsters expanded remarkably. In the summer of 2002, *SunnydaleU* discovered fanfiction, including slash fan-fic, and some members were wild for it. Those who didn't care were not posting, or "lurking." Simon and I, not particularly interested and feeling the need to save space on our YahooGroups site (no longer an issue), banned the regular posting of fan-fic, though not discussion of same. Eventually, list-members who wanted to discuss characters other than Spike, or who had differences of opinion regarding Spike's place in the Buffyverse, fell largely silent — at least on those topics — though some continued to post on other issues, such as technology, related books or movies, etc.

In my experience — supported by studies of similar "virtual communities" (Turkle; Bell & Kennedy; Wexelblat) — most such lists will inevitably develop a high percentage of "lurkers" — members who rarely or never participate, for various reasons. *SunnydaleU* now has approximately sixty percent of its members set at "no-mail" or "digest" options, indicating pretty clearly that they don't intend to participate regularly. In 2002, a few (three) *SunnydaleU* members offered representative reasons: *"more than a season behind in our viewing"* in the UK ("milligirl"); busy with other things in off-line life (Albert); or *"some of us are intimidated"* by posters perceived as more articulate ("capreacula").[12] *SunnydaleU* continued to be a fairly active list — only dropping below 400 postings during months when no new *Buffy* or *Angel* episodes are broadcast (summer 2003; December 2003, January 2004) — but from May 17–May 23, 2004, eight members produced almost all of the 184 messages posted to the list, with one or two appearances by nine other list-members, most of whom had not been heard from for weeks or months — a pretty typical week in the that year. Without definite feedback, it is impossible to determine, but some of the silent list-members may have felt a bit like Willow in *Prophecy Girl*: "it wasn't our world anymore. They made it theirs. And they had fun" (Season 1, Episode 12). Or, they may simply be busy with other things (Albert), enjoying "lurking" and agreeing or disagreeing silently with the posts that appear.

In summer 2004, Whedon fans in North America faced a fall television season without a Whedon series, *Angel* having been cancelled unceremoniously in the second half of its fifth season. The *SunnydaleU* administrators polled the members: "'Where should *SunnydaleU* go from here?'" (*"BtVS* and *AtS"*). Posts had dropped over the summer to under 200 per month, and only twenty-four members responded. Ten respondents chose the option "Major in fiction/fantasy/speculative TV/Fiction/Movies." None wanted to "stop the list." Posting did not increase significantly. We polled the members again in March 2005: "What should the remit of this list be?" Although fewer members responded, the overwhelming majority (eighteen of twenty-one) chose "Extend its remit to all audio-visual entertainment (Movies, TV, Comics, Radio) except music." Postings went over 600 in April and May 2005, as people discussed *Lost, Dr. Who, Farscape, Serenity,* and the new *Battlestar Galactica* series. *House, Veronica Mars,* and *The Closer* have also become frequent topics, along with Harry Potter movies and *Pirates of the Caribbean.* Nevertheless, postings fell under 100 per month from January to August,

2006, although new science-fiction/fantasy television series such as *Heroes*, *Blood Ties*, and the *Dresden Files* seem to have revived the list somewhat, along with historical series such as *Rome* and *The Tudors*: posts from September 2006–July 2007 averaged 166 per month, and went over 200 for May–July. A few members have left the list; a few have joined because they have just discovered *Buffy* or *Firefly*. Anything James Marsters does is likely to be noted, but his recent appearance in an episode of *Saving Grace* elicited the comment, "*I've about decided I don't give a fig newton about JM, but I sure do miss Spike*" (Wyman, "JM guest-appearance") and several replies indicating general agreement.

I admit that one reason I agreed to co-moderate a *Buffy* e-list for Dorothy Dunnett readers was that I wanted to discuss the show with people who loved it as much as I did. As time went on, many of those who joined *SunnydaleU* seemed actually to come to dislike *Buffy*—both the show and the character—or to want it to be something that it was not and, for various reasons it seemed to me, would never be. At times, Simon and I—like all list-moderators—have felt somewhat beleaguered; and we know some list-members have been fairly annoyed with us, too. Many of the most active members have found other lists or boards where they feel as or more comfortable posting about *Buffy* and *Angel* (and *Firefly/Serenity*) as they do at *SunnydaleU*—and yet they still make regular appearances on our list and as far as I know, there's nowhere else online where one can be sure people will understand if one posts, "To all intents and purposes..., Xander is Jerott" (nantague).[13] At the same time, without *SunnydaleU* and the provocative discussions there, I might never have gone as deeply into "*Buffy* Studies" as I have done, and I believe the list has encouraged others as well, at least two of whom have published or presented their "Whedon studies" work, which is not to say they would not have done that in any case, of course![14] *SunnydaleU* began as a unique segment of the *Buffy/Angel* fan community, and now represents a microcosm of that community, though it remains a small, obscure list and has expanded into general discussion of television and film. Moderating it has been an educational experience in many ways, and despite the implications of my somewhat facetious title, the list has been a great source of friendship, ideas, and support, and I would not want to do without it.

Notes

1. The title comes from a passage in *Queens' Play*, the second volume in Dunnett's Lymond Chronicles, referring to the court of French king Henri II: "When he was King, he kept a court still of marzipan and kisses, but a tough, esoteric, gamey core also persisted: the patronage of scholars and master craftsmen; the habit of good talk and private accomplishments, with the poet and the professor familiarly at the elbow" (35).

2. Random selection of off-topic post subject lines from September 2001: "Ferrets & weasels," "Greek & Roman films," recommendations for other books, "Tastee Freeze," etc.

3. To the best of my knowledge, Dorothy Dunnett is the only historical novelist to have had three fan conventions or "Gatherings" organized in her honor — two in Edinburgh (1999 and 2000), one in Philadelphia (2000) — which led to the formation of the Dorothy Dunnett Readers' Association (DDRA). Based in the U.K., the DDRA "aims to promote interest in [Dunnett's] novels and the historical background in which they take place ... [and] encourages ... meetings at which members ... discuss Dorothy Dunnett's work and, often, listen to expert speakers on topics if historical interest." Since its founding in 2001, the DDRA has held an annual meeting in Edinburgh as part of a weekend of Dunnett-related events. Since the large conventions in 2000, many smaller get-togethers of fans from Marzipan and at least two other Dunnett e-lists with overlapping memberships have occurred, in places as diverse as Rye and Oxford, England; Munich, Germany; Sydney, Australia; Dublin, Ireland; Toronto, Canada; and various states in the U.S. The most recent international gatherings were held on the island of Malta (the setting of one of the novels), in 2005 and at Saddell Castle, Scotland, in 2007.

4. "Edinburgh 2000" — the second international Dunnett Readers' Gathering (see note #3).

5. We have not been able to discover which writer this was. We suspect either Jane Espenson, an English major with an M.A. in linguistics, or Marti Noxon, famously known as the "pain and chains girl," but have not been able to track down confirming documentation.

6. Several *SunnydaleU* members took part in Edinburgh and/or Philadelphia productions of *The Nikado*. My sister was one of the "three little maids of Naxos," and I was a member of the "Scottish jury" chorus in the Philadelphia production — we have the t-shirts (Hedges, *Nikado*).

7. This is not the place to discuss the validity of such labels. The vast majority of Dunnett e-list members are women; and most of us have found Dunnett novels suitable reading for just about any place and time.

8. If I recall correctly, among the first *SunnydaleU* members who had either seen every episode or been fans from the beginning of the show (besides me), were Simon Hedges, Connie England, and Nancy Wyman.

9. The "casting game" is a frequent pastime on Dunnett e-lists, though most agree that making a film based on even one of the complex, densely plotted novels would be — to put it mildly — insane. To even come close to doing justice to Austen's *Pride and Prejudice*, A&E needed a 12-hour mini-series. Each of Dunnett's historical novels is nearly 500 pages long, with a cast of hundreds (not to mention thousands of extras, though CGI would help, in the battles and crowd scenes), and settings that may range — in *Scales of Gold*, for example — from various places in northern Europe to coastal and inland central Africa to desert Timbuktu to the Mediterranean. The mind reels.

10. The "spiral" idea lay dormant, however, until 6.18 "Entropy," which ultimately inspired my essay "Yeats's Entropic Gyre and Season Six," presented at the Blood, Text and Fears: Reading Around *Buffy the Vampire Slayer* conference and now forthcoming in an anthology of essays on seasons six and seven of *Buffy*.

11. Available as a "special feature" in the BtVS Season Six DVD set. Nancy and the other *SunnydaleU* members do not appear.

12. Requests for comments from the membership as I was revising this paper elicited exactly nothing, so I am on my own as far as more recent excuses for lurkerdom.

13. Jerott Blyth, introduced in *The Disorderly Knights*, third in the Lymond Chronicles, becomes one of Lymond's close friends and admirers, an officer in his mercenary troop, and a key character. Whether he really *is* like Xander, however, remains an open question.

14. Dawn Heinecken, author of *The Warrior Women of Television: A Feminist Cultural Analysis of the New Female Body in Popular Media*, and Mara Schiffren, who analyzed the visual and narrative structures of *Angel* in "On Escherian Dualism and the Metaphysics of the Middle Way: Interpreting the Spatial Architecture of *Angel the Series*." presented at the first *Slayage* Conference on Buffy the Vampire Slayer in 2004.

Works Cited

Albert, Sharron. "Re: question about lurkers." Online posting. 19 Nov. 2002 <http://tv.groups.yahoo.com/group/sunnydaleu/message/9972>.

Barlow, Linda. "Re: Does anyone read..." Online posting. 19 Oct. 2001. *Marzipan.* 20 May 2004. <http://groups.yahoo.com/group/marzipan/message/48>.

beerforsammy. "Spike." Online posting. 4 Dec. 2001. *SunnydaleU.* 20 May 2004. <http://tv.groups.yahoo.com/group/sunnydaleu/message/762>.

Bell, David, and Barbara M. Kennedy, eds. *The Cybercultures Reader.* New York: Routledge, 2000.

Bloody Awful Poet Society. 20 May 2004. 23 May 2004. *http://www.bloodyawfulpoet.com/*

Bristow, Mary. "OT: Totally and Absolutely OT." Online posting. 4 Oct. 2001. *Marzipan.* 20 May 2004. <http://groups.yahoo.com/group/marzipan/message/49478>.

capreacula. "question about lurkers." Online posting. 18 Oct. 2002. *SunnydaleU* <http://tv.groups/yahoo.com/group/sunnydaleu/message/8805>.

Dorothy Dunnett Readers' Association. 2 Aug. 2007. <http://www.ddra.org/>.

Dunnett, Dorothy. The House of Niccolo.

______. *King Hereafter.* New York: Vingage/Random House, 1998.

______. The Lymond Chronicles.

______. *Queens' Play.* 1964. New York: Vintage/Random House, 1992, 1997.

______. *Scales of Gold.* 1991. New York. Vintage/Random House, 1999.

Hedges, Simon. *Dorothy Dunnett.* 17 June 2007. 2 Aug. 2007 <http://www.simonhedges.com/>.

______. *The Nikado.* 4 Aug. 2001. 2 Aug. 2007. <http://www.simonhedges.com/>.

______. "Re: Re: OT: Totally and Absolutely OT — Buffy." Online posting. 5 Oct. 2001. *Marzipan.* 20 May 2004. <http://groups.yahoo.com/group/marzipan/message/49503>.

______. "RE: Re: Polls." Online posting. 15 June 2002. *Marzipan.* 20 May 2004. <http//: groups.yahoo.com/group/marzipan/message/53971>.

______. "The Story of Austin Grey." *Y'allSpit* (Austin Grey Slides). 3 May 2003; updated 1 Jan. 2004. 20 May 2004. <http://www.simonhedges.com>.

Joss' Stakehouse at yahoogroups. 20 May 2004. <http://tv.groups.yahoo.com/group/the_stakehouse/>.

Lane, Claudia. "Re: OT: Buffy." Online posting. 4 Oct. 2001. *Marzipan.* 20 May 2004. <http://groups.yahoo.com/group/marzipan/message/49482>.

Macdonald, Andrea. "Uncertain Utopia: Science Fiction Media Fandom and Computer Mediated Communication." *Theorizing Fandom: Fans, Subculture and Identity.* C. Harris and A. Alexander, eds. New Jersey: Hampton Press Inc., 1998. 139 ff.

mack29. "REALLY late to the party...*g*" Online posting. 27 Oct. 2001. *SunnydaleU.* 20 May 2004. <http://tv.groups.yahoo.com/group/sunnydaleu/message/113>.

______. "Re: My Second Day on the Set — Long-moderate spoilers, one major spoiler." Online posting. 9 Aug. 2002. *SunnydaleU.* 20 May 2004. <http://tv.groups.yahoo.com/group/sunnydaleu/message/7331>.

Malcolm, Anne. "Dorothy Dunnett's Excellent Adventures." New York Times on the Web. 24 Dec. 2000. 2 Aug. 2007. <http://www.nytimes.com/books/00/12/24/reviews/001224.24malcolt.html>.

Marshall, Bill. "Bibliography: Introduction." *Dorothy Dunnett.* 20 May 2004. <http://www.dorothydunnett.co.uk/dubibliointro.htm>.

Marydot. "Re: Spike & Drusilla." Online posting. 10 Oct. 2001. *SunnydaleU.* 20 May 2004. <http://groups.yahoo.com/group/sunnydaleu/message/24>.

Marzipan. 20 May 2004. <http://groups.yahoo.com/group/marzipan/>.

McMillan, Ann. "Re: OT: Totally and Absolutely OT." Online posting. 3 Oct. 2001. *Marzipan.* 20 May 2004. <http://groups.yahoo.com/group/marzipan/message/49440>.

Meyer, Heike. "Re: Re: OT: Buffy." Online posting. 5 Oct. 2001. *Marzipan.* 20 May 2004. <http://groups.yahoo.com/group/marzipan/message/49524>.

milligirl. "Re: question about lurkers." Online posting. 19 Oct. 2002. *SunnydaleU.* 20 May 2004. <http://tv.groups.yahoo.com/group/SunnydaleU/message/8836>.

Monash, Curt. "Re: Hi All." Online posting. 8 Oct. 2001. *SunnydaleU.* 20 May 2004. <http://tv. groups.yahoo.com/group/SunnydaleU/message/11>.

nantague. "Re: But he's still hooked." Online posting. 25 Mar. 2002. *SunnydaleU.* 2 Aug 2007. <http://tv.groups.yahoo.com/group/sunnydaleu/message/4264>.

nethy. "OT: Totally and Absolutely OT." Online posting. 3 Oct. 2001. *Marzipan.* 20 May 2004. <http://groups.yahoo.com/group/marzipan/message/49436>.

_____. "RE: Re: OT: Buffy." Online posting. 5 Oct. 2001 *Marzipan.* 20 May 2004. <http:// groups.yahoo.com/group/marzipan/message/49523>.

Pen. "Re: OT: Totally and Absolutely OT." Online posting. 4 Oct. 2001 *Marzipan.* 20 May 2004. <http://groups.yahoo.com/group/marzipan/message/49454>.

"Prophecy Girl." 1012. Joss Whedon. Dir. Joss Whedon. *Buffy the Vampire Slayer.* WB. 2 June 1997.

Rambo, Elizabeth. "OT: Invitation to *SunnydaleU.*" Online posting. 5 Oct. 2001 *Marzipan.* 20 May 2004. <http://groups.yahoo.com/group/marzipan/message/49529>.

_____. "Re: Latecomer." Online posting. 12 Oct. 2001 *SunnydaleU.* 20 May 2004. <http:// tv.groups.yahoo.com/group/sunnydaleu/message/29>.

_____. "Yeats's Entropic Gyre and Season Six." Forthcoming in Edwards, et. al. *At Sixes and Sevens:* Buffy the Vampire Slayer *in the UPN Years.*

Schiffren, Mara [alcibiades]. "Buffy/DD." Online posting. 20 Nov. 2001 *Marzipan.* 20 May 2004. <http://groups.yahoo.com/group/marzipan/message/387>.

_____. "On Escherian Dualism and the Metaphysics of the Middle Way: Interpreting the Spatial Architecture of *Angel the Series.*" The Slayage Conference on Buffy the Vampire Slayer. Middle Tennessee State U. Nashville, TN. 27–30 May 2004. Available online as: "Spiraling and Spinning: The Escherian Idiom of AtS." <http://www.teaattheford.net/conversation. php?id=975#16551>.

_____. "Re: Angel 3 Spoiler." Online posting. 19 Nov. 2001 *SunnydaleU.* 20 May 2004. <http://tv.groups.yahoo.com/group/sunnydaleu/message/358>.

_____. "Re: Welcome Mara." Online posting. 7 Nov. 2001 *SunnydaleU.* 20 May 2004. <http://tv.groups.yahoo.com/group/sunnydaleu/message/225>.

"Smashed." 6009. Drew Z. Greenberg. Dir. Turi Meyer. *Buffy the Vampire Slayer.* UPN. 20 Nov. 2001.

Tabula Rasa. 2 Aug. 2007. <http://www.btvs-tabularasa.net/>.

Turkle, Sherry. *Life on the Screen: Identity in the Age of the Internet.* New York: Simon & Schuster, 1997.

Wexelblat, Alan. "An Auteur in the Age of the Internet: JMS, *Babylon 5,* and the Net." *Hop on Pop: The Politics and Pleasures of Popular Culture.* Ed. Henry Jenkins, Tara McPherson, and Jane Shattuc. Durham, NC: Duke U P, 2002.

Williams, Rebecca. "'It's About Power!' Executive Fans, Spoiler Whores, and Capital in the *Buffy the Vampire Slayer* Online Fan Community." *Slayage: The Online International Journal of* Buffy *Studies* 11–12 (April 2004). 20 May 2004. <www.slayage.tv>.

"Wrecked." 6010. Marti Noxon. Dir. David Solomon. *Buffy the Vampire Slayer.* 27 Nov. 2001.

Wright, Nancy G. "My second day on the set — long — moderate spoilers." Online posting. 9 Aug. 2002 *SunnydaleU.* 2 Aug. 2007. <http://tv.groups.yahoo.com/group/sunnydaleu/message/ 7323>.

_____. "Re: Gloominess." Online posting. 20 Mar. 2003 *SunnydaleU.* 2 Aug. 2007. <http:// tv.groups.yahoo.com.group. sunnydaleu/message/12765>.

Wyman, Nancy. "Re: JM guest-appearance on 'Saving Grace.'" Online posting. 31 July 2007 *SunnydaleU.* 2 Aug. 2007.

<http://tv.groups.yahoo.com/group/sunnydaleu/message/26559>.

_____. "Re: Spoiler B6 (was Re: Why we watch)." Online posting. 23 Nov. 2001 *SunnydaleU.* 20 May 2004. <http://tv.groups.yahoo.com/group/sunnydaleu/message/416>.

Buffy, Angel, and the Creation of Virtual Communities

Mary Kirby-Diaz

"The Internet, you know.... The bitch goddess that I love and worship and hate. You know, we found out we have a fan base on the Internet. They came together as a family on the Internet, a huge, goddamn deal. It's so important to everything the show has been and everything the show has done — I can't say enough about it" [p. 10].

Introduction

This study was completed in 2004, and was the first in a series of short sociological studies that explored and described diverse areas of the Buffy-verse Internet fandom. Although it has been substantially revised, the report's hypotheses, findings, and conclusions remain the same. The general goal of the study was to expand our learning, our understanding, and our explanations for Internet fan behavior.

The specific goal of *this* research project was to explore some of the virtual communities produced by the Buffyverse fandom in order to ascertain if any were, in fact, "true" communities. In other words, this study placed special focus on the *virtual community* (a.k.a. *virtcom*). Although Internet communities are *virtual,* it is the hypothesis of this paper that the virtcom can become a *real* community, by means of which Buffyites and Angelites can regularly interact.

The Internet helps to feed the multi-million dollar business enterprise that is *Buffy the Vampire Slayer* and *Angel: The Series.* Internet fans communicate with each other through virtual communities — called "virtcoms" — that are real-time chat rooms. Although they are technically "virtcoms," the members usually refer to them as fan boards or fan forums. Virtcoms maintain loyalty to the show, the characters, the creators of the show, and the actors. In some cases, virtcoms extend beyond the boundaries of fandom into the creation of an actual community without borders, creating a "real" virtual community. Registered members converse with other registered members to discuss issues that are important to them.

Reality and Television

Sociologists study "the things" which are produced by — and in turn produce — social life. Sociologists view "these things" with the assumption that people create, identify, use, and repeatedly use "those things" until they have created a pattern that creates our reality. Reality, then, is socially constructed, made up of "the things" we do repeatedly enough to create that pattern we call "reality." (Hence, those phenomena we encounter rarely are often referred to as "unreal," "surreal" — i.e., not "real" enough.)

When we become engaged in a specific behavior for a long period of time, we *invest* in the behavior — we become involved with it, and it become important to us (Ryan and Wentworth, 16–17). Eventually it becomes a part of our every day life — our reality.

The social phenomena that make up the reality of everyday life in the United States includes the popular culture medium of television. Television creates a significant impact on our society and our concept of reality. The current data on television viewing indicates that the average American television viewer watches four-to-six hours of television every day, almost 1,500 hours every year, twenty-five percent of her/his waking time, watching television. This is a significant amount of time.

Indeed, one might expect more sociological research on the impact made by an activity upon which we spend twenty-five percent of our waking time. Any activity that takes up one-quarter of our active life would seem to be important to study. However, academia — and society in general — has generally regarded the role of television as relatively insignificant.

Surprising too, how few studies have been done on the people who actively consume popular culture and mass media — the fans. Most studies on fandoms have heretofore been conducted by scholars in media studies, communications, and journalism. It is surprising how few *sociological* studies have been done on the subjects of popular culture and mass media, especially on television's impact in our lives.

For viewers who are intensely interested in a particular kind of television program (sports or horror or fantasy shows) that four-to-six hours a day can serve as a mechanism for transporting the viewer to a reality where the television programs watched — their characters, actors, writers, directors, story arcs, etc., assume a priority in their lives.

In fact, the act of watching the show becomes an important focus on their real lives. Lives come to revolve around watching the show, talking about the show with others who watch, discussing the scripts and dialogues, learning the names of actors, writers, and directors of the show. It becomes important to not miss an episode of that show. Fans want to see the show "fresh," not taped (although many will tape the show for later re-watching) because the subject of the show — and the loyalty to the show — are strong in their lives.

It's literally possible to spend more than four hours a day living in the television show's "universe," i.e., a world created by producers and writers, buttressed by make-up artists and special effects artists, actors, musicians, etc. Genre fans' lives, therefore, become what they visualize — peopled by characters reminiscent of those in the TV-verse, with pop cultural references, a vocabulary and language gleaned from episodic dialogue. Thus, can a fan move their *weltanschauung* from the world familiar to non-genre universe viewers to the world of what exists on television. Talking with other 'verse fans is *of the good, insane troll logic* need not apply ("Of the good," and "insane troll logic" are Buffyisms).

For example, Internet fans of *Buffy the Vampire Slayer* and *Angel: The Series,* can quote dialogue from entire episodes. They weave "Buffyisms" and "Angelisms" into their everyday language. Buffyites and Angelites often compare real life situations to those in the episodes, and compare people they know in real life with characters on the shows.

Buffy the Vampire Slayer + *Angel the Series* = *The Buffyverse (or the Jossverse)*

One of the most prominent "universes" in popular television is that of "the Buffyverse," a universe created by Joss Whedon, writer and creator of three remarkable television series: *Buffy the Vampire Slayer, Angel: The Series,* and *Firefly.* The former series,' *BtVS* and *AtS,* have received cult status since their premieres on March 10, 1997, and October 5, 1999, respectively. Their fans watched each program, digested dialogue, and then popped onto the 'Net immediately after each episode to discuss, digest, and deconstruct each episode. Even now, with *BtVS*'s and *AtS*'s run of new episodes finished, many Internet fans continue to attend fan conventions, read Buffy and Angel-centered fan fiction, purchase BtVS Season Eight comics and remain steadfast fans.

The long-running *BtVS* series ended its seven-season run in May 2003; *AtS* ended its five-season run in May 2004. However, syndication assures that new generations of Buffyites and Angelites will generate indefinitely. *Buffy the Vampire Slayer* and *Angel: The Series* are a global phenomenon, with an extensive international fandom in Canada, the UK, Ireland, Australia, New Zealand, France, Germany, Italy, Spain, Turkey, and in much of South America.

Today, many of the Internet fans who were members of the various fan boards studied owned DVDs of every season of *BtVS* and *AtS* (thirteen seasons, 254 episodes, combined). At the initial writing of this article, the Internet fans under study not only owned the DVDs, but would watch episodes re-run in syndication. Result? Buffyites and Angelites often watched their hero and heroine, their friends, their lovers, and their epic stories, for a total of fifteen hours a week — in addition to re-watching episodes at their leisure via DVD. Anecdotally, in the United States, many Buffy and Angel fans still re-watch episodes that air in syndication five days a week, Monday through Friday. "I always have my breakfast with Buffy," one fan told me.

In 2004, when this study was originally completed, *BtVS* had ended and *AtS* was about to end its run of new episodes, many *BtVS* and *AtS* Website boards included threads for a particular season or show. Discussion threads also included specific characters, and regular, recurring, and guest characters from both series (Fan board discussions specifically limited to one topic are called "threads").

Loyalty to *Buffy* generally includes its spin-off, *Angel: The Series*. The devotion fans previously accorded only to *BtVS* stretched in 2004 to include *AtS*, especially so at the beginning of *AtS* Season five, when Buffy's most popular character (excluding Buffy herself), Spike the Vampire (a.k.a. William the Bloody) joined the cast of *Angel*, offering that show a re-charged mission and an increase in viewers, many of whom followed the charismatic character (and the actor who plays him) to *AtS*. Many of the formerly only *BtVS* virtcoms then followed each new episode of *Angel: The Series*, with a formal review and discussion on the boards, much as they did new episodes of *BtVS*.

Buffy the Vampire Slayer and *Angel: The Series* are a multi-billion dollar business, and its fans not only watch the show, they also purchase the goodies. In other words: they *watch*, they *read*, they *listen* — they are surrounded by, and live in, a universe which, at the same time that it is enriching its makers, is also enriching the lives of the millions of fans who populate it. It's a mutually reinforcing circle of life. And this does not include the profound place of *BtVS* and *AtS* on the Internet. Indeed, it might be said that, without the Internet, specifically the virtual community, the Buffyverse might never have spread so wide, so far, so deeply into the realm of the cult TV show, and American industry (It's called show **business**, but that's another study).

Of course, there are also books, fan fiction available on the Internet, board discussions, *BtVS* and *AtS* soundtrack music available on three separately-issued CDs to play in one's car or at home, collectible major character dolls, two RPG's (Role-Playing Games), video games, comic books, graphic novels, collectible cards and plates, souvenir items, T-shirts, key chains, bumper stickers, and all sorts of other goods and wares, and regularly-scheduled Fan Conventions (called "fancons").

Until 2006, there were regularly issued *Angel* and *Buffy* magazines. There were also two streaming radio (Internet radio programs, each dedicated to discussions about the series, the writers, the cast, and crew, and the music played on *Buffy* and *Angel)*. Their titles: *The Succubus Club* and *Radio Buffy*.

Interestingly, none of the billions of dollars made for, around, and through the Buffyverse includes include that ubiquitous piece of high-tech business and high-tech life in our society: the Internet, which feeds the business of Buffy and Angel memorabilia, DVDs, CDs, graphic novels, novels, and etc.

In conclusion, Buffyites and Angelites take part in the business of BtVS and AtS. They purchase DVDs, novelizations, action figures, and other merchandise. They go to the movies to watch Buffy's and Angel's actors in different roles, but do so as part of their loyalty to the fandom. They attend concerts and fan conventions that feature their favorite character's actor or actress. The *coups* at such events — an autograph or autographed picture, attendance at a "Q & A" are highly treasured.

Fan conventions significantly feature as their main draw a session — usually one hour in length — that features one of the major characters from either/both series. For a (sometimes huge) fee, the featured actor appears as "himself" or "herself" on stage, and answers fans' questions on any topic. Public appearances by featured actors created create intense posting by fans.

Enter the Virtual Community

The Buffyverse exists nowhere as profoundly as the Internet. It can be said that the true Buffyite and Angelite exists in a Buffyverse made unique and richer by the (sometimes) synergistic energy of fan fic writers. Fan fic writers — who write without remuneration — post their tales on the Internet fan boards. Fans write the fan fiction; other fans read the fan fiction; loyalty for the series' is maintained through the energy and creativity of the fan ficcers and their readers — all through Internet fan boards.

Fan boards provide fans with a way to check-in daily with other fans. They help to create and maintain a sub-culture of people (commonly called a "cult fandom") that metaphorically lives in the Buffyverse. Members discuss upcoming 'verse-related events, such as concerts, or new work obtained by the casts and the writers of the shows. They post new pictures of the actors and writers.

Prior to the Internet, fan fiction was available to fans through 'zines — periodicals that published fan fiction. Enter the Internet, and enter the realm of real social change. Because of the Internet, fans read fan fiction through the Internet, not in a hard-copy format. It's accessible; it's cheap, and it works to help keep the fandom going. Fandoms and Internet fan fiction are mutually-reinforcing. Each keeps the other going, in a circle of energy and engagement that reinforces the importance of the virtual community as agency through which the fandom is maintained.

Millions of people spend time every day chatting with others through the medium of the Internet. The Internet has often been criticized for replacing real-life social interaction. However, through the modality of the virtual community the Internet has become a means of encouraging and enabling people to cross sometimes vast territorial boundaries to form communities of people who share the same interests, fears, loves, and experiences. Age, gender, race, class, national origin, native language, *appearance* — all unimportant — on the Internet you can make friends and create a community where you can feel you belong (Rheingold, 1988).

Nowhere is this phenomenon of the virtual community manifested more clearly than in the fan virtcoms ("the boards") supporting genre television. The fan support is such that, in Britain such TV shows — and their fans — are referred to as "cult TV." In the United States, cult status had, prior to *BtVS* and *AtS*, been limited to the *X-Files*, *Star Trek* and *Star Wars* phenomena. Today, television shows actively seek out genre/cult status. They *want* those fans — those fans who are engaged, committed, and ready to invest time and money in their series-related merchandise.

Community

It is salient to review the definition of "community." The two social sciences that use that term most are anthropologists and sociologists. When anthropologists use the term community, they often use the term territorially, such as when studying contemporary societies bound by specific physical boundaries. However, this researcher is a sociologist, so the definition to be used here would be sociologically-defined. The dilemma is that sociologists are not in total agreement as to the definition of a community.

A community is described sociologically as ... well, it isn't described sociologically. Indeed, there is not any *one* single *definition* of community that is accepted in sociology. There are, instead, *definitions* of community.

From its formative years as a science, sociologists have been interested in the idea of "community"—studying communities, writing about communities, teaching about communities. "Community" is one of the most important concepts in sociology—we sociologists agree on that (Nisbet, 1966). The problem is, definitions and theories proliferate in sociology, and there is not one definition that satisfies everybody.

One of the earliest sociologists to write about community was Emile Durkheim. To understand Durkheim's theories on community, we need to understand that for Durkheim, religion was the key to community. Religion held society together in a web of social affiliations, beliefs, and social camaraderie. He focused on the need people have to belong to something greater than themselves. Through the aegis of religion, he theorized, people established bonds with each other. These bonds were reinforced every time they encountered each other. Hence, religion established a community of believers who reaffirmed and reinforced their beliefs each time they met. So, for Durkheim, "community" has a religious underpinning; beliefs strengthen the bonds between people, the constant repetition of which reinforces the individual's sense of belonging to that community.

But, what if a group of people do not share a religious belief? Could there still be a community? Yes, because what is a community of believers share may not be so much a "religion" as a commonly held system of beliefs about "something," or "anything." After all, Durkheim believed that society was God, that people's belief in the society *was* the true belief. In other words, Durkheim theorized that communities are groups of people who share the same perspective about life (Durkheim 1965).

Georg Simmel took the opposite viewpoint. Simmel did not theorize about what a community is; he looked at what communities were not. He did not write so much about the necessity for community or its roots in religious belief, but rather about the isolation the individual faces in modern life. Ironically, Simmel was not writing in the twentieth or twenty-first centuries, but in the nineteenth century. He wrote profoundly about the problems of the individual in the metropolis, and of the characteristic isolation and impersonalization that is endemic in large cities then—and now. He used the term, *blasé*, to encompass that sensation of not caring or being interested in anything or anyone beyond the self. He wrote about city life. One of the hallmarks about Simmel's writing about city life is that for him, community is not important: living in an urban setting—surviving in an urban setting, was key (Simmel 1971).

Simmel's observations of social types—the stranger, the miser and the spendthrift, the adventurer—reveal his acute understanding of the various kinds of people that stand out in society. For Simmel, "community" was not an appealing concept. Where Durkheim saw "community," Simmel saw modern city life and loneliness. While Durkheim looked at what unites us and encourages us to conform to society, Simmel looked at what makes us stand out and stand apart from the crowd. While it is helpful to us to understand both concepts in order to understand "community," neither presents us with enough information to form a solid concept of "community."

Simmel's sublime essay *The Stranger*, reminds us that strangers are often trusted with secrets because they are strangers — because they do not know anyone in the community (Simmel, 143–150). This essay comes closest to Simmel's theories about community. A stranger, he reminds us, is one who is "estranged" from the earth; a stranger is one who is without roots. For Simmel, therefore, "community" is related to having roots — to being rooted in a territory, with a group of people who know you — and know you well. We will return to this concept.

About the same time, Ferdinand Tonnies was exploring the differences between life in a village and life in a metropolis. Villagers know each other a lifetime and their interactions with each other are personal and profound. People in small town — in villages — have time for each other, and treat each other with respect. This is not true of those who live in cities, where there are so many people, we don't have time to treat them with respect. The characteristic quality of modern city life, Tonnies said, was the impersonality of the relationships. Thus, Tonnies and Simmel would agree on what a community is not: it is not impersonal; it does not disrespect the person. Community is a place where people take time for each other (Tonnies 2004).

For Durkheim, Simmel, and Tonnies, community was not so much territorial, but rather the result of a complex web of social relationships found within a territory. Respectful, personal, caring — a community was depicted as a group of interacting individuals who regard each other as individuals, rather than roles, within a specific (and very real) space.

The next group of sociologists who explored the concept of community were two sociologists who worked in Chicago in the early twentieth century: Robert Park and Ernest Burgess. They focused on community as defined by geography and structure. They paid special attention to the size of communities and to the demographic changes in communities over time. Park and Burgess explored the relationship between social activities such as business, neighborhoods, and factories and their relationship in a geographic landscape.

While their independent studies expanded our learning about the spatial qualities of communities, the definition of "community" still remained unclear. Although their work was invaluable in aiding our understanding of city processes, it did little to help clarify the definition of community.

Burgess and Park's influence was such that community sociology drifted to the background, and urban sociology took the research lead. Sociologists increasingly concentrated on research projects that emphasized the alienation and impersonalization of mass society and the geographic and spatial development of large communities. By the early 1960s, many sociological studies seemed to indicate that "community" was a concept antithetical to twentieth century life.

A separate conception of community began in the late 1930s at the tail end of the Great Depression, on the east coast, about 1,500 miles away from Chicago — in another urban center: Boston. William Foote Whyte developed a theory about communities as a result of his study of a working-class community in South Boston. He observed the solidarity between neighbors who lived in a small neighborhood of South Boston. Foote Whyte was intrigued by the confluence of communities that made up a large city; he saw the city not as an undifferentiated mass, but as an accumulation of neighborhoods, each a small community in itself (Foote Whyte 1943).

The success of his work initiated an era of community studies that concentrated on increasing our understanding of communities by exploring the neighborhoods of larger cities. For several decades, there was a division between those sociologists who studied big cities, a la Park and Burgess, or observed small neighborhoods for "slice of life" community studies, like Foote Whyte.

By the 1960s, Robert A. Nisbet referred to community as *the* most basic concept in sociology. Furthermore, he defined community in almost lyrical terms: ..." a fusion of feeling and thought, of tradition and commitment, of membership and volition" (Nisbet 48) "It is where we live..." according to W. Allen Martin (Martin xiv).

Gans' work in the 1960s identified types of people who live in urban areas, concentrating on ethnic enclaves. Gans' work called to mind Tonnies' observations about social interaction in villages — and Gans demonstrated that village life (i.e., community) exits in the large city (Gans 1962).

By the 1970s, sociologists had rediscovered the idea of community, even if they could not necessarily agree on a definition of it. Sociologists today often use the term, "community." However, that term is often applied ambiguously, expanded to include both people who live within specific territorial boundaries as well as citizens of an online community.

Remember Durkheim, Simmel, and Tonnies' depictions of community and extend the concept of "territory" beyond geography. What if a community were territory-less? What if there were not any geographic boundaries to a community? What if the boundaries were infinite?

The Internet community is not a geographic entity. The Internet community — the virtual community (virtcom) — unlike *real* communities — is boundaryless; it is theoretically infinite.

The Virtual Community

What are virtual communities? They are non-geographic, non-territorial places where strangers meet and talk and become friends. How did the concept of a "virtual" community develop? What are its roots?

The idea of a virtual community developed in the late 1970s. Writing in 1979, Barry Wellman and Barry Leighton reconceptualized the model of community. They moved it away from the fixed territorial and physical reference points that were so important to Burgess. Leighton and Wellman developed a concept of a community that was bound by the territory of social relationships, social ties and social bonds (376–379).

Instead of physical boundaries, they suggested a reformulation of neighborhood and community into a new concept. In their reformulation of community, people were not geographically limited in their choices of relationships, and were free to create their own communities, based on their social relationships and social interests. By so doing, Wellman and Leighton believed that people would be expanding their opportunities to become engaged in a social community unlimited by spatial boundaries.

Three years later, Claude Fischer's research on social spaces and social relationships in California supported Wellman and Leighton's suggestion that community was more socially constructed than geographically constructed. People, according to Fisher, were more interested in hanging out, spending time, socializing, and just generally interacting with others who shared their socioeconomic status, education, and interests (Fischer 1982).

It is useful to stop a moment and recall that, until the development of the railroad and the automobile, most people interacted only with others who lived within a five-mile radius. People were born, married, lived, and died within a five-mile territory. Everybody really did know everybody else. Every day was pretty much like the day before it and the day that followed. New experiences were rare, and strangers rarer.

Autos, trains, telephones, radio, television, and then the wondrous Internet, all stretched our possibilities for meeting, greeting, bonding, and friending. With the Internet, we can literally make friends with people half-a world away, who have interests and passions like our own. Members of a community offer each other support. When someone in a citizen's family dies, when someone is about to lose their job, when they have work or school or family or health problems? The members of the board are there to offer solace, advice, and support.

The last century's *public* is today's *virtcom*. That is, a virtcom is really more or less a twenty-first century manifestation of what sociologists used to call a *public*—a group of people united by a common interest/passion. There is an important difference, however: members of a public rarely communicate with each other — and when they do, that communication is likely to be formal, via mailed correspondence. Virtcoms, on the other hand, encourage communication — both formal and informal — between members. There are literally hundreds of thousands of virtcoms on the Internet.

Virtual communities "can gather strangers from the far reaches of cyberspace and throw them together in the real world" (Metz 134). This can be temporarily, or for long, long, periods of time; long enough to create real and lasting relationships. Relationships in the virtcom reflect relationships in the real world. Polite hellos are quickly replaced by a sharing of opinions, ideas, fears, happiness and secrets. Citizens of virtcoms use personalized avatars (personal icons), emoticons, and animated and static imported images, to overcome the anonymity of invisibility. These enable the citizens of virtcoms to interact at deeper levels at a faster pace than might be appropriate in real life.

Board posting does have its problems, since communication is chiefly through a visual vacuum. 'Net users can't see each other. The chief problem is that the written word does not afford a glimpse of recipients' body language, facial expression, and general mien. Regionalisms, communicating across national and linguistic boundaries, etc., make virtcom communication a challenge.

Emoticons, and other images such as those noted above, and shorthand phrases (Like *lol* [lots of laughs], *ROTFL* [rolling on the floor laughing], *ITA* [I totally agree], *IMHO* [in my humble opinion], *FWIW* [for what it's worth], and *IIRC* [if I remember correctly]) help, but board conflicts can be common and hard to forget. It is not unusual, for example, to get caught up in one's desire to make a point, tell a joke, or add color commentary to a subject under discussion only to find that one has offended at least one person, and perhaps a sizeable number of persons. Then, it's not unusual for others to jump right in, in full attack mode (called "a flame"), before the original poster has a chance to even respond, clarify, apologize, or delete.

Remember the discussion above, on Simmel's *The Stranger*. Who is a stranger? A stranger is a person without roots; one who is not tied to territory or geographic place. Why do people trust strangers with secrets? Why do people interact with strangers? Because, Simmel would say, they are not the people we see every day. They are not tied to the same web of social affiliations; they are without roots.

Who are we that communicate online? We are people living in contemporary society — a society characterized by impersonalization, alienation, constant change. *We* are without roots: *we* do not occupy a physical territory; *we* are not an everyday part of each other's (real) lives. Hence, we are strangers to each other, and we meet, as strangers, online. And it is online where, as strangers, we create a community that is without boundaries and without territory.

Remembering Durkheim's theory, every time we meet, we build solidarity. Every time we meet, we reaffirm our beliefs — especially our belief in each other. Every time we meet, as Simmel would say, we are establishing roots; we are becoming less impersonal. Every time we connect online with another person in a chat room, in a fan board or fan forum, we have the opportunity to bond with others. Our online conversations (a.k.a. computer-mediated communication) can create a territory that is boundaryless; we *can* create a community in cyberspace. So: here is a definition of a virtual community: A virtual community is a non-geographic, non-territorial place where strangers meet and talk and become friends.

Hypothesis and Method

The Buffyverse was chosen for four reasons: (1) the deep loyalty Buffy and Angel fans have for the show, its cast and crew of writers; (2) a prior review of the literature on genre fandoms indicated that genre series fans are generally more engaged with their favorite shows than are non-genre fans; (3) the researcher is a Buffyite who has some previous knowledge of the Buffyverse fandom; and (4) The *BtVS* and *AtS* fan communities occasionally engage in face-to-face activities designed to afford citizens an opportunity to meet face-to-face (sometimes with citizens of cast and crew) at fancons (fan conventions), social events, and events designed to raise money for charity.

The charity events sponsored by most of the fan boards studied grew directly out of large boards, such as *City of Angel,* the *Bronze Beta Board,* and the *Soulful Spike Society.*[1] How large and powerful is the Buffyverse virtual community? Well, all of the major characters (and actors) (and some minor recurring characters) have websites dedicated to them. *Many* websites dedicated to them. Many of these Websites (not all) also have boards.

For our purposes, Websites dedicated to the series' *actors* were not included in the study. Actors' websites may extend beyond the series to include movie work and theatre work, thus taking the study beyond the confines of the universe of *Buffy* and *Angel.* For our purposes, the focus was on the *characters* portrayed.

There are Websites dedicated to the major characters: Angel, Buffy, Cordelia, Spike, and Willow. There are Websites dedicated to the love relationships (called 'ships) of the major characters: Buffy/Angel, Buffy/Spike, Cordelia/Angel, Willow/Tara, for example. There are also Websites dedicated to what are called "unconventional," i.e., non-canonical 'ships, such as

Spike/Anya and Spike/Angel. There are Websites dedicated to specific episodes of BtVS and Angel, such as *Once More with Feeling, Chosen,* and *Are You Now or Have You Ever Been.* In addition, there are thousands of sites maintained by fanfic writers who support various 'ships. Each of these sites may/may not have a fan board.

Such is the loyalty toward the 'verse that even *minor* recurring characters may have their own websites. Warren, a character from *BtVS* season five, who became a villain in season six, had a website dedicated to him that included fanfiction adventures. The same is true for Gwen Raiden, a *Rogue*-like character who appeared in several episodes of *AtS* season four. Finally, a mention should be made of the Website devoted to the Hyperion Hotel, (*Hyperion's Attic*) Team Angel's Art Deco base of operations for AtS Seasons Two through Season Four.

With so many possibilities, which virtcoms were to be observed in-depth? One might think that Alexa.com, an amazon.com company, and Google.com, which periodically posted statistics on the 100 most frequently visited sites (called a "traffic post") in the Buffyverse, would be useful. However, their statistics were not useful for this study, except as noted below. Alexa and Google count visits, not *postings,* and many of the sites listed in Alexa and Google do not have fan boards.

Private boards, of which there are thousands, were also not included in this study. Such boards are small, with size limited by founders. These are the elite boards; free speech is a given. For purposes of this study, small boards would not be germane. Such boards are more properly defined as a clique or circle of friends, rather than a true virtcom. For example, during the observation period, one board had one citizen, but logged in twenty-eight visits and not one *visitor* posted (Information on this URL is provided in the Appendix).

The Bronze Beta board was also eliminated from inclusion. The Bronze Beta is arguably the most famous fan board in the 'verse. Scholars have written articles about the influence of the Bronze board. Celebrities post there. The producer and the writers of both *BtVS* and *AtS* post there — and still occasionally do so, despite the fact that the series finished three years ago. It seemed "over-exposed," so it was eliminated from the study list. The final list included boards that seemed less self-conscious, less aware that others were reading their postings.[2]

I used three methods. First, I needed to derive a listing of fan boards. Alexa.com and Google.com, being the major source for statistics on Web traffic, were still the places to go to derive an initial listing of fan boards. Consequently, my first step was to configure a listing of the major *Buffy* boards according to Alexa.com and Google.com. From their lists, I derived a random list of twenty-five fan boards. From these twenty-five, I derived another twenty fan boards that I obtained from the links they provided to other fan boards.

From these three lists of links: alexa.com, google.com, and the random list of twenty-five fan boards, I derived a total of forty-five fan boards from which to choose a microcosm of the Online Buffy 'verse: four fan boards that would be observed.

The boards randomly chosen for inclusion in this study were based on (1) facility of posting and (2) regularity of posting. Fan boards which had been randomly selected, but had not received regular postings in the first week of June 2003 were not included in the study. That left seventeen boards.

My next step was to randomly choose four boards of the remaining seventeen for daily observation via the traditional "paper sack method." For those unaware, the paper sack method requires a paper sack and small pieces of paper. Seventeen identically-sized pieces of paper were cut; each fan board's name was written on one of the precut pieces of paper, then folded and dropped into the paper sack. Four pieces of paper were drawn — each with the name of a different board. The results of the drawing were the names of the four fan boards to be observed. The boards observed were (in order of choosing) (1) thebigbad.net, (2) soulfulspikesociety, (3) hellmouthcentral. com, and (4) cityofangel.com.

Two of the chosen boards were "general" boards — CityofAngel.com and hellmouthcentral.com; two were character-specific (Spike) — thebigbad-board.net, and the soulfulspikesociety.net. Looking at the four pieces of paper, I recall pondering the paper sack method with a renewed trust in the method, and a renewed wonder at the mathematics of probability.

Regular posting was defined for purposes of this study, as having at least five messages posted for each day in the first week of June 2003. Observation began the following week. I registered and lurked at each site for at least an hour each day, every day, six days a week over a five month period, starting with June 8, 2003 through October 31, 2003. While I did occasionally post, the only board at which I posted with any frequency was the S^3 (The Soulful Spike Society board is referred to as S^3 by its citizens). In addition to the four in-depth boards, I observed an additional fifteen boards, checking in every two days for at least an hour. This was a time-consuming method, but it garnered me an appreciation of the Buffyverse fandom, and the people who love and support the creative staff employed by Joss Whedon and the folks at Mutant Enemy, the producers of BtVS and AtS.

A caveat on SoulfulSpike. I fought with myself on including it because I was a frequent poster there. By the end of August, I was considering eliminating SoulfulSpike from the observation list. In doing research on virtcoms,

I had found a home for myself—hence, I felt the need, for purposes of objectivity, to eliminate my home community from the base of those being observed. Still, that board was growing, dynamic, and very active—easily the most active, per citizen, of any of the observed boards. How could I eliminate the board that was appearing to be the closest to the virtcom ideal? How could I withhold the data, the knowledge, of an active, **real** virtcom in fandom? Because it is the board at which I posted most frequently I did want to eliminate it from the study, but the results were such that I **had** to include it. I decided, therefore, to continue to include the board, but to eliminate any mention of specific board conversations and controversies in the written report **for all fan boards**. Fan boards are rife with controversy, most of which stem from communication problems noted above.

Members of virtcoms are often called "citizen" in the literature. We can approximate the level of virtcom involvement per citizen by a simple arithmetical formula. This can be done arithmetically, by dividing the number of posts by the number of citizens (Let P=Posts and C=Citizens, so: P_C). The resulting number will yield the number of posts per citizen (P_C= # Posts per Citizen).

The number of posts per citizen is an indication of commitment to the online community. The greater the number of posts per citizen, the more likely the board is to be a true virtcom. The fewer the posts, the less involved the person, and the less likely the board is to be a true virtcom. The results were somewhat surprising, as we will see.

Methodological Weaknesses and Strengths

There are two major weaknesses to the methodology. First, it is important to remember that although boards are *maintained* by a half-dozen people (all of whom are volunteers), they may be *visited* by thousands each week. In the thirty-six hours following a new episode of AtS, thousands of fans may be trolling the boards, reading reviews and looking for an opportunity to chat about the episode which has just been broadcast.

Many visitors to a site lurk and read; few post. Where registration is required prior to posting, many do not bother to register; other may register, post, then move on to another board, and never post at that board again. Since we are looking at the numbers of *regular* posters, we are interested in the forum as a *community*, not solely a means of information. Second, the number of boards studied is microscopic compared to the number of boards that exist. Undertaking a study of the top 100 boards would have necessitated a cadre of trained observers—which was beyond the scope of this study.

The strengths of the methodology are that, by limiting the number of boards studied to four, *and* by focusing on each board for a minimum of eight hours a week, I could gain both a better depth of understanding of the concept of a virtual community *and* the depth of involvement in fandom on the part of the citizens of those communities. Of course, it is all about the mission — and the mission — (learning more about fandom) could be kept on track with a smaller, more intense observation, as opposed to a larger, more diffuse observation.

Expectations

Beginning my observations soon after the finale of *BtVS*, I hypothesized that much of the board communications concerning *Buffy* would be about the finale, *Chosen*. By mid-summer, discussion of *Chosen* had trickled out and speculation concerning *AtS* Season five was exploding.

The popular and highly original *AtS* spin-off ended its fourth season at the same time that *BtVS* was ending permanently. There was some question as to whether or not *Angel* would be renewed for a fifth season. Producer Joss Whedon shot a new concept finale, and all parties reached a five-point accord, as noted in the following section.

(1) Spike, the other vampire with a soul, would be added to Angel's regular cast. The WB's demographic research revealed that Spike was the most popular character in the Buffyverse, much to the chagrin of some fans. The character of Spike was initially an evil vampire in a romantic relationship with another evil vampire, Drusilla — his sire.[3] However, due to a chip, then a soul, Spike threatened to stake (kill) Drusilla for his (now) true love, Buffy. Eventually, Spike died to save Buffy and the world. It was Spike's fans The WB was hoping to entice as new AtS viewers.

(2) Angel would return to a Monster of the Week (MOTW) format, thus enabling new viewers to catch onto the premise more easily. *Angel's* ratings had fallen drastically during Season Four. A subsequent survey revealed that for many fans, Season Four was their least favorite season. Many fans reported that they stopped watching the show that year.

Season Four was highly innovative; the entire season was based on a complex, interconnected series of episodes. Like *24*, each episode takes place over a small period of time — two weeks. Like *24*, viewers who missed an episode often felt confused when catching the episode following the one that they missed. The opening trailer for the show grew more protracted as the season progressed.

Fans left *en masse* when Angel's son, Connor, began a sexual relationship with Cordelia, whom Angel also loved. Fans' dislike was intense because their relationship (Cordelia's and Connor's) was more Jocasta/Oedipus relationship than Romeo/Juliet.

(3) The cast location would be removed from a demon detective agency housed in a 1950's *noir*-style hotel to an evil law firm whose Los Angeles branch is housed in a contemporary skyscraper. Fans loved the hotel, called The Hyperion, and many online fans were concerned that the characters' relationships would change with a new venue.[4] Of course, the functionalist architecture of the evil law firm also symbolized the impersonal, blasé, uncaring nature of its business (evil), but the online fans indicated that would miss the old Hyperion.

The old hotel may have been difficult to light, and it may have been difficult to script scenes there, but the characters had more opportunities to interact in the old set than in the new skyscraper setting. The new set was a contemporary, functionalist-style skyscraper in downtown Los Angeles — a radical departure from the art deco Hyperion fans had loved in Seasons Two through Four.

(5) Two popular female characters were eliminated and replaced by different female characters. Although many online fans claimed to "have nothing against" the two new female actors, they loved the female actors — Charisma Carpenter and Stephanie Romanov — who were being replaced. Many online fans expressed disappointment and anger with the decision to remove characters (and actors) they cared about and liked. Some fans threatened to stop watching the show; some wrote to the show's producers to complain. The two characters eliminated were played by actresses in their early thirties; the new characters were played by actresses at least ten years younger. Many female fans were outraged by that, believing the substitution to have been done to increase ratings with the desired male demographic.[5]

Observations

For the purposes of this study, I was particularly delighted about the choice of two Spike-centric boards in the study; it was inclusion of the character of Spike that was creating speculation throughout all the boards. As both a fan of BtVS and a sociologist, I knew the Spike-change would have an effect on board posting, or at least, reading the postings about it was bound to be interesting, as well as fun.[6]

The WB and ME (network and the production company) hoped these changes would result in higher ratings for the critically-acclaimed spin-off series. The anticipated changes in AtS created a buzz in the boards. Each day's circuit of observation included a growing thread regarding rumors and "spoilers" about the season's opener and the role that Spike would be playing in the series. Always a controversial presence in the lives of Buffy and the Scoobies in Sunnydale, Spike had appeared on Angel several times, each appearance bringing energy, a quality of gleeful mayhem to each of his appearances there. So much so, that many long-time AtS viewers were concerned that his character would overshadow that of Angel or over other characters who had been on the series longer.

In the months that followed, the presence of Spike proved to be a catalyst of change for the series. The Monster of the Week format had a tag-along, but subtle seasonal arc, replete with red herrings of evil puppets, warlocks, demon clan fights, parasitic worms, Nazis, and cyborgs. The new location allowed the writers to focus on corporate evil and the dangers of succumbing to its temptation. Ratings shot up thirty-six percent; several national critics listed it as one of the ten best shows on television, and stated that the scripts were better than ever. The fans were gleeful; the cast and crew relieved; the sponsors happy. Of course, the next thing the network did was to cancel the show.[7]

During the period of observation, the four most popular topics on *BtVS* fan boards (commonly called BuffyBoards) were: (1) The attempts by BtVS viewers to catch up on the storyline for AtS; (2) the projected changes in *Angel: The Series*; (3) the addition of two new female recurring characters; and (4) deletion of two popular female characters, Cordelia Chase and Lilah Morgan.

(1) Online *BtVS* fans scurried to rent, borrow, and if necessary — buy — four seasons' worth of *Angel* DVDs and/videotapes. Conversations buzzed as fans e-mailed postal service addresses and exchanged more personal, RL (real life) information to expedite the transfer of the treasured DVDs and videotapes.

(2) Fans — especially the fans of James Marsters — speculated about possible storylines, plot arcs, and 'ships that might occur once Spike was on the scene as a regular addition to the cast. A new 'ship emerged: Spike/Fred, which hypothesized that once Winifred Burkle (a.k.a. Fred) met Spike (and vice-versa) they would fall in love. Fred would see Spike as the hero he really was, and Spike would adore Fred because she would adore him and treat him with respect. Two new Websites, devoted to Spike/Fred fan fiction opened; by the time Season Five premiered, the Spike/Fred 'ship was in full sail.

Fans speculated that Cordelia might come out of the coma she had been left in at the end of Season Four, and once again take Angel to task whenever he strayed from the path of righteousness. They also speculated about what had happened to Connor. Had he been truly killed? Not a fan favorite, especially since his pairing with Cordelia, many expressed satisfaction with his leaving the series.

(3) A recurring character in BtVS Seasons One through Five, Harmony became a vampire the day she graduated from Sunnydale High School, in Season Three. That same year, she entered into a sexual relationship with Spike that lasted intermittently through *BtVS* Season Five. In between, Harmony had guested once on *AtS* in Season Two.

Many fans — especially males — loved her (and the actress who played her). Many fans — especially female fans of Spike (and James Marsters) — were not fond of the character, though they liked the young actor that played her (Mercedes McNab).

There was repeated speculation among the fan boards that Harmony may have been brought onto *AtS* to resume her relationship with Spike. It was this possibility that most concerned Spike's fans. They did not want to see him paired with Harmony again.

There was much speculation, too, about the character that would replace Lilah Morgan, everyone's favorite evil attorney. The new Liaison for the Senior Partners — Eve — would be played by a female actor unknown to most of the members of the fan boards. Most of the speculation swirled around what her relationship would be to Angel, and whether or not Wesley (who had been in a relationship with Lilah) would remember Lilah after the "mind wipe" at the finale of Season Five.

(4) Lastly, fans of both genders were angry that the characters of Cordelia Chase and Lilah Morgan were eliminated. Cordelia had been a regular on BtVS for three seasons, and then made the move to AtS when that show's pilot was shot. The actress, Charisma Carpenter, played the character for seven years, and was very popular with fans. Popular opinion was that her character was being written out of the show because the actress was pregnant during Season Four. Others speculated that, for some reason, there was disharmony between the actress and the producer. Stephanie Romanov was a recurring cast member for four seasons, and her character — the amoral, evil, Lilah Morgan — was a favorite with many fans, both male and female.

Gossip and rumors eddied about, from early in the morning through late evening. The boards were never quiet, as fans discussed all the permutations and combinations of interactions and plot devices. Many fans claimed they would not return to *AtS* because of the deletion of the characters of Cordelia and Lilah; others claimed they wouldn't return to watching *AtS* because of the inclusion of Spike. Still others said that Spike's inclusion on the show would spark their becoming a regular viewer of the show. These events were all discussed, digested, pondered, debated and meditated upon in the active boards.

Following is list of the major boards observed, including the four that were examined in-depth, in descending order.

Using this measure, the boards that are closest to a true virtcom are those that have over one hundred posts each citizen. That would include the following boards: the Soulful Spike Society, Hellmouthcentral, Buffyworld Forum, Buffymania.net, and Buffy-vs-Angel.com. Of those listed, only four—the Soulful Spike Society, Hellmouthcentral, CityofAngel, and The Big Bad—were part of the in-depth study. There were also very few Off-Topic conversations during the observation period at the boards studied less intently. There was only one board that had conversations that were continually off-topic (off-topic being defined as not germane to the Buffyverse)—and that was the Soulful Spike Society.

Buffyite Fan Boards (Virtcoms)

Soulful Spike	106,850 posts/169 citizens = 632 posts ea. citizen
Hellmouth Central	231,041 posts/677 citizens = 341 posts ea. citizen
Buffyworld Forum	622,693 posts/2,205 citizens = 282 posts ea. citizen
Buffymania.net	10,668 posts/41 citizens = 260 posts ea. citizen
Buffy-vs-Angel	30,258 posts/207 citizens = 146 posts ea. citizen
Smg.fan	233,097 posts/2,502 citizens = 93 posts ea. citizen
Totally DB.uk.com	3,936 posts/49 citizens = 80 posts ea. citizen
Buffy.com.au	114,939 posts/1651 citizens = 70 posts ea. citizen
Stranger Things	27,778 posts/2,324 citizens = 62 posts ea. citizen
Charisma Carpenter Forum	37,080 posts/1,035 citizens = 36 posts ea. citizen
alysonhannigancorner.com	11,579 posts/441 citizens = 26 posts ea. citizen
marstersmobsters.com	9,985 posts/494 citizens = 20 posts ea. citizen
sparklies.com	29,508 posts/1,999 citizens = 15 posts ea. citizen
charismacarpenter.com	19,077 posts/1,433 citizens = 13 posts ea. citizen
The Big Bad	12,650 posts/1,300 citizens = ~10 posts ea. citizen
davidboreanaz.com	12,471 posts/3,380 citizens = 2 posts ea. citizen
CityofAngel.com	129,360 posts/156,000 citizens = 1 post ea. citizen

Note: number of posts ÷ by number of citizens = number of posts each citizen

At the Soulful Spike Society, fan board members discussed their private lives, their fears, their hopes and dreams for themselves, their families and friends. Virtual prayers were sent for citizens experiencing hard times. Child-rearing tips were exchanged. Books and movies were discussed, as were television shows other than *BtVS* and *AtS*. People posted about work, vacations, and what they did in Real Life.

Members were supported, nurtured, and encouraged. Unlike many of the boards observed, disagreements were quickly settled, with all parties moving on to positive interaction quickly, usually due to the intervention of a small group of females and two males. They carefully watched all the posting, and if there was any likelihood of controversy, disagreement, or "hurt feelings," they acted promptly to smooth everything out. Respect for each other was treated as importantly as the board's *raison d'etre*: an appreciation of the character of Spike and indeed, all the characters of the Buffyverse.

Mixed in with the personal exchanges were the On-topics specifically related to the two series, their characters, myths, episodes, music, and etc. Unlike other boards, their 'verse discussions often related to the philosophical, psychological, and even anthropological aspects of the characters and their stories. Here was that rare commodity: a real virtual community! The conversations were of a type not usually seen in the larger boards, with topics rarely seen in the larger boards. Here was that *Eldorado* promised in the literature: a true virtual community. Eureka!

The update on The Soulful Spike Community, reviewed as a lurker, rather than a citizen, during the period June 1, 2007, through July 7, 2007, indicates that its status as a true virtcom remains in good stead. As of July 7, 2007, a review of SoulfulSpike's fan board indicates a total of 2,033 topics, with 483,854 posts by 230 members. The community contains Archives, for those who want to catch up on the community's history, recommendations for fan fiction — both authorized novelizations and comics, as well as Internet fan fiction, links to fan conventions and scholarly conferences, and episode reviews for all three of Whedon's TV series.

By adding new cult TV series — *Lost, Battlestar Galactica, Heroes, Veronica Mars, Firefly, Smallville, Dr. Who,* and *Torchwood* to its territory, the Soulful Spike Society has maintained interest by its membership, which has increased thirty percent since 2004, the finale year for *Angel*. Like Angel, the Soulful Spike Society will likely not fade away.

Demographics

According to the information available about citizens' gender at the boards observed, and during the time period observed, most of the online Buffyverse fans were females. Although more males were registered at AtS and Jossverse boards, females predominated there, too. This is in line with the two series: Buffy is about a young female super-heroine; Angel is about a young male superhero (well, young-looking; after all, he is a vampire). Angel is aimed at a male audience, and it also delivers male citizens to its boards, according to the boards' rosters of members and observation of posters.

Many of the women are married, with children; whereas, the many of the males are single. At the major boards, where citizens average one hundred postings or more, female citizens are more likely to be older. Most of the females are over twenty-five years of age, college-educated or with some college background, middle-class, white-collar workers, professionals and semi-professionals.

Many of the men are thirty-five years old or younger. Younger males are likely to be college students. Older males are likely to be college-educated, and like their female counterparts, they are likely to be middle-class, white-collar, professionals and semi-professionals.

Not surprisingly, many of the citizens are very computer-literate, capable of answering complicated questions to help other citizens with computer problems. One board (Soulful Spike Society) includes a large number of lawyers and teachers.

Many citizens are lovers of science fiction and not only watch science fiction fantasy programming and movies, but also read science fiction. Older citizens initiate younger citizens into science fiction reading, movies, and television programming. This is one area where you will not find a generation gap; the Buffyverse brings the generations together.

Conclusions

Conclusions, while always tentative, indicate that, despite its rarity, the true virtual community does exist online. It was not what was expected. In my enthusiasm for online living, I had expected to find that at least half of the four fan boards studied would be virtcoms, and that as many as one-half of the less-intensely-observed forums would also be virtcoms. From the research, this was not the case.

The Internet, in fact, continues to feed the multi-billion dollar enterprise that is the Buffyverse. Although thousands of fans still communicate via fan boards, blog sites such as LiveJournal, InsaneJournal, GreatestJournal, and JournalFen appear to have increased in popularity as fan boards have closed and/or diminished in popularity. The ability of blog owners to lock posts, restricting communication to those who also have blogs is changing the Internet's computer-mediated communication. This change to fan blogs is currently under study.

This study began as part of a larger endeavor to learn more about cult TV fans and the fandom experience. It accomplished that goal. More short studies are planned; hopefully each project will add to the knowledge base about the Buffyverse fandom.

Appendix

Following is a listing of major virtual communities in the Buffyverse, as of May 30, 2004. Those still active as of August 25, 2008, are asterisked (*).

The Big Bad *http://www.thebigbad.net*
Buffy mania. Italian site. *http://www.buffymania.net*
Buffy-vs-Angel *http://www.buffy-vs-angel.com/cgi-bin/sunnydale/ikonboard.cgi*

Buffy world *http://www.buffyworld.com* *
City of Angel *http://www.cityofangel.com* Although the forum is closed, the site is still relatively active, with news posted periodically.
The Council of Watchers *http://www.protej.com/Buffy/*
Hellmouth Central *http://www.hellmouthcentral.com* *
More Than Spike *http://www.morethanspike.com* *
Soulful Spike *http://scubiefan.proboards18.com/index.cgi* *
Sparklies *http://www.sparklies.org*
Stranger Things *http://www.stranger-things.net/forum/**
Totally David Boreanaz *http://totallydavidboreanazuk.com*
Whedonesque *http://www.whedonesque.com* *

Following are the websites created to celebrate specific episodes of BtVS/AtS: As of August 25, 2008, all were closed.

http://musical.chosentwo.com/main.html Once More with Feeling
http://www.aynohyeb.moonlitviolets.com Are You Now or Have You Ever Been
http://www.hyperion.moonlitviolets.com Hyperion Hotel
http://chosen.blueberry-scone/com Chosen
Eternal Flame (one member, 28 postings).

Flash mobs: all still open as of August 25, 2008.

http://www.flashmob.com
http://www.flashmob.co.uk

Buffy Radio Stations:

http://www.thesuccubusclub.com A radio program focused on Buffy and Angel series
Since the end of the series, it's now a Buffy and Angel website, complete with chat room.
http://www.radiobuffy.nu French Buffy radio program.

Notes

1. The exception in fund-raising is the very successful Make-a-Wish-Slay-a-Thon, which has been running a marathon benefit every summer since 2003. Slay-a-Thon did not emanate from a fan board, but from the work of a Buffy and Angel fan, Kelly Creamer. For more information, go to slayathon.org.

2. This turned out to be a serendipitously wise decision, as I later learned that Asim Ali was involved in a nearly decade-long study of members of the Bronze — called *Bronzers*.

3. His first sire was revealed to be Angelus, in BtVS, Season 2, School Hard. However, three seasons later in BtVS, Season 5, Fool for Love, it was revealed that Drusilla, his lover, had sired him. Angelus had apparently "raised" him.

4. They had reason to fear: the characters' relationships did change, but that was clearly part of Whedon's intended plot arc for Season Five.

5. "The desired male demographic" is a single male, 18–49 years of age.

6. "What this place needs is a lot less ritual and a lot more fun!," Spike, BtVS, *School Hard*, 2.02.

7. The decision, according to spokespersons from The WB, was based on demographics. The target audience for AtS was 18–49 year old males, whereas most of the viewers were outside this demographic. What WAS outside the demographic? Females. The audience was mostly 18–49 year old females. And we know that women don't have the buying power of males of the same age group. In other words, it wasn't enough that the series' rating were the best they'd been; the audience just wasn't the right kind of people.

Works Cited

Durkheim, Emile. *The Elementary Forms of the Religious Life*. New York: Free Press, 1965.
_____. *Moral Education*. New York: Free Press, 1962.
_____. *Suicide: A Study in Society*. Trans. J. A. Spaulding and G. Simpson. New York: Free Press, 1952.
Fischer, Claude. *To Dwell Among Friends: Personal Networks in Town and City*. Chicago: University of Chicago Press, 1982.
Flanagan, William G. *Urban Sociology: Images and Structure*. 4 ed. Boston: Allyn and Bacon, 2002.
Ken P. "An Interview with Joss Whedon." June 23, 2003. January 5, 2004. *IGN Entertainment.* *http://tv.ign.com/articles/425/425492p1.html*
Martin, W. Allen. *The Urban Community*. Upper Saddle River: Pearson/Prentice Hall, 2004.
Michelson, William H. *Man and His Urban Environment: A Sociological Approach. with Revisions*. Reading: Addison-Wesley Publishing Company, 1976.
O'Neill, J. M. "Pop Culture Cracks College Curriculums." January 20 2004. 1 January 2004. Philadelphia, PA: *Knight Ridder Tribune Information Services*. <http://www.whedon.info/Pop-culture-cracks-college.html> <http://www.freerepublic.com/focus/f-news/1047649/posts>
Palen, John J. *The Urban World*. 5 ed. New York: McGraw-Hill, 1997.
Rheingold, Howard. *The Virtual Community*. 1998. 12 December 2003. <http://www.rheingold.com/vc/book/>
Ryan, John and William M. Wentworth. *Media and Society: The Production of Culture in Mass Media*. Boston: Allyn and Bacon, 1999.
Simmel, Georg. *On Individuality and Social Forms*. Donald N. Levine, Ed. Chicago: University of Chicago Press, 1971.
_____. "The Stranger." Ed. Donald Levine. *On Individuality and Social Forms*. Chicago: University of Chicago Press, 1971. 143–150.
Tonnies, Ferdinand. "Community and Society *(Gemeinschaft und Gesellschaft)*," Trans. and Ed, Charles P. Loomis, from *The Urban Community*, ed. by W. Allen Martin, Upper Saddle River: Pearson/Prentice Hall, 2004. 21–32.
Wellman, Barry and Barry Leighton. "Networks, Neighborhoods, and Communities: Approaches to the Study of the Community Question." *Urban Affairs Quarterly* 1979. 14: 363–390.
Whyte, William Foote. *Street Corner Society: The Social Structure of an Italian Slum*. Chicago: University of Chicago Press. 4 ed. 1993.

RL on LJ: Fandom and the Presentation of Self in Online Life

Rebecca Bley

Introduction

"That thing I try desperately to avoid."

"The boring bits."

"Stuff that is not fictional and not on the internets."

"You could find me (and murder me in my bed!) using the information."

"All the boring, lonely, pathetic hours I'm not on-line."

These are some of the answers that arose when a group of media fans on LiveJournal.com was asked to define "Real Life" (or "RL") (*fan_research*, December 2–6). It is a term that is frequently bandied about on the Internet, at times quite matter-of-factly, yet in some corners it still arouses controversy. It is often understood as meaning time that is spent offline, or in "meatspace" as opposed to "cyberspace." Some fans describe it as anything outside of fandom, while some use it to refer to anyone they have met in person, fan-related or not. Some fans are offended at the implications of the term, inferring an invalidity to their online experiences. Consequently, the various personal interpretations of the term, "Real Life," as well as the concept of "Real Life," can lead to complex presentations of self in the online world.

When Erving Goffman wrote *The Presentation of Self in Everyday Life* in 1959, he claimed an interest in the structure of social interaction when people enter one another's immediate physical presence (254). Online interaction complicates this idea and requires people to negotiate *both* their physical and non-physical existences. This article takes Goffman's theoretical approach and applies it to the Digital Age, using his framework to analyze the ways in which members of media fan communities, particularly those of Joss Whedon's *Buffy the Vampire Slayer* and *Angel: The Series*, resolve their online and offline selves on the personal blogging web site, LiveJournal.com ("LJ"). Live-Journal's unique structure allows its users to define very specific audiences for individual posts, creating unusual opportunities for audience segregation and overall modern management of personal representation.

First, the LiveJournal "stage" and its technical features are described, with an emphasis on what sets it apart from other blogging web sites. This article then explores social interactions commonly seen in media fandom (specifically, Buffyverse fandom) as an example of one common type of online community. Finally, this article looks at the intersection of these ideas, using survey results to identify trends and show how *Buffy* and *Angel* fans on Live-Journal are a manifestation of Goffman's principles at work in modern society.

LiveJournal

Goffman defined a "social establishment" as "any place surrounded by fixed barriers to perception in which a particular kind of activity regularly takes place" (239). LiveJournal clearly falls within these guidelines, with its fixed location and methods of interaction defined by its technological infrastructure, and its regular social interaction. At a time when blogs are nearly ubiquitous on the Internet, LiveJournal stands out with its social networking and advanced capabilities for customized levels of privacy. Like any common blogging service, LiveJournal allows for users with very little technical skill to create and regularly update their own web sites. These journals are usually filled with commentary on the author's everyday life, social engagements, professional experiences, family experiences, and hobbies. In addition to these personal journals kept by individual users, LiveJournal is made up of "communities," which are special journals in which any community member can post. These communities are devoted to shared hobbies, media texts, celebrities, geographical locations, medical conditions, etc. They are one way users forge new links after joining the LiveJournal service. In fact, the main feature touted by LiveJournal in its attempt to lure in new users is that of a "True Community." On its "Take a Tour" page, LiveJournal promises, "From art to zombies, if you can think of it, there's probably a community about it" ("Quick Tour").

In addition to communities, LiveJournal stimulates social networking through the use of a threaded commenting system. While the popular blogging site "Blogger" uses a commenting system that results in one continuous mass of comments on each post, arranged only in chronological order, Live-

Journal creates "conversations," where users can respond to specific comments and create message threads that branch off from one another (Blogger). The conversation threads are visually delineated on the screen through indentation and automatically-created child pages for longer threads. Participants can also elect to be notified through email, text message, or Instant Message when someone responds to comments they have made, even in another user's journal. Every comment from a LiveJournal user who is logged in contains the user's name and personal icon, or "userpic" (a 100x100 pixel square of graphical material chosen by the user). The name is also a hyperlink to that user's journal, and the official LiveJournal graphic next to the name is a link to that user's profile. This technical structure is more conducive to community-building than that of Blogger and other similar sites. The commenters engage with each other as well as the original poster, creating and maintaining personal links outside of their respective journals.

Another quality unique to LiveJournal is the ability to "lock" certain posts, or even entire journals, changing the public nature of LiveJournal blogs. LiveJournalers ("LJers") can set their posts to be visible only to designated (logged-in) LiveJournal users, or even only to themselves if they wish to keep a private journal. This element works in tandem with another distinctive LiveJournal feature, which is the "Friend" function. Creating a LiveJournal account and being Friended by another user works as a password of sorts, allowing access to material that is not visible to the general public. Users are able to designate each other as official Friends, a framework that functions on two levels. First, the LiveJournal posts of those on one's "Friends List" are automatically aggregated onto a single web page (one's "Friends Page") in reverse chronological order, creating a personalized experience for each user.

To illustrate the Friends Page function, one can imagine the hallway of an average college dormitory. There are whiteboards attached to each bedroom door, and one can walk down the hallway, searching for the rooms of acquaintances and reading the messages on each board in turn. This is the way the average blog system works. LiveJournal's Friends Page is the equivalent of someone asking which whiteboards are to be read, collecting the messages on each of those, and copying them onto a single whiteboard that is brought directly to one's own doorstep. This feature increases the sense of a single LiveJournal community as opposed to a succession of separate and individual sites.

The second major use of LiveJournal's Friend feature is the ability to create Custom Friends Groups and use them to either further customize a Friends Page view, or to define different privacy levels for each post in one's own LiveJournal. The first case is akin to having several collated whiteboards delivered directly to one's doorstep, perhaps one featuring posted messages of female friends and the other with messages of male friends. If one just wanted to read the message of female friends, one could read only a single whiteboard of collected messages and ignore the other. The second way in which Custom Friends Groups are employed is especially relevant to this article. The ability to lock individual posts in one's LiveJournal is the equivalent of using special "invisible" ink on one's whiteboard. Only people with specially tinted glasses can read messages written in this invisible ink. There can be many different "colors" of this invisible ink, each requiring their own specific, uniquely tinted glasses. Those who write the messages choose exactly who gets each pair of glasses. If a dorm resident writes a message on her whiteboard complaining of her homework for the evening, she might use the *blue* invisible ink, and give pairs of blue glasses only to the people on her dormitory floor. If she wishes to complain about her floor's Resident Advisor, however, she may use the *red* invisible ink and ensure that said Advisor does not have a pair of red glasses (thus filtering him out, one reason Custom Friends Groups are often called "filters"). The average visitor walking by her door sees nothing, because he does not possess any of the glasses that match her invisible ink.

As an example of these ideas in practice, theoretical LiveJournaler, "Jane" could create a filter for "*Buffy* fans," one for "Family," and one for "Academic" friends. The morning after a new episode of *Buffy* airs, Jane might use her "*Buffy* fans" filter to view her Friends Page, so that all other journals on her Friends List do not appear and she can focus her time on this fandom. The next day when posting about her grandmother's birthday party, she might limit viewing access to this post to those people on her "Family" filter, to protect her grandmother's privacy. Anyone who is not on her "Family" filter cannot see that post, even if they are on her Friends List. Finally, she might post a notice about an upcoming academic conference and limit viewing access to those on her "Academic" filter, so as not to bore other readers or clutter their Friends Pages with irrelevant material. LiveJournal allows her to have several different faces and adjust her behavior according to whichever identity she is "wearing" at the time. Thus, it provides a unique opportunity to explore audience segregation in action. By creating various filters, a fan on LiveJournal "ensures that those before whom he plays one of his parts will not be the same individuals before whom he plays a different part in another setting" (Goffman 49). LiveJournal uses filters to offer its users this measure of region control.

Fandom

LiveJournal has become a popular site for media fan activity. The community "fandom_counts," intended as a census of sorts to show the potential power of fandom on LiveJournal, boasted over 34,000 members in July of 2007 (*krisomniac, vichan*). Fans use their LiveJournals to share commentaries on movies, books, television shows, and even computer games. They write stories (called "fan fiction" or "fanfic") using the characters and environments from the original texts.[1] These stories range from mild "G" ratings to hard "NC-17" ratings, self-rated as such occasionally for violence, but more often for graphic sexual content. They also create fan art, both by hand in traditional manners and by using computer technology to manipulate photographs and screen captures.[2] Again, fan art can be innocuous or strongly sexual; content varies. Sometimes art is created as an illustration for a fanfic, or used as "desktop wallpaper" or icons/avatars for LiveJournal and message board communities. Fans also create "filk," which are fan-composed songs or lyrics to pre-existing songs revised to apply to specific movies, television shows, etc.[3] Finally, fans create "vids," in which they take video clips from films, television shows, or games and edit them together to create music videos.[4] These fan vids can be tributes to particular characters or romantic combinations of characters, or they might deal with general themes from the original texts, or even just be humorous in nature. Clearly, fan creativity has many outlets.

The legality of these outlets has repeatedly been questioned by both corporate lawyers and fans themselves. In nearly every case, characters and concepts have been copyrighted, and fans do not have explicit permission from the creators or distributors to use them. Although there is yet to be a precedent-setting court case to settle the matter, fans continue to include legal disclaimers at the start of their fanfics, fan art, filk, and fan videos. For example, LiveJournaler *Bibliophile20* includes a representative example in her profile, "All of the characters, plotlines and other ideas derived from the books that served as sources for these fics are the property of the authors of those books, their publishers and their distributors. I claim no ownership thereto. None of the writing on this journal was intended for profit, and no money had been or will be accepted for it" (*Bibliophile20*). Additionally, many fans use the Internet to trade copies of the original texts, posting digital versions of clips or entire episodes and films for each other to download. Of course, the legality of this particular practice is hardly a gray area.

One legal issue that *is* somewhat gray is sexually explicit fanfic or fan art featuring illegal sexual acts, or involving underage characters. In May of 2007, this gray area exploded in controversy. Over the Memorial Day weekend, LiveJournal employees abruptly suspended approximately 500 accounts that they claimed "expressed an interest in" or otherwise encouraged illegal behaviors, particularly pedophilia (*ashenseraph*). LiveJournal usernames belonging to the 500 deleted LiveJournals appeared with a line through the letters, in effect, "striking them out"; hence, LiveJournalers refer to this as "LJ Strikethrough."

Along with journals that promoted pedophilia, LiveJournal employees suspended journals belonging to survivors of molestation and incest, to those interested in discussing Vladimir Nabokov's novel *Lolita*, and to those engaged in fan activities (catrinella). Those journals engaged in fan activities included journals containing sexual fan fiction or those kept solely as "Role-Playing Game" character journals. Role Playing Game character journals are journals written from the points of view of various characters and can include those of "villains," and such villains can/might include pedophiles. The crackdown many had feared for some time had arrived; while some suspended accounts were reactivated upon further consideration, many were not, and the possible legal ramifications of fan activity on LiveJournal became strikingly apparent.

Finally, fanfic is sometimes written not about the characters themselves, but the actors and actresses portraying the characters (these stories are labeled "Real Person Fiction").[5] It is not known whether Sarah-Michelle Gellar would appreciate a story detailing a romantic relationship between her and co-star Eliza Dushku, but one can imagine how discomfiting such a thing could be, and why an actor might be compelled to take action against it. These murky legal waters, along with a general societal disdain for the stereotypical "Trekkie," frequently compel fans to shroud their activities in secrecy. After all, the average high-powered executive is not often eager to be "outed" as a person who can quote entire episodes of a "teen" series called *Buffy the Vampire Slayer*. This can lead to double (or even triple, etc.) lives carried out online, with some fans doing everything possible to separate their fannish identities from their "Real Life" ones.

Life, The Buffyverse, and Everything

"I have a life. I simply choose to spend it online," insists one LiveJournaler's icon. It is a sentiment strongly felt in the Buffyverse fandoms, and has been for years. "The Bronze" was a linear message board on the official *Buffy the Vampire Slayer* web site from 1997 to 2001 (Tuszynski 5). "Bronzers," as the board's participants called themselves, developed famously powerful social connections, online and off. In 2003, Stephanie Tuszynski conducted a study of these fans in her investigation of the boundaries between online and "virtual" life, a project that was part of her dissertation and later developed into a documentary film, *IRL (In Real Life)* (2006). A number of her respondents spoke to the unusually strong links maintained after the message board was no longer in existence. "It's changed your life," said one. "You stay in contact with these people because they're not fans of a show like you any-more, they're just your friends. They're just your friends" (Tuszynski 4). This was a pattern Tuszynski observed repeatedly throughout her research. "[I]dentifying as a Bronzer meant something more than simply being a *Buffy* fan. The identity is more complex and is almost entirely rooted in the group of people who made up the community, rather than being attached solely or primarily to the television show" (4). Blurred boundaries such as these naturally lead to complicated sets of Custom Friends Groups when the interaction is taken to LiveJournal.

Whedonverse fans are plentiful online, and LiveJournal is no exception. On July 25th of 2007, a search for the term "Buffy" among official LiveJournal Interests produced 375 communities alone, thirty-three of which had been updated in the previous twenty-four hours. "Joss Whedon," the creator of *Buffy the Vampire Slayer*, and *Angel: The Series*, appeared as an Interest in 399 communities, featuring names such as "Joss_is_God" and "I_heart_Joss." One such community was "The Sunnydale Herald," which acted as a "fandom newsletter" for *Buffy the Vampire Slayer* and *Angel* fandoms; it was a near-daily collection of links to notable fan fiction, graphics, discussions, and fandom news on LiveJournal, along with outside links to series-related news (*lostakasha, piratesword, spuzz*, and *sweptawaybayou*). In its first three years of existence, it collected over 1,100 official readers, and an unknown number of "lurkers." In 2007, four years *after* the series finale of *Buffy*, the community was linking to approximately twenty posts of interest daily. It billed itself as a "selective" newsletter, meaning it was not even a collection of *all* Buffy-verse-related LiveJournal activity — only the editors' top choices.

In fact, it would be almost impossible to accurately estimate the Buffy-verse-related activity that still takes place on LiveJournal on a daily basis. In 2006, a doctoral student at the University of Illinois at Urbana-Champaign conducted an online survey of over 1,500 fans, 55 percent of whom reported having LiveJournal accounts (Buffyverse Fandom Survey). According to Google, the term "Buffy" was used on LiveJournal's domain over 11,000 times from April to October of 2007. LiveJournal fans like these volunteered when the survey for this article was taken. Clearly, despite the cancellation of their shows, Buffyverse fans continue to forge and maintain social links on Live-Journal. The survey conducted for this article is an attempt to explore those social links and their position within Goffman's framework.

Methods

This article is a result of general anecdotal observations collected during three years of participation in fandom on LiveJournal, but more directly, of a survey conducted in December of 2006. Fans of many media texts participated in the survey, with the Buffyverse strongly represented. As of July 2007, nearly half of the respondents still listed at least one of Whedon's series in their LiveJournal Interests, and many listed all three of Whedon's series (including *Firefly* [Fox, 2003]), and even the phrase "Joss Whedon," as one of their LiveJournal Interests. From this point on, this article refers more generally to LiveJournal users who responded to the survey, with the understanding that a significant portion of these respondents were Buffyverse fans.

The survey was posted in a LiveJournal created specifically for this project, using LiveJournal's built-in "Create a Poll" feature, which would be familiar to most participants. The survey was a combination of thirty-two fixed-response and free-response questions, and garnered 352 replies. Approximately 35 percent of respondents identified themselves as between nineteen and twenty-four years old, with another 35 percent identifying as between twenty-five and thirty-five years of age. The next most common demographic was between thirty-six and forty-five years old (16 percent), followed by between thirteen and eighteen years old (9 percent) and between forty-six and fifty-five years old (5 percent), and capped off by one respondent over the age of fifty-five. About 29 percent of respondents had been on LiveJournal for between two and three years, followed by 24 percent at between three and four years. The remaining 46 percent was about evenly split between less than two years and more than four years. Over 94 percent of respondents spend at least thirty minutes per day actively reading or posting on LiveJournal, with a majority (57 percent) spending between one and three hours per day, and another 21 percent spending more than three hours daily on LiveJournal. These survey demographics are in keeping with general observations of fandoms as a whole on LiveJournal.

Respondents were recruited by posting notice of this survey in a popular LiveJournal community named "fanthropology," made up of LiveJournalers (both academic and non-academic) who are interested in academic study of fan activity. As of December 2006, there were 1,416 LiveJournal users who watched this community, with an unknown number of people who watched the community, but did not join or participate in it (*dragonscholar* and *sailormac*). The survey was also announced in an individual personal journal, which was watched by 172 LiveJournal members and an unknown number of non–LiveJournal readers. The survey was then linked to by the editors of the LiveJournal community "metafandom," which is a thrice-weekly collection of links to posts of "interesting discussion in fandom," and had 2,224 watchers at the time (*cathexys*, et. al). Thanks to these three "advertisements," responses from over 350 people were collected in a very short period of time. Over 100 people filled out the survey in the first ten hours, and that number passed 200 by the next day. The survey had over 330 respondents by the fourth day, when participation abruptly slowed.

This is typical of the "lifecycle" of a post on LiveJournal, where most activity is high-volume, fast-paced and extremely current. Posts rarely receive attention after the initial flurry of responses because readers have already moved on to the plenitude of other material being posted at every hour of the day. The strong response to the survey is indicative of the navel-gazing that is characteristic to fandom, especially on LiveJournal. The existence of communities like "fanthropology," "metafandom," and many others shows the drive within the fan community to analyze and understand itself. This article is in service of that end.

"Friends Locking" and the Back Region

As Goffman pointed out, "Although particular performances, and even particular parts or routines, may place a performer in a position of having nothing to hide, somewhere in the full round of his activities there will be something he cannot treat openly" (64). This claim fits with reported use of LiveJournal's "Friends lock" feature; almost 65 percent of respondents to this survey reported locking at least some posts, and over 18 percent reported locking *all* of their posts. Goffman's concept of "front" and "back" regions can be applied to this situation.

Many fans treat their locked posts in general as "back" regions where "the impression fostered by the performance is knowingly contradicted as a matter of course" (112). They might put forth a certain image in their public, "front" posts or comments (for example, a strictly heterosexual female), but when they relax in the "back" region of their locked posts, "dark" secrets may be revealed (for example, that the poster actually identifies as a bisexual person) (Goffman 141). They have different faces for different audiences.

This idea of regions is especially relevant considering the demographic make-up of Whedonverse fandoms. For example, in the Urbana-Champaign "Buffyverse Fandom Survey" mentioned earlier, of the respondents who claimed to be members of a *cultural* minority, 52 percent (over 200 fans) listed "sexual orientation" as the minority group in question.

Among the backstage behaviors observed by Goffman, evidence of "reciprocal first-naming" can be seen in the use of LiveJournal usernames and pseudonyms; "profanity" that would not normally appear in more dignified, "safe to view at work" unlocked posts; "open sexual remarks" in the form of sexual commentary or sexually explicit fiction; "elaborate griping" often aimed at colleagues, politicians, and the creators of the media texts; "use of dialect" seen in prevalent fandom and/or LiveJournal slang and punctuation practices; "playful aggressivity and 'kidding'" aimed at other LiveJournal friends; and "inconsiderateness for the other" often at work in posts secretly complaining about mutual acquaintances in fandom (Goffman 128).

Interestingly, while in Goffman's model higher status means *less* time spent "backstage" (133), in this social establishment, higher status in fandom usually entails *more* time "backstage." Some fans, often dubbed "Big Name Fans," carry higher status than others due to their popularity and influence in the fan community. When the average fan with little stature in the community makes a controversial unlocked post, not many people take notice. If a "Big Name Fan" makes the same unlocked post, a storm of debate can follow; thus, fans of high status often find themselves locking more posts than they did in their days of obscurity. In any case, for a majority of the fans who responded to this survey, there was *something* in their lives worth hiding from *someone*.

In an attempt to identify those elements, the survey asked respondents to check off the various types of posts that they lock, selecting as many as applied from a list of ten fixed choices with an option to specify an "other" answer. The most popular answer was "any post that I do not want others to publicly link to" (40 percent). This can be seen as a reflection on the public/private nature of communication on LiveJournal. Despite the many built-in functions that attempt to connect people and make social links, there is sometimes a wish for the discussion to remain "in the family," so to speak. This means that the original poster does not want her journal's regular readers to bring in new ones for this particular post, especially if the content is inflammatory or in reference to other fans who might take offense. The next most popular response (at 33 percent) was "any post that contains photographs of me or my friends and family," likely showing respondents' desire to keep online and offline lives separated and a knowledge of the possible havoc that could be wreaked by an enemy with digital imaging software. At 30 percent was "Other," and submitted answers included references to media sharing (another "dark secret" worth protecting), possibly offensive posts, possibly controversial posts, original or adult-oriented fiction, and financial discussion. One fan claimed she simply locked "[a]nything where someone Googling their name or organization could find the entry and not be pleased." Remaining selected answers included posts that reference jobs (25 percent) and love lives (20 percent), and at 18 percent each were "references to people I know in 'Real Life,'" "an embarrassing story about me," and "I lock all of my posts." Posts containing "discussion of another fan or group of fans" came in at 14 percent, but more interestingly, "any post that is not about fandom" was the least popular selection, at only 11 percent. While many fans describe efforts to keep their fan lives separate from their offline lives, only a total of thirty-five respondents reported doing so in this somewhat simple fashion. There apparently remains a wish for some elements of the non-fannish self to be presented alongside the fannish self.

"Filters" and Audience Segregation

It is almost as if LiveJournal programmers were in conversation with Goffman when they created the "filtering" capabilities on their web site. "Incapacity to maintain this [region] control leaves the performer in a position of not knowing what character he will have to project from one moment to the next, making it difficult for him to effect a dramaturgical success in any one of them," argued Goffman (137). This difficulty prompts the performer to seek ways to separate (or "segregate") his audience into specific groups. On LiveJournal, filters grant this control to the user and thus increase her chances of successfully navigating among the numerous characters she plays. Nearly 87 percent of respondents reported using filters, with a plurality (39 percent) citing controlled reader access as the primary motivation to do so, while only 21 percent use filters primarily to control their Friends page views. The remaining 27 percent used filters for both purposes. When asked how many filters they used, "7+" was the most common answer at 30 percent. With such widespread use, patterns are likely to emerge.

The most popular type of filter was "an interest-specific filter — e.g., only people in specific fandoms or hobbies," with 60 percent of respondents selecting that option. The next most popular answer was "a 'Real Life' filter — only people who know me offline" (45 percent) and "a 'quick' filter — when I have time to read only the most essential journals and communities" (42 percent). The first and third answers imply use related to one's own Friends page views, while the second seems to most often refer more to controlling access to locked posts (although one fan did describe a "locals" filter, "people with whom i might soon be physically interacting [so information is time-critical and reading first could be important]"). Many fans described having "levels" of filters according to how close they felt to various people, and how much they trusted them with more personal or "Real Life" issues. One fan went so far as to declare having "one filter for every person so [she] can choose exactly who reads [her] posts." This relates to another common answer to the question of filter types, which was "a filter that specifically blocks certain people on my [Friends List] (e.g., a romantic partner)" (37 percent). This type of filter follows the practice Goffman observed of a user "exclud[ing] from the audience those before whom he performed in the past a show inconsistent with the current one" (137–138). Segregation of audiences is as much a matter of who is *excluded* as who is included.

In fact, some fans choose to bypass the use of filters all together and create entirely separate journals for different elements of their lives. Nearly 29 percent of respondents reported having done so, with the most frequent genres being "one fannish, one personal or 'Real Life.'" Many reported having specific journals for their writing (both original and fan fiction), for fan art, or for recommendations of others' work. Some had special journals for use in Role-Playing Games, in which they took on a different kind of separate identity. One fan who claimed a separate journal for "fic, meta and stuff that I want people to see" explained that she created the journal at a time when she wanted to keep her fannish activities secret from those in her "Real Life," but that it did not matter anymore. Other fans mentioned owning separate journals, "but it's a hassle" or that they "haven't looked at [them] in more than a year." Their intentions to present different versions of themselves had diminished over time. Although the survey asked respondents to treat separate journals as filters for the remainder of the questions, one fan pointed out that they are *not* interchangeable, and that they are "set up specifically to follow different rules." Another fan said that she had no desire to lock any of her posts, only to segregate her audiences. She did not mind if unknown fans read her fannish posts, only that her "Real Life" friends did not. Having separate, unlinked journals allowed her a specialized version of impression management — she could post publicly while still presenting different selves to different audiences.[6]

"Real Life" and the Self as Performed Character

In his book, Goffman differentiates between two parts of the individual: the *performer*, "a harried fabricator of impressions involved in the all-too-human task of staging a performance," and the *character*, "a figure, typically a fine one, whose spirit, strength, and other sterling qualities the performance was designed to evoke" (252). The difficulty in identifying these different aspects of the self is reflected in the challenge of defining the common Internet term "Real Life." Is "Real Life" the "character" behind a LiveJournal user, or is it just a different performance? Can these two aspects ever be thought of independently?

When the survey asked respondents to define "Real Life," some fans answered simply and briefly, while others took the opportunity to protest popular usage of the term. The word "offline" was used in a vast majority of the free-response answers, followed by answers along the lines of, "That which is not fandom," as one fan declared. For these respondents, their lives are a dichotomy in which everything can be classified as fandom or non-fandom; it is the determining factor in how they interpret their experiences. Some fans pointed to the original circumstances under which they met the people in question when deciding whether they are part of their "real lives." Many of these same respondents had included "face to face interaction" as part of their definitions, but since their fannish activities had brought them into physical contact with other fans, they wanted to clarify that these interactions were still different from "Real Life." For others, these fandom-induced physical interactions were just as "real."

One fan summed up her feelings by defining "Real Life" as "All of my life. I segregate by Online and Offline lives. Just because it's online doesn't make it not real." This was a sentiment expressed by many respondents uncomfortable with the term, "Real Life." One fan in particular posted a longer comment in response to the survey as a whole, explaining her view of the situation. She was house-bound, on medical retirement from her job.

> "I'm real when I'm on-line, on LJ, etc." she claimed. "I don't suddenly become a different person, thus it is my 'real life'.... Do you know of people in your non-on-line world who talk about their 'real life' as opposed to their hobbies and interests? I certainly don't."

Fans who have conducted romantic relationships online or primarily online were particularly upset about the term. For some, rather than "Real Life" and "Non-Real Life" filters, they had something like "Close" and "Closer" filters, disregarding the online/offline status of the relationships and relying solely on levels of personal trust. Explained one fan, her "Real Life" consisted of "People, interests, and activities that I would still be involved with if my Internet connection went down forever." For these fans, the Internet does not differentiate between types of friends; it only facilitates the friendships. The "performer" and the "character" are inextricably linked.

While 45 percent of respondents claimed to have a "Real Life" filter, there were also 24 percent who claimed to have a "Non-Real Life" filter ("only people who do *not* know me offline"). The uses of these two types of filters are related in an intriguing way. The survey asked this group of respondents to elaborate on how they used their "Real Life" and "Non-Real Life" filters. While it was expected that some fans would classify certain things as "too private for Internet-only acquaintances" (also 24 percent), another 19 percent of the group designated some things as "too private for people who know me in Real Life." To them, there are some things you can only say to people you will not have to confront in the morning; a faceless Internet can be a great confidant to many people. The other 57 percent said that they used their filters for both reasons, depending on the topic. Extremely personal issues, family, and work complaints topped the list of posts locked under "Real Life" and "Non–Real Life" filters.

For some fans, participation in "slash" fandom was reason enough to lock posts from the eyes of certain readers. "Slash" is usually defined as homosexual romantic pairings of characters (or actors in Real Person Fiction), and makes up a significant portion — if not the majority of many media fandoms' fan fiction, fan art, and fan vids. For some fans, there are people on their Friends Lists who would not understand or approve of slash discussion or fiction. These fans sometimes choose to either hide their slash activity for their own comfort of self-presentation or simply decline to discuss it in deference to their readers' sensibilities. At times, use of these filters is purely a matter of public relations. "I think of my LJ as semi-professional," explained one fan. "As in, if I ever become a famous writer, people could come back and read my old archives. Therefore I lock whatever I would not want known to the general public." Her "performer" is protecting the future reputation of her "character."

When Goffman described the individual as performer, he depicted that performer as sometimes having fantasies and dreams "full of anxiety and dread that nervously deal with vital discreditings in a public front region." The performer has a "capacity for deeply felt shame, leading him to minimize the chances he takes of exposure" (253). Along these lines, this survey asked respondents whether they maintained filters to hide certain aspects of their lives from people on their Friends List (as opposed to hiding things from the general public). Examples provided with the question were "sexual orientation or participation in NC-17 fandom." Only 25 percent of respondents reported having such a filter, although another 13 percent said they had considered it. Types of "hiding" filters included ones that specifically excluded individuals, such as family members. For example, one fan did not want her mother reading that she was failing certain subjects in school. Another fan said, "I don't think my roommate needs to get details on my sex interests." Several people listed "slash" or sexual filters (including "porn" and "kink"), offering reasons such as, "I keep real life people out of the sexuality stuff because it would be embarrassing to see them in person knowing they knew that about me." Some respondents cited a concern that certain readers do not approve of certain activities, and these respondents feared losing certain "Real Life" friends if they explained their fannish lives. One fan who did not use "hiding" filters but had considered it defended them by saying, "Anything one can use to feel more open to freely express themselves, at least in this small way, is something worth considering." In her view, closing down audience access can open up performances.

When asked to explain why they did *not* use such filters, some fans were offended by the idea. "I don't friend people that I feel wouldn't accept me as a person," said one fan. Another fan agreed, saying simply, "I am who I am.

Why hide it?" Others were concerned about the security of information posted on the Internet, even under supposedly private conditions. "If I wanted to hide something, I wouldn't mention it ANYWHERE online!" declared one respondent. One fan believed that "your interests on LJ are abundantly clear from looking at your friends and communities, so it's pointless [to try to hide things]." Several fans pointed to a feeling of "we're all here for the same thing," or "we're all a bit deviant here on LJ anyway, so why bother?" One fan said that filters felt "dishonest" to her and that she found them "distasteful" all together. If the self as a performed character is "a dramatic effect arising diffusely from a scene that is presented" (253), she desired to present that scene as honestly as possible.

"Opt-in Filters," Pseudonyms, and the Role of the Audience

"Friends locking" and filters would likely be defined as "defensive practices" by Goffman, or "strategies and tactics to protect [one's] own projections." Yet Goffman also spoke of "protective practices" or "tact," which he defined as "when a participant employs [these strategies] to save the definition of the situation projected by another" (13–14). With this he acknowledges the active role often played by the audience in their reception of a performance. On LiveJournal, there are some situations where the audience member has the opportunity to shape his own segregation and avoid the "difficult problems in impression management that arise" when "an outsider happens upon a performance not meant for him" (139). These cases are usually called "opt-in" (or "opt-out") filters, wherein the LiveJournaler asks her readers whether they would prefer to be included in or excluded from certain filters. The idea is to avoid "boring" or offending readers with posts about jobs or controversial activities (such as drug use or Bondage & Domination/Sadism & Masochism experiences). Some fans feel freer to post about these topics if they know their readers have specifically requested hearing about them, or they feel secure in the knowledge that they gave the readers the opportunity to avoid hearing about them.

About 15 percent of respondents reported having such a filter, although another 17 percent had considered it. Popular types of "opt-in/out" filters submitted to the survey included ones about jobs, academia, fandom in general, specific fandoms, "Real Life," writing, weight loss, politics, religion, and pornography. One fan clarified that while she makes all of her filters "opt-in," she retains the right of "final say." Some fans spoke of attempts to create "opt-in" filters, but no longer used them. "I *used* to have a slash filter, and I feel better now I don't use it anymore," stressed one respondent. Another respondent tried to make a filter about her studies, but claimed that everyone had "opted in," so she never created it. In her case, audience segregation was simply not necessary.

Similarly, even when reading public (unlocked) posts, it is customary for many users to comment on the post and let the author know that they are now reading or that they have Friended the author. This practice is similar to the warning messages, knocks, or coughs described by Goffman when watching the Shetland crofters approach each others' homes, prompting the homeowners to fix "proper expressions" upon their faces (229). Despite the fact that the post is not locked, the author has little reason to assume that many non–Friends will stumble upon her journal and begin reading. This courtesy can be a result of a desire on the reader's part to have the same courtesy extended to her by new readers of her own journal. As Goffman explained, one motivation for tact is the audience's "immediate identification with the performers" (232). The audience can thus take an active role in its interpellation as both reader and segregated reader.

Sometimes the audience has a more indirect effect on the LiveJournal post. Possible online and offline effects on the lives of the discussed prompt some authors to use caution. Many LiveJournalers choose not to use real names when discussing people online, instead electing to assign pseudonyms or just initials. Over 58 percent of respondents in this poll acknowledge following this practice, with many qualifying that they usually do so only for people without LiveJournal usernames to employ instead. Overwhelmingly, the reason given for this practice was "to protect privacy." Most reasoned that while *they* had chosen to share personal accounts with others, their friends and family "haven't signed up to have their lives posted on the internet." Some respondents were concerned about embarrassing their "Real Life" acquaintances and family, or endangering their jobs. A few respondents noted that it seemed "rude" to use real names, and that they were simply following custom. This is similar to the individuals whom Goffman observed acting in specific ways because "the tradition of [their] group of social status require[d] this kind of expression" (6). One fan claimed she used pseudonyms and initials for "plausible deniability," implying a tendency to speak ill of people and a wish not to be held accountable.

Some respondents disagreed with the practice of excluding "real" names. "I'm not in high school," asserted one fan. "I friend lock my posts and I am aware of who reads them. Initials or pseudonyms are cop outs." One fan claimed that filters were a better outlet for fears that lead to pseudonym use. Others said they did not post anything that would embarrass them if the person discussed were to find out, or that they did not post about other people at all. Whether they choose to follow these conventions or not, LiveJournalers constantly take their possible audiences into account. Another reason for the tradition was explained by this respondent: "I think it's easier for people to relate to a story about people they don't know if I use a pseudonym." For this fan, the ultimate goal of the post is not necessarily to inform others about her life, but to tell engaging stories. She is accounting for both the audience she is discussing *and* the audience who happens to be reading, and allowing both to guide her performance.

In the End

As Goffman mused, "All the world is not, of course, a stage, but the crucial ways in which it isn't are not easy to specify" (72). Goffman's stage is vast indeed. He used dramaturgical terminology to analyze face-to-face social interaction, taking a few-to-many situation and using it to analyze a one-to-few situation. Applying his work to the Internet and specifically LiveJournal blogs returns the interaction to a one-to-many scenario. The management of audience is complicated on the Web by a lack of knowledge about that audience.

Annie Sewell-Jennings assumed that she was just posting to her friends when she joked in an unlocked LiveJournal post about her anger at President Bush and what she wished would happen to him. A few weeks later, the Secret Service appeared on her doorstep, "tipped" that Sewell-Jennings had threatened the President by another LiveJournal user — with a grudge. Sewell-Jennings posted about her experience, warning other LiveJournalers, "I want people to be aware that what they say on their LJ can cause problems for them in RL, because I love all of you and I don't wish what happened to me on you" (Sewell-Jennings). Hers was a harsh lesson to learn.

The average blogger has no idea who might be reading. The blogger on LiveJournal, however, has a unique opportunity to define her audience and exert control over it. Finally, the media fan on LiveJournal may have more reason than most to thoughtfully coordinate and delineate her various online identities. "Jane" might not choose to have her colleague or her daughter read the pornographic Xander/Spike fanfic she wrote the night before; she also might balk at her friends in the Xander/Spike pornographic fanfic community discovering her offline occupation of kindergarten teacher in Pleasantville, Colorado. The agency over presentation of self that is lost in the move from meatspace to cyberspace is returned to her by LiveJournal's Friends locking and filtering features. They grant her a multiplicity of customized stages on which to perform.

Notes

1. For example, see: "FanFiction.net." *http://www.fanfiction.net*
2. For example, see: "Michelle Rodriguez Underground Fan Hub." *http://www.mclaughlinlabs.com/leigh/fans/artwork.htm*
3. For example, see: DAG Productions. "Filk.com." *http://www.filk.com/*
4. For example, see: "sisabet.com: Elephant Momentum!" *http:3/www.sisabet.com/*
5. For example, see: shirasade. "Monaboyd.net — for all your Dom/Billy needs." *http://monaboyd.net/*
6. Of course, the use of multiple identities is not unique to LiveJournal; countless New Media scholars have investigated the ways in which individuals manipulate their many online profiles in message board communities, bulletin board systems, chat rooms, Massively Multi-player Online Games, etc. LiveJournal simply offers a new framework.

Works Cited

ashenseraph. "LJ Strikethrough: Info for Scholars and Reporters." *LiveJournal.com*. 20 May 2007. 02 August 2007 <http://ashenseraph.livejournal.com/98293.html>.

bibliophile20. "bibliophile20 Profile." *LiveJournal.com*. 2005–2006. 02 August 2007 <http://bibliophile20.livejournal.com/profile>.

Blogger. 2007. Google. 14 October 2007. <https://www.blogger.com/>

"Buffyverse Fandom Survey." 02 August 2007 <http://www.geocities.com/ljficwriters/>.

cathexys, fabu, fairestcat, inalasahl, isiscolo, lim, lonelywalker, and oulangi. "metafandom Profile." *LiveJournal.com*. Created January 2005. 02 August 2007. <http://community.livejournal.com/metafandom/profile>.

catrinella. "'Permanent Suspensions,' or Strikethrough2007." 31 May 2007. *LiveJournal.com*. 14 October 2007. <http://catrinella.livejournal.com/151812.html>.

DAG Productions. "Filk.com" 2006. 02 August 2007 <http://www.filk.com/>.

dragonscholar and sailormac. "fanthropology Profile." *LiveJournal.com*. November 2005 <http://community.livejournal.com/fanthropology/profile>.

fan_research. "Poll #888504: LiveJournal, Filters, Fandom, and 'Real Life.'" 14 December 2006. Survey conducted by author via *LiveJournal.com*. 02 August 2007 <http://www.livejournal.com/poll/?id=888504>.

"FanFiction.net." 02 August 2007 <http://www.fanfiction.net>.

Goffman, Erving. *The Presentation of Self in Everyday Life*. New York: Doubleday, 1959.

krisomniac and vichan. "fandom_counts Profile." *LiveJournal.com*. 30 May 2007. 02 August 2007 <http://community.livejournal.com/fandom_counts/profile>.

Leigh. "Michelle Rodriguez Underground Fan Hub." *MRU*. 2006. 02 August 2007 <http://www.mclaughlinlabs.com/leigh/fans/artwork.htm>.

"LiveJournal Home Page." *LiveJournal.com*. 2007. SixApart. 14 October 2007. <http://www.livejournal.com/>.

lostakasha, piratesword, spuzz, and sweptawaybayou. "The Sunnydale Herald Profile." *LiveJournal.com*. 03 August 2007. 03 August 2007. <http://community.livejournal.com/su_herald/profile>.

"Quick Tour." *LiveJournal.com*. 2007. 14 October 2007. <http://www.livejournal.com/tour/>.

Sewell-Jennings, Annie. "a word to the wise." *LiveJournal.com*. 27 October 2004. 02 August 2007 <http://anniesj.livejournal.com/331112.html>.

shirasade. "Monaboyd.net — for all your Dom/Billy needs." 16 November 2006. 02 August 2007 <http://monaboyd.net/>.

Sisabet. "sisabet.com: Elephant Momentum!" November 2005. 02 August 2007 <http://www.sisabet.com/>.

Tszuynski, Stephanie. "IRL (In Real Life): Breaking Down the Binary of Offline vs. Online Social Interaction." Dissertation, Graduate College of Bowling Green State University. May 2006. 02 August 2007 <http://www.ohiolink.edu/etd/send-pdf.cgi?bgsu1143431168>.

Acknowledgments: The author wishes to acknowledge Professor Christine Garlough for her guidance in the research for this article, as well as Randy Wedin, Carla Lee, and Keith D. for their help in the preparation of the final manuscript. The author also wishes to thank the members of the Media and Cultural Studies area in the Department of Communication Arts at the University of Wisconsin — Madison for their input on this project.

So, What's the Story? Story-Oriented and Series-Oriented Fans: A Complex of Behaviors

Mary Kirby-Diaz

Introduction

What happens if you don't like the plot of your favorite TV show? Do you take it in stride? Complain to the network or the show's producers or creative team? Do you go online to one of the show's fan boards and complain? Do you search for Internet fan fiction that will change what you didn't like? Will you write fan fiction to re-write the show's mythos to one that is more to your liking? How invested are you in the fandom of your favorite TV show? How committed a fan are you? Are you a story-oriented fan or a series-oriented fan?[1]

Previous research on fandoms has noted that most fans view a TV series' episode, and then forget about it.[2] Occasionally, a show will engender such interest that it may become fodder for the "water cooler"—it will be discussed at work, at school, and in social gatherings. However, for some fans—particularly Internet fans—their favorite TV series is not just fodder for the water cooler—it is a way of life, a sub-cultural community that has an impact on their lives.

Internet fandoms are relatively easy to create: Take one inventive television series with clever writing and direction, add telegenic actors, a series website and a fan board. Advertise, broadcast, and wait. Voilá! A fandom is created. What sustains a television fandom? *Buffy the Vampire Slayer* ended its first-showing run in May 2003; the following year, *Angel: The Series* was cancelled. Their combined fandoms continue. What sustains this fandom? Who are the fans? How does the fandom continue when both series are over, and the actors and creative staff have moved onto other series?

But are fandoms an undifferentiated mass or are there different groups of fans that comprise a fandom? If there are different groups of fans, how do some fandoms maintain themselves despite the differences between them? The answers to these two questions are the goals of a long-term study on the Buffy and Angel 'verse Internet fandom.

Goals of the Study

This article will focus on the following question: are there different groups of fans that comprise a fandom? It is one of the hypotheses of the long-term research project this article emanates from that fandoms are maintained by at least two groups of fans: story-oriented fans and series-oriented fans. The goal of this particular research project is primarily descriptive — an exploration of two types of fans: story-oriented and series-oriented.

Most studies on fandoms have not included much research by sociologists, despite the impact of the media in our lives. This study is the exception; it is sociologically-based, rather than emerging from the usual background of Fandom Studies, Cultural Studies, Media Studies or Journalism. Sociological concepts referred to herein are sociological concepts — via Durkheim (Durkheim, rep. 1971) and Simmel (Simmel, rep. 1971) — who wrote in the nineteenth century — and whose works are still relevant and still resonate with import for studies of groups in today's society.

Production of Culture vs. Consumption of Culture

The community of story-oriented fans is supported by *production of culture* — specifically fan fiction and fan vidding, which serve to maintain the *mythos* of the series. However, the community of series-oriented fans is supported by activities that are designed to *consume* and maintain the *series* — concerts, fan conventions, video games, and comic books. There is considerable overlap; fans who are story-oriented also love the series, and fans who are series-oriented also love the mythos. However, most fans can be categorized as belonging primarily into one of these two categories. Together they provide the momentum needed to maintain a fandom long after a series has been cancelled or has ended its run. Much has been written about the role of production of culture in maintaining fandoms (Jenkins, 1992; Hills, 2002; Bacon-Smith, 1992, and others), but for a fandom to survive, it must not only provide for the *production* of culture but the *consumption* of culture. Fortunately, there are fans more (or less) interested in each process.

Audiences Become Fandoms

Until the late 1990s, audiences were considered to be essentially passive, non-cohesive publics, moving somewhat willy-nilly, as television executives created and canceled series (Lewis, 1992). If fans were attached to a particular series, it was held to be a transient attachment. Shortly after a series' demise, it was believed fans would move onto The Next Big Series Hit and forget about the series of the past. However, research by Jenkins, MacDonald, Gillilan, and Benshoff, indicate that the obverse is true. TV audiences are not passive, and indeed, often take an active role in not only participating in the life of an ongoing series, but in maintaining a series long after its demise, going so far as to actively produce fan art that would perpetuate the series' stories (Jenkins, 1992).

The original *Star Trek* television series ran for three seasons, starting in 1966. Thirty-eight years later, the *Star Trek* franchise demonstrates the power of fandoms. Five separate series, eight feature films, and hundreds of scholarly articles later, we have evidence that fans don't give up — they hang on — and on and on. Lest we think the *Star Trek* franchise is an anomaly, there are other fandoms that persist. Unlike *Star Trek*, which lasted three seasons (eighty episodes), *Firefly* barely lasted one season. Thirteen episodes were shot, ten were broadcast, and the fandom went wild when it was canceled. Three years later, the fans' wish was granted: the movie, *Serenity*, continued *Firefly*'s story on the big screen. Not content with that story, *Firefly*'s saga continues in comic book form.

We see it also in the Buffy and Angel fandom. *Buffy the Vampire Slayer* and *Angel: The Series* were both produced and created by Joss Whedon. *BtVS* ended its seven seasons run in 2003. *AtS* ran for five seasons, ending its run in 2004. Although their fans now view other TV shows, and have become invested in newer series — *Veronica Mars, Heroes, Lost, Dr. Who, Torchwood, Battlestar Galactica, Bones* — many remain a part of the Angel and Buffy fandom.

Social Cohesion

Classical Durkheimian theory regards social cohesion as the glue that holds society together. When we use the term, "social cohesion," we are referring to the bonds between people in a society. The tighter the bonds, the harder it becomes for people to leave the society, or to act in ways that are not socially approved. The looser the bonds, the easier it is to leave the society, the easier it is to act in ways that are not socially approved. Viewed from this perspective, communities are tightly bonded groups that "hold fast." Few members leave the group, and when they do leave, they miss the group, and the feelings of community they shared with the group. Thus, social cohesion is a major component in an individual's sense of community. Without a strong sense of social cohesion, communities cannot maintain themselves.

Fandoms — particularly Internet fandoms — are communities composed of individual fans who are socially bonded by their experiences as fans of specific TV series, movies (like *The Fast and the Furious*), books (like the *Harry Potter* series), musicians, and sporting teams. Internet fans can become a community through repeated, intense communication with others on subjects of interest to them; this has been demonstrated by previous research by Kirby-Diaz, Ali, Coon, and others.[3] Computer-mediated communication has altered the face of interpersonal communications — people living thousands of miles apart can easily communicate with each other, and a common icebreaker is a TV series' fan board, wherein fans begin communicating with each other about a particular episode and sometimes stay to chat about other issues that are important in their lives.

According to sociological researcher Don Dillman, Internet users tend to be more committed — and that commitment is more intense — than those who do not regularly use the Internet (Dillman, 2000). This commitment and intensity operates regardless of the reason for the Internet usage. Sports fans, working people, cult TV fans, researchers — tend to communicate more intensely over the 'Net — and for this reason, Internet surveys can oftimes produce more powerful responses from participants than surveys gleaned from respondents chosen "off the street."

Internet Fans Cross the Border

Most fans of TV series don't automatically watch a show, and then search for other fans on the Internet with whom to chat. "Something" impels them to seek out others to discuss the series, the plot, characters, mythos, cast, and/or the writers. A fan must literally "cross the border" — that is, must consciously make the effort to find a fan board, seek feedback, and reaffirm their status as loyal fan.

What brings a fan to cross the border and communicate with others on the Internet is still subject to discussion and research. What we do know is that, generally speaking, many fans who do "cross that border" report that their lives are never quite the same again.[4] If a fan "crosses the border" are there other behaviors that accompany that crossing? If so, what are the other behaviors?

What separates the "ordinary" fan that enjoys a show, then forgets about it until the next episode, from the fan who participates in the fandom as a member of the more intense Internet fandom community? What separates the fan who attends a concert or movie primarily because one of the featured performers is an actor in a TV series of which she/he has become a fan from the moviegoer/concertgoer who is not there to see the featured TV actor? Who creates fan art — be it a drawing or illustration of a character in the series, a video inspired by the show, a piece of fan fiction that tells the story the fan wants told? What is the relationship between the fan who, involved in one/all of these activities, becomes *invested* in the fandom?

For members of an Internet fandom, watching each episode — as broadcast on TV, as well as via DVD — becomes a central point in their lives. Their loyalty to the series remains strong and committed well past the show's lifetime. An Internet fan's *Weltanschauung* expands to include the culture of the fandom. It has been noted that many Internet fans continue to attend fan conventions, produce fan culture — such as fan fiction, fan videos, and fan art, purchase DVDs and comic books, long after a series' cancellation. Years later they remain invested fans.

Much research attests to the necessity of the Internet for the preservation and expansion of the Buffy and Angel fandoms.[5] Fan boards provide fans with a means by which they can "check in" daily with other fans; it creates a sub-culture commonly called a "cult fandom," that metaphorically lives in the Buffyverse and Angelverse. Members discuss upcoming 'verse-related events, such as concerts, or new work obtained by the casts and the writers of the shows. They post new pictures of the actors and writer, as well as information about upcoming movies and TV shows which the actors and writers will be associated with.

Story-Orientation and the Production of Culture; Series-Orientation and the Consumption of Culture

The fan frustrated by the killing of a favorite character, or the fan whose 'ship has been destroyed by the show's writers, can seek out fan fiction that will re-tell the story to the fan's liking. Such fan fiction can relieve the frustration caused by an unpopular plot point.

Prior to the Internet, fan fiction was available to fans through 'zines — periodicals that published fan fiction. Today fans rarely publish stories in 'zines; they produce fan fiction (fan fic) and post it directly to the Internet via blogs such as LiveJournal, GreatestJournal, InsaneJournal, and JournalFen. Today, fans read fan fiction through the Internet, rather than in hard-copy format. It's accessible; it's free, and it works to help keep the fandom going. Fandoms and Internet fan fiction are mutually-reinforcing. Each keeps the other going, in a circle of energy and engagement that reinforces the importance of the virtual community as agency through which the fandom is maintained.

It can be said that the true Buffyite and Angelite exists in a Buffyverse made unique and richer by the (sometimes) synergistic energy of fan fiction writers. Fan fiction writers — who write without remuneration — post their tales on Internet fan boards, blogs, Internet fan fiction archives, and writer's personal archives. Fans write the fan fiction; other fans read the fan fiction; loyalty for the series' is maintained through the energy and creativity of the fan ficcers and their readers — all through Internet fan boards.

Although the role of fan fiction is significant in maintaining (and increasing) a fandom, it is not the only culture produced by fans. Many fans are accomplished in creating short videos that visually perform the same service for fans as fan fiction.

However, the same can be said for fan conventions, scholarly conferences such as the various Popular Culture Association conferences and The Slayage conferences, concerts and performances by series' actors and musicians, and the continuing availability of series-related merchandise, such as comics, figurines, and video games. These items of *consumption* also serve to maintain the fandom. Series-oriented fans abound at conferences and conventions, attend plays and concerts featuring the regular (and guest) actors, and purchase the never-ending supply of merchandise that is series-related. Of course, communication about these activities is transmitted via fan boards, blogs, and e-mail. The Internet is a key factor in creating a fandom community and maintaining it.

It is not the sole efforts of fans that produce culture that maintains the fandom; it takes more than fan fiction to keep a community alive. Rather, it is the *combination* of activities — the synergy of consumption and production that provides the energy and momentum that keep the fandom active, alive, and interested in the series' long after it's ceased to be syndicated. Next we must ask: who are story-oriented fans and series-oriented fans, and what are the differences between them?

Story-Oriented Fans and Series-Oriented Fans

Who are the fans that care so passionately about a series that they won't let it die? For some fans — particularly those who interact through the Internet, membership in a fandom is actually a membership in a *community* of fans who become engaged in a complex of behaviors that serve to intensify the fandom experience. This intensification leads to continuing engagement with the series — and the fandom — long past a series' demise. Fans become *invested* in a series or in the characters' mythos — and keep "hangin' on." This complex of behaviors that was discussed above creates the fandom community relies on fans being story-oriented or series-oriented.

Story-oriented fans are attracted to the mythos — the plot lines, plot arcs, characters, heroes, villains and archetypal patterns of the series' canon.[6] Story-oriented fans care passionately about the mythos of the series. They are intensely interested in relationships (called 'ships) between characters.

As such, story-oriented fans are fascinated by "the story" more than the overall concept of "the series." They are not particularly interested in the actors, writers, and creator's version of "canon." If a plot line or plot arc is not to their liking — for whatever reason — they are more likely to seek out or even re-write what they don't like to please their sense of storyline. If a plot point displeases them, they will look for — and sometimes re-write — the story as *they* want to read it. They are more likely to produce their own episodes via fan fiction, fanvidding, and filks, than are series-oriented fans. Story-oriented fans are more likely to look for Internet fan fiction, read fan fiction, and write fan fiction than series-oriented fans.

Story-oriented fans produce their own culture, in the forms of fan fiction, fanvideos, filks, poetry, and fan art. Story-oriented fans often perceive a series as raw material from which to garner plot ideas for fan fiction and fanvidding. They have a unique awareness of the *potential* for plot arcs, plotlines, relationships, and character growth and development.

'Ships and Fics

'Ship refers to romantic relationships between fictional characters (Generally, the dominant character's name is "slashed" first). There are lots of 'ships in the Buffy and Angel 'verse — fifty-three 'ships were identified for purposes of that survey, and many participants added 'ships to their questionnaires that were not originally included. It was demonstrated that fandoms are enhanced by 'ships and fan fiction.

Fan fiction (or *Fics*) is the oftimes controversial telling and re-telling of the stories and adventures of characters previously encountered in other forms. Fan fiction in the world of Buffy and Angel may include the writing of "missing" scenes from an episode or the telling of a new tale that involves characters from the series.

Fan fiction is an old type of storytelling. Shakespeare's *King Henry V*, is an example of what fan fiction writers call RPF (Real Person Fiction) — stories about real people, re-told by someone who wasn't there. Nicholas Meyer's *Seven Percent Solution*, and Caleb Carr's *The Italian Secretary*, are two more examples of fan fiction — this time, a tale about Sherlock Holmes that wasn't penned by Sir Arthur Conan Doyle.

Professional writers (i.e., those who write for monetary compensation) sometimes debate the ethics of fan fiction, since the fan fiction writer doesn't create new characters. That debate is irrelevant here, since examined fans' reading habits, and much of their reading was (and remains) fan fiction of Buffy and Angel characters. Of course, professional writers are paid to write authorized fan fiction — that is, novelizations and movie/TV tie-ins. The difference seems to be one of use value and exchange value.

Use value and exchange value are terms that reflect the value of a work based on *why* it is produced, rather than how or where.[7] Work that has use value is produced for oneself or for the enjoyment of others. The creator of such a work does not seek nor want remuneration. Exchange value, on the other hand, refers to work that is produced for compensation. In other words, fan fiction produced by fans for fans, and without remuneration has use value, whereas, fan fiction (such as *The Italian Secretary*, or *The Seven Percent Solution*, or *King Henry V*) produced for compensation has exchange value.

Internet fan fiction is written without compensation and for the entertainment and amusement of friends, clearly has "use value"; whereas novelizations and other authorized fan fiction, novels like *The Seven Percent Solution* and *The Italian Secretary*, are written for "exchange value" — for monetary compensation.

Fans write fan fiction to "correct" what they perceive as poor script writing and incorrect characterization, to deepen a relationship they'd like to see — or see sub-textually, on the shows they are engaged in, and to amuse/entertain themselves and other fans. Fans who may/may not write fan fiction, will often read fan fiction to see what they want to see happen with the characters they love on the series they follow.

Consequently, fans who would like to see particular relationships occur — or who want to read more about a particular relationship, will search for, read, and sometimes write fan fiction. Fan fiction — which is available on the Internet, for free — thus reinforces 'ship loyalty.

'Ship loyalty created major schisms in the fandom, particularly among fans 'shipping four of the major characters in the series — Buffy, Angel, Spike, and Cordelia. There were two major schisms: Angel/Buffy and Spike/Buffy. During Angel's third season, a third major 'ship emerged — Angel/Cordelia; then in Angel's fifth season, Angel/Spike 'ships emerged, creating new schisms among Internet fans. Fans loyal to one of these four 'ships were generally not interested in reading or following any other 'ships. In fact, there are 'shippers (as they are called) who indicated that they did not talk to other fans who 'shipped differently.

These divisions were put aside temporarily for the Save Angel campaign, which emerged in the Spring 2004, in an attempt to prevent cancellation of *Angel: The Series*. The coordination and effort of nearly 200,000 fans was ineffective; the series was cancelled; the fandom continues.

'Ships and Fics: A Previous Study of Buffyverse Online Fans' Reading Habits

A previous survey examined two aspects of Buffyite and Angelite fan behavior:

(1) 'ship loyalty and preference, and (2) fan fiction reading habits. An examination of both preferences and fan fiction reading habits were seen as a reflection of demographic correlates: age, education, and marital status.

Among those involved in the previous study of 'shippers and fan fiction, almost ninety percent of the participants read fanfic, most of it unauthorized, and straight off the Internet. Fourteen percent of them read between seven-to-fifteen hours of fanfic weekly. On average, they spent one-to-three hours a week reading fanfic. They did not generally print out the fanfic; they saved them to their hard drives or CDs.

Participants in the earlier study of 'shippers and fan fiction readers indicated that their reading interests were broad; they were not all interested in sexy reading matter. Many like romances, but just as many liked adventure and comedy stories.

This earlier study of Internet fans generally attracted older fans, well-educated, and working in career-oriented occupations and professions. The fans who participated in both studies are not "young adults"; eighty percent are older, mostly over twenty-one, mostly over thirty years of age. They wanted adult reading — in plot, characterization, and sex. They were not interested in stories about Buffy and the Scoobies attending the prom! All of those who read fan fic intend to continue to read fan fic, even though both series ended and there aren't any plans to continue with mini-series, spin-offs, or MfTV ("Made for TV") movies.

It was evident from this study that fan fic readers are all about the story. Only about twenty-five percent of the participants had attended a fan convention. This means that about seventy-five percent of the respondents had never attended a fancon. This, we shall see, indicates a major difference between series-oriented fans and story-oriented fans.

Series-Oriented Fans

Series-oriented fans are all about the series, *sui generis*: the plots, the characters, the actors — they care passionately about the series. It is not so much the *story* that enthralls them — it is the series' *total "package"*: story, characters, settings, mythos, cast and crew. If a plot line or plot arc is not to their liking, they care — but their concern will not move them to read/write fan fiction to correct what they didn't like. They are not especially interested in the production of fan culture — theirs or others. It is the *series* they are interested in, and it is the series as a whole to which they are loyal.

Consequently, series-oriented fans are more likely to follow a specific actor's career, to attend a performance in which he/she is featured, to attend a concert given by a series performer or guest artist. Series-oriented fans see themselves as loyal to the *series*; whereas story-oriented fans see themselves as loyal to the story, the characters, and/or the relationships.

Series-oriented fans are passionate about *the series* — the story, the actors, the writers, the guest stars, the plot lines, etc. However, they do not seek out fan fiction or fanvids to correct a story line they don't like. For them, "it's a television show"; their passion remains limited to accepting the storyline as presented, and not changing it. Series-oriented fans are often more passionate about particular characters than they are of specific plotlines.[8] Series-oriented fans are more likely to purchase tickets to a movie in which one of the series' actors appears. They are "fans of the shows" which means that they accept "annoying" storylines without trying to change them. It's possible that series-oriented may move on to other series more easily than story-oriented fans, although that might be the subject of future research.

Both series-oriented fans and story-oriented fans are generally congenial in their relationships with each other. Both groups agree that the key is to maintain the fandom — to keep the series they both love alive, even though it's accessible only through DVDs, comic books, and re-runs at 7:00 on cable stations. Both groups of fans possess a high degree of social cohesion, necessary to any community, whether "real" or virtual.

Methodology

Three years ago, I began studying Web blogging as a means by which fans communicate and create fan fiction. I had just completed a study of Internet fanboard communities, and wanted to expand the study to include newer means of communication — viz., blogging.

At the same time, with I distributed three Internet surveys. After reviewing several strategies for hypotheses-testing, and with a battery of hypotheses to test, the best solution seemed to be a survey. The use of a survey did raise an important question: Just how valid and reliable is a survey of Internet fans? For such a survey to be both reliable and valid one might assume a cost of thousands of dollars and a sampling size of at least 1,000 respondents would be the starting point. I did not have access to the resources required for such an endeavor.

Fortunately, Don A. Dillman, a specialist in Internet surveys, had already responded to that concern. One would only need 100 carefully-chosen volunteers. Thus, the survey method was chosen for testing of these hypotheses.[9] A solicitation for volunteers was sent to eight fan boards across the Internet, during the summer of 2003. Fan board moderators were notified of the survey, and participation was requested by a posting for volunteers directly by me or indirectly through the board's moderators. All postings would be identically worded. All volunteers would be instructed to contact me via my e-mail address for a copy of the survey.

Solicitations for volunteers were sent to Buffistas.com, All Things Philosophical on Angel and Buffy, Slayage.tv, and the Bronze; these either did not respond to the solicitations or refused to post them. Solicitations to participate in the 'Ships and Fics survey were also sent to four other significant Buffyverse fanboards: The Big Bad Board (now defunct), Soulful Spike, Angel: Carpe Noctem (now defunct), and City of Angel (now defunct, though the site's archives are still available). All responded positively, excluding Soulful Spike, from whom I never received an official response. However, members of Soulful Spike did respond to the survey, as they had learned of it from their participation in other boards, and because solicitation for volunteers was posted there without a special thread or other notification coding.

The Big Bad Board, Angel: Carpe Noctem, and City of Angel gave permission to post an invitation to their members to volunteer to participate in a survey that asked questions about 'ships they followed and fan fiction they liked to read. A notice was also sent to Slayage Online — the International Online Journal of Buffy Studies. Slayage Online is not a fan board, but hundreds of fans and academic scholars stop by the site periodically for news about academic research related to Buffy, Angel, Firefly, and Whedon studies. Slayage Online posted the solicitation notice within fifteen minutes of my e-mailing them.

In fact, Angel: Carpe Noctem and Slayage Online — the International Online Journal of Buffy Studies, posted a banner at their site that linked directly to my official e-mail address. This enabled volunteers to contact me directly to request a copy of the survey.

My gatekeeper with other fanboards was the moderator/administrator/host of Angel: Carpe Noctem.[10] She created a banner and separate page at the

A:CN (Angel: Carpe Noctem, hereinafter referred to as A:CN) site just for The Fandom Project's research. A liaison for fourteen fanboards, and an influential member of the Save Angel Campaign, she took the solicitation for participation to thirteen other boards — who in turn responded by posting the announcement.

The response was phenomenal and a testament to the speed of the Internet. I had predicted that it would take me twelve weeks to garner 100 completed questionnaires for the first survey. Thanks to the gatekeeper's efforts on behalf of the study, all *three* surveys were completed in four months.

Solicitations for volunteers were sent to fourteen fan boards using the same methodology used previously. One hundred twenty-two volunteers completed the survey. Most of the participants were from the United States, although a few fans were from Australia, New Zealand, Canada, Great Britain, Ireland, Italy, Russia, Finland, and Peru. Most of the respondents were female.

Dillman notes that the reliability of online surveys is related to the sophistication of survey populations with high rates of computer use. "There is no other method of collecting survey data that offers so much potential for so little cost as a Web survey" (Dillman, 2000). The survey's participants who responded to the call for volunteers were experienced Internet users, mostly college graduates and graduate school graduates, sophisticated in the use of computers.

This article's data was derived from some of the findings of the second survey, which focused on favorite characters and plot lines that frustrated fans. The purpose of that particular survey, completed in the summer of 2004, was to elicit solely descriptive data, which was subsequently reported, presented, and/or published in other venues.[11] Subsequently, it became apparent that the data could be re-used in a secondary analysis to test hypotheses about story-oriented and series-oriented fans. Therefore, this is a secondary analysis of data originally collected in the summer of 2004, after both series were off the air, but while fandom issues were still fresh.

For purposes of this research project, thirty-two surveys were deleted from the study. Six surveys were deleted because they were returned with strange markings, or in a font below a seven-point pitch, rendering them uncodable/unreadable. Seven were returned incomplete, or were uncodable because the participants did not follow the instructions. Finally, the numbers of male respondents were of insufficient numbers for the purposes of this study, so those nineteen male surveys were eliminated. At some point in time, it will be interesting to analyze the data therein, but this is not the venue for that investigation. Eighty-five surveys remained — all females.

Each questionnaire offered forty-four plotlines that had been the subject of online board discussion threads for both series. Participants were asked to choose five plotlines that bothered them the most, indicating the one that most bothered them with an asterisk. Subsequently, they were asked what their response was to that plotline. They were offered three choices: (1) write to the show's producers, creator, and writer; (2) look for fan fiction that solved the dilemma to their satisfaction; or (3) go online and discuss the issue on a fan board.

Coding their surveys revealed that there were, as hypothesized, two groups of fans: those that were story-oriented and those that were series-oriented. Their predominant interests — story or series — influenced their fandom activities, although both activities perpetuated the fandom. The more committed and engaged the fan — the more invested the fan in the fandom, the more likely they were to choose *all three* activities.

Hypotheses — Expectations

My hypothesis was that Internet fans could be categorized by at least two types — story-oriented and series-oriented. Both groups of fans are invested fans who are immersed in the Internet community of Buffy and Angel fans. That is, because they have spent considerable energy and time communicating about and writing about the Buffy and Angel 'verse, they have become invested in the online community of Buffy and Angel fans.

Story-oriented fans would be more likely to use the Internet for creative purposes, such as to read and post fan fiction. Series-oriented fans, however, would be more likely to use the Internet for more practical reasons, such as discussing an episode or upcoming personal appearances of the featured actors, or to discuss behind-the-scenes gossip or news about an upcoming event. For the series-oriented fan, fan boards were (and still are) a means of learning news about their favorite shows, rather than a place to complain about the series. For the story-oriented fan, fan boards were (and still are) a place to express oneself creatively. Series-oriented fans would be more likely to attend a fan conference, a concert by one of the featured actors, and to purchase movie tickets to view a movie that includes one of the series' actors. Series-oriented fans would be less likely to search for fan fiction.

Both groups of fans, I further hypothesized, would be equally likely to participate in the Save Angel Campaign. The series-oriented fan would participate because she/he wanted the series to continue, whereas the story-oriented fan wanted more of the story to be told. Each would also be equally likely to purchase authorized fan fiction, though story-oriented would be more likely to do so.

I predicted that story-oriented fans would search for fan fiction; they would be more likely to go online to discuss the plotline; they would be less likely to attend a fan convention/comic convention; and less likely to attend a concert. Although it might seem that series-oriented fans would be more likely to purchase DVDs, I predict that story-oriented fans would actually be more likely to purchase the DVDs. My reasoning for this was that for story-oriented fans, it's all about the story, and the DVDs enable them to continue the story. Lastly, I predicted that story-oriented fans would be more likely to write to the show's creator, producers, and writers to complain about the plotlines that concerned them.

Findings and Observations

A review of the tables that appear in the Appendix will provide more information; however, what follows is a discussion of the relevant data on the findings and observations of that data. As we review the data, the differences between story-oriented and series-oriented fans will become clearer.

Demographic Data

Marital Status. Almost half of the participants in the study were single. Over half (53 percent) of the story-oriented fans were single, whereas less than half (43 percent) of the series-oriented fans were single. Therefore, we can state that single fans are more likely to be story-oriented than series-oriented.

Age. Age does not appear to be a significant factor in a fan's being story-oriented or series-oriented. Regardless of age, there is no relationship between age and a fan's orientation toward story or series.

Unlike the findings reported previously by Pugh (Pugh, 2005), the Internet fans that participated in all four studies would seem to be atypical. Much has been written about teens' involvement in Internet production of fan culture, but that was not evident in this study. Sixty-four percent of the participants were between the ages of 20–39, and twenty-six percent were over 40. It was not teens who sought fan fiction solutions. It was not teens whose fandom activities can be examined as a complex of behaviors characteristic of invested fans. Teens accounted for only ten percent of those who sought fan fiction in this survey.

Most of the participants in the four studies that were completed during 2003–2004 were not teen-aged females, but women between the ages of twenty and fifty-nine. It might be that my population is somehow skewed toward the mature age range; it might be that others' findings are generalizations for the entire universe of the fandom. That is, when one includes Internet fans, *as well as* all those who watched the series, but didn't go online, then it is quite possible that the average fan may have been a teen-aged girl. At the same time, as a series matures, so does its audience. The fan who was sixteen years-old in 1997 would have been twenty-three in 2004.

Education. If we compare participants who completed college with those who completed graduate school, there appears to be no difference in their probability to be story-oriented or series-oriented. However, if we start by looking at series-oriented/story-oriented participants, we will immediately note that *almost* half (47 percent) of the story-oriented fans are college graduates, whereas *over* half (55 percent) of the series-oriented participants are college graduates. The difference is slight — therefore, we should state that college graduates are *slightly* more inclined to be series-oriented than story-oriented.

When we examine graduate school graduates, we note that they are more likely to be series-oriented. Over one-half (67 percent) of the graduate school graduates score as series-oriented, whereas only one-third (33 percent) of the graduate school graduates are story-oriented.

Lastly, in examining *current students*, we see something a bit more interesting: college students are more likely to be *story-oriented*, whereas graduate school students are more likely to be *series-oriented*. This may be a function of the responsibilities of graduate school; there's little time for production of fan culture when there are papers to be written, theses to be developed and dissertations to research, write, and defend. It may also be a function of the size of the cell: Only twenty-four percent of the participants were active students (20/85), so the cells were small. This is a variable that needs to be examined more in subsequent studies. Anecdotally, it often seems, based on my studies of blogs, as though a large number fan fiction writers are graduate students; this has yet to be empirically tested.

Parental Status. More participants were non-parents (59/85) than parents (25/85). If we look at the participating fans who are parents (25/85), the percentages are nearly equal (12/25, 13/25). However, thirty-eight percent of the story-oriented fans were parents, compared to twenty-five percent of the series-oriented fans. Consequently, we can state that parents are more likely to be story-oriented than series-oriented. However, because of the greater proportion of childfree fans in the survey, we still must assert that both series-oriented and story-oriented fans are predominantly childfree.

What do the results of this survey tell us about online fandoms in general, and the Buffyverse online fans who participated in this survey?

Fans who enjoy and are engaged in the Buffyverse fandom (and perhaps other fandoms as well; this may be determined in a future survey) are probably female, between the ages of twenty-one through forty years, single, highly-educated career professionals. They like to read, and are willing to spend hours every week reading Internet (read: free) fan fiction that involves their favorite characters from their favorite TV shows. Being career professionals and highly-educated, they have a large disposable income, which they are willing to spend on paraphernalia that is fandom-related. Cult-TV fans do not necessarily fit the stereotype of an adolescent/post-adolescent, computer-geek male who can't find a date and can't interact successfully with others.

Invested Fans: Story or Series?

Fan Fiction. A crucial difference between the story-oriented fan and the series-oriented fan is the fan's attitude toward the production of culture. Does the fan read fan fiction? Does she look for fan fiction on the Internet or does she only read authorized fan fiction?[12]

It was my hypothesis that story-oriented fans, would seek out fan fiction to correct plotlines that nagged at them. Being oriented toward the production of culture they would seek out original solutions to what they perceived as story dilemmas. They would look for — or write fan fiction to solve their uncomfortabilities with unhappy plotlines, confusing plot arcs, relationship zigzags, and what they perceived as out-of-character shifts.

Participants' responses to the question, "Did you look for fan fiction that would correct the plotline?" was the key factor in the initial categorization of story/series orientation. Those participants that responded positively were categorized as "story-oriented." Those that did not respond positively to the questions were categorized as "series-oriented." This categorization based on the answer to one question was demonstrated to be valid, since the remainder of participants' answers could be reliably estimated based on their answer to that one question.

Of the eighty-five participants in this survey, thirty-two (35 percent) of the participants replied that they did search for fan fiction, with several responding that they also wrote fan fiction to relieve their unhappiness with the plotline. These were the participants denoted as "story-oriented." A review of the remaining two surveys will be completed in the future to further substantiate these initial findings.

Story-oriented fans were more likely to purchase authorized fan fiction than series-oriented fans. If we look at fans that purchased authorized fan fiction, those who were series-oriented seemed to be slightly more likely (51 percent vs. 49 percent) to purchase such books. When we explore story-oriented fans, the story changes; seventy-two percent of the story-oriented fans purchased fan fiction, compared to forty-five percent of the series-oriented fans.

Fan board discussions. Fifty-six percent of the participants who indicated that they had taken part in online fan board discussions were series-oriented. If we reexamine the data by story-orientation and series-orientation, the result is quite different. Seventy-five percent of the story-oriented went online, as compared to fifty-nine percent of the series-oriented. This indicates that story-oriented fans were more likely to discuss story-related issues than series-related fans in this survey.

Save Angel Campaign. As expected, a majority — sixty-seven percent — of both groups of participants took part in the Save Angel Campaign. By examining both story-oriented and series-oriented, we note that for both groups, participants were more likely to have joined the campaign than not to have joined.

Fan Cons & Concerts. Most of the participating fans, regardless of series-orientation or story-orientation, do not attend fan conventions, comic conventions, and/or concerts performed by featured actors or guest actors in the series. However, seventy-one percent of those who *do* attend such events are series-oriented.

Movie Tickets. Most of the participating fans, regardless of orientation, purchased movie tickets for movies that featured series' actors. Although most of the ticket-purchasers were series-oriented; the percentage of participants was close: seventy-seven percent series-oriented and sixty-nine percent story-oriented.

Purchased Authorized Fan Fiction. In looking at all of the participants who purchased authorized fan fiction, story-oriented and series-oriented fans were almost equally likely (49 percent: 51 percent) to purchase novelizations. However, in looking at responses to this question a bit differently, if we look at the responses of story-oriented and series-oriented fans separately, story oriented fans were much more likely to purchase novelizations. In fact, while over seventy percent of the story-oriented fans purchased novelizations, well less than fifty percent (45 percent) of the series-oriented fans did. Therefore, we can conclude that story-oriented fans are more likely to publish fan fiction than series-oriented fans.

DVDs. Not surprisingly, over ninety percent of the participants had purchased DVDs of the series. The seven percent that had not purchased the DVDs were categorized as series-oriented fans. In other words, *all* of the fans that were story-oriented had purchased the DVDs, whereas slightly *less than ninety percent* of those that were series-oriented had purchased the DVDs.

Officially Writing to Complain About Plotlines or Characters. Six participants wrote to the series' producers, writers and/or series creator. All six were story-oriented fans.

Conclusions

From a review of the data, we can conclude that there were two often distinct categories of fans noted from this survey: story-oriented fans and series-oriented fans. Demographically, both groups of fans were more likely to be single, between the ages of 20–49, and child-free.

Both groups were highly educated. There were few who had only graduated from high school; most graduated from college and/or graduate school.

The key to determining story-orientation and series-orientation could not be found in this set of demographics, but rather in the behaviors of fans. There are other variables than education, marital status, age, and gender that might explain participant's behavior in the fandom as story-oriented or series-oriented.

Crucial factors seemed to be whether the fan focused on the mythos or on the series. Crucial to the story-oriented fan seemed to be intense interest in the mythos of the series, whereas series-oriented fans were less involved with the story, and more involved with the series. Those who sought out fan fiction were more likely to purchase DVDs, participate in on line fan boards, and to purchase novelizations (authorized fan fiction). Those who did not seek out fan fiction were more likely to attend cons, concerts, purchase tickets that featured actors from the series. Finally, the six participants who wrote to the series' creator, producers, and writers to complain about plotlines were story-oriented fans, who had turned to Internet fan fiction to work out the plot knots that had frustrated them. While there was considerable overlap, there was significant enough differences to warrant continued use of the categorizations.

Methodological Weaknesses and Strengths

No research study is perfect, and this study certainly had weaknesses. The survey was not funded, nor did the researcher have the assistance of eager students to code the data. There was not any funding for computer coding of the surveys; all data had to be hand-coded. The study used recycled data from a previous study; original data was not used, and the parameters of the original survey's territory were stretched.

Because the original survey was designed to elucidate information for descriptive purposes only, it was difficult to wrest explanatory observations. At the same time, the original survey yielded such fruitful data that one could re-use the data for at least three more surveys and still yield valid and reliable information.

One of the most difficult research tasks to achieve is a true random sampling of Internet fans in any television fandom. First, only those fans who are most intensely engaged with a television series will search for a fan board to take part in online discussions related to a favorite television series. Once such a fan board is located, only the most committed (i.e., invested) fan will "cross the border," de-lurk, then participate in order to maintain online commitment to a TV series.

Second, Internet surveys of fans are, perforce, socio-economically biased toward those fans who can afford computers and online servers (be they DSL, Wi-Fi, etc.). Such fans also tend to be more highly educated than the rest of the population. As a result, although the statistics herein reflect these biases, they are nevertheless *reliably representative of the participants studied*.

Finally, with the passage of time (three years), it would seem that another survey of fan behavior is necessary to double check the reliability and continued validity of the findings. However, with many fan boards closed, and fans now more active on *LiveJournal*, *GreatestJournal*, *InsaneJournal*, and *JournalFen*, it would be difficult to repeat the study and find the same number of participants so quickly. Further study of the complex set of behaviors observed in the invested online fan is necessary to assert the continued reliability and validity of the research.

Appendix

The following tables indicate the numbers and percentages of participants' responses to the survey, based on being categorized as "story-oriented" and "non-story-oriented." Percentages have been rounded to the nearest whole number, consequently true percentage totals may vary from 99.5 to 101.

Marital Status

Marital Status	Story-Oriented	Series-Oriented	Σ N=85
Single	17 (53% of 32)	23 (43% of 53)	40 (47% of 85)
Cohabiting	4 (13% of 32)	7 (13% of 53)	11 (13% of 85)
Married	10 (31% of 32)	18 (34% of 53)	28 (33% of 85)
Divorced	1 (3% of 32)	5 (8% of 53)	6 (7% of 85)
Total	32 (100% of 32)	53 (100% of 53)	85 (100% of 85)

Age Ranges

Age Ranges	Story-Oriented	Series-Oriented	Σ N=85
15–19	3 (9% of 32)	1 (2% of 53)	4 (5% of 85)
20–29	10 (31% of 32)	19 (36% of 53)	29(34% of 85)
30–39	10 (31% of 32)	17 (32% of 53)	27 (32% of 85)
40–49	6 (19% of 32)	11 (21% of 53)	18 (21% of 85)
50–59	3 (9% of 32)	5 (9% of 53)	8 (9% of 85)
Total	32 (100% of 32)	53 (100% of 53)	85 (100% of 85)

Education 1

Education	Story-Oriented	Series-Oriented	Σ N=85
High School completed only	7 (22% of 32)	7 (13% of 53)	14 (16% of 85)
College completed only	15 (47% of 32)	29 (55% of 53)	44 (53% of 85)
Graduate School completed only	8 (25% of 32)	16 (30% of 53)	24(28% of 85)
Unanswered	2 (6% of 32)	1 (2% of 53)	3 (4% of 85)
Total (completion only)	32 (100% of 32)	53 (100% of 53)	85 (~100% of 85)

Education 2

Education	High School	College	Graduate	Unanswered	Σ N=85
Story-Oriented	7 (50%/14)	15 (34%/44)	8 (33%/24)	2 (67%/3)	32
Series-Oriented	7 (50%/14)	29 (55%/44)	16 (55%/24)	1 (33%/3)	53
Total	14 (100%/14)	44 (100%/44)	24 (100%/24)	3 (100%/3)	85

Student Status 1*

Education	Story-Oriented	Series-Oriented	Σ N=20
High School Student	1 (13% of 8)	0 (0%)	1 (5% of 20)
College Student	3 (38% of 8)	2 (17% of 12)	5 (25% of 20)
Graduate School Student	4 (50% of 8)	10 (83% of 12)	14 (20% of 20)
Total	8 (100% of 8)	12 (100% of 12)	20 (100% of 20)

Student Status 2*

Student Status	High School	College	Graduate School	Σ N=20
Story-Oriented	1 (100%/1)	3 (60%/5)	4 (29%/14)	8 (40%/20)
Series-Oriented	0	2 (40%/5)	10 (71%/14)	12 (60%/20)
Total	1 (100%/1)	5 (100%/5)	14 (100%/14)	20 (100%20)

Parental Status

Parental Status	Story-Oriented	Series-Oriented	Σ N=85
Parents	12 (38% of 32)	13 (25% of 53)	25 (29% of 85)
Non-Parents	20 (63% of 32)	39 (74% of 53)	59 (69% of 85
Unanswered	0	1 (2% of 53)	1 (2% of 85)
Total	32 (100% of 32)	53 (~100% of 53)	85 (100% of 85)

Some participants indicated that they are currently enrolled in an academic program. They may also have indicated graduation from HS and College.

Looked for Fan Fiction on the Internet That Would Re-Tell the Storyline to Participants' Satisfaction by Story-Oriented/Series-Oriented

Looked for Fan Fiction	Story-Oriented	Series-Oriented	Σ N=85
Yes	32 (100%)	0	32 (35% of 85)
No	0	53 (100%)	53 (64% of 85)
Total	32 (100%)	53 (100%)	85 (100% of 85)

Participated in Online Discussions in a Series-Related Fan Board by Participation

Participation In Online Fan Board	Yes	No	Σ N=85
Story-Oriented	24 (44% of 55)*	8 (27% of 30)	32 (~38% of 85)
Series-Oriented	31 (56% of 55)*	22 (73% of 30)	53 (62% of 85)
Total	55 (100% of 55)	30 (100% of 30)	85 (100% of 85)

Participated in Online Discussions in a Series-Related Fan Board by Story-Oriented/Series-Oriented

Participated in Online Fan boards	Story-Oriented	Series-Oriented	Σ N=85
Yes	24 (75% of 32)	31 (59% of 53)	55 (65% of 85)
No	8 (25% of 32)	22 (42% of 53)	30 (45% of 85)
Total	32 (100% of 32)	53 (100% of 53)	85

Participated in the Save Angel Campaign

Save Angel		Yes	No	Σ N=85
Story-Oriented		23 (40% of 57)	9 (33% of 27)	32 (38% of 85)
Series-Oriented		34 (60% of 57)	18 (66% of 27)	52 (61% of 85)
Unanswered	1	-		1 (1% of 85)
Total	1	57 (100% of 57)	27 (100% of 27)	85 (100% of 85)

Some participants indicated that they are currently enrolled in an academic program. They may also have indicated graduation from HS and College.

Participated in the Save Angel Campaign
By Story-Oriented/Series-Oriented

Save Angel	Story-Oriented	Series-Oriented	Σ N=85
Yes	23 (72% of 32)	34 (64% of 53)	57 (67% of 85)
No	9 (28% of 32)	18 (32% of 53)	27 (32% of 85)
Unanswered	0	1 (2% of 53)	1 (1% of 85)
Total	32 (100% of 32)	53 (100% of 53)	85 (100% of 85)

Attended Fan Conventions/Comic Cons
by Story-Oriented/Series-Oriented

Attended Cons	Story-Oriented	Series-Oriented	Σ N=85
Yes	8 (25% of 32)	25 (47% of 53)	33 (39% of 85)
No	24 (75% of 32)	28 (53% of 53)	52 (61% of 85)
Total	32 (100% of 32)	53 (100% of 53)	85 (100% of 85)

Attended Fan Cons/Comic Cons by Attendance

Fancons	Attended	Not Attended	Σ N=85
Story-Oriented	10 (29% of 35)	25 (47% of 53)	35 (41% of 85)
Series-Oriented	25 (71% of 35)	28 (53% of 53)	53 (62% of 85)
Total	35 (100% of 35)	53 (100% of 53)	85(100% of 85)

Attended at Least One Concert by (1)
BtVS/AtS Guest Performers/Actors 1

Attended Concert(s)	Yes	No	Σ N=85
Story-Oriented	8 (38% of 21)	24 (37% of 64)	32 (38% of 85)
Series-Oriented	12 (57% of 21)	40 (63% of 64)	52 (61% of 85)
Unanswered	1 (5% of 21)	-	1 (1% of 85)
Total	21 (100% of 21)	64 (100% of 64)	85 (100% of 85)

Attended at Least One Concert by (1)
BtVS/AtS Guest Performers/Actors 2

Attended Concerts	Story-Oriented	Series-Oriented	Σ N=85
Yes	8 (25% of 32)	12 (23% of 53)	20 (24% of 85)
No	24 (75% of 32)	40 (75% of 53)	64 (75% of 85)
Unanswered	0	1 (2% of 53)	1 (1% of 85)
Total	32 (100% of 32)	53 (100% of 53)	85 (100% of 85)

Purchased Tickets for Movies Featuring Series Actors 1

Purchased Movie Tickets	Story-Oriented	Series-Oriented	Σ N=85
Yes	22 (69% of 32)	41(77% of 53)	63 (74% of 85)
No	10 (31% of 32)	11(21% of 53)	21 (25% of 85)
Unanswered	0	1 (2% of 53)	1 (1% of 85)
Total	32 (100% of 32)	53 (100% of 53)	85 (100% of 85)

Purchased Tickets for Movies Featuring Series Actors 2

Purchased Movie Tkts	Yes	No	Unanswered	Σ N=85
Story-Oriented	22 (35% of 63)	10 (48% of 21)		32 (38% of 85)
Series-Oriented	41 (65% of 63)	11 (52% of 21)		52 (61% of 85)
Unanswered	-	-	1 (100% of 1)	1 (1% of 85)
Total	63 (100% of 63)	21 (100% of 21)	1 (100% of 1)	85 (100% of 85)

Purchased Authorized Fan Fiction 1

Purchased Authorized Fan Fiction	Story-Oriented	Series-Oriented	Σ N=85
Yes	23 (72% of 32)	24 (45% of 53)	47 (55% of 85)
No	9 (28% of 32)	29 (55% of 53)	38 (45% of 85)
Total	32 (100% of 32)	53 (~100% of 53)	85 (100% of 85)

Purchased Authorized Fan Fiction 2

Purchased Authorized Fan Fiction	Yes	No	Σ N=85
Story-Oriented	23 (49% of 47)	9 (24% of 38)	32 (38% of 85)
Series-Oriented	24 (51% of 47)	29 (75% of 38)	53 (62% of 85)
Total	47 (100% of 47%)	38 (100% of 38)	85 (100% of 85)

Purchased Series DVDs 1

Purchase Series DVDs	Story-Oriented	Series-Oriented	Σ N=85
Yes	32 (100% of 32)	47(89% of 53)	79 (93% of 85)
No	0	6 (11% of 53)	6 (7% of 85)
Total	32 (100% of 32)	53 (100% of 53)	85 (100% of 85)

Purchase Series DVDs 2

Purchased DVDs	Yes	No	Σ N
Story-Oriented	32 (41% of 79)	0	32 (38% of 85)
Series-Oriented	47 (59% of 79)	6 (100% of 6)	53 (62% of 85)
Total	79 (100% of 79)	6 100% of 6)	85 (100% of 85)

Notes

1. Acknowledgment must be given to Lindlof, Coyle, and Grodin (1998) whose earlier study of science fiction readers prompted curiosity about the kinds of fans needed to maintain a fandom.

2. See the Bibliography section of this book for more information on audiences and fandoms.

3. Kirby-Diaz has been studying the BtVS online fandom since 2003; Ali has been studying the Bronzers community for nearly a decade. Finally, David Alan Coon's, *An Investigation of Friends Internet Relay Chat As A Community*, was published in 1998.

4. Anecdotal research of Internet blogging and fanboards indicates that the experience of seeking out Internet discussions of TV series may be an activity that is more "natural" to audiences under thirty-five than over thirty-five. Older fans, while seemingly less likely to "cross the border" to post comments on fanboards, nevertheless report that the experience has in some way "changed" them about being a fan.

5. See the Bibliography section of this book for more information.

6. Canon is usually defined as "the official story"—found in a series' transcripts—not the scripts (which are often edited during shooting, and which may also be changed in post-production). Hence, what is *broadcast* becomes canon; the rest, as one fan fiction writer told me anonymously, "is hearsay."

7. Use value and exchange value are terms that are used throughout the social sciences, originating with Karl Marx's *Capital*.

8. As an example, Spike the Vampire (aka William the Bloody), was found to be the most popular character in the online surveys I distributed. Spike was not a leading character in either BtVS or/and AtS. Still: it is Spike's fans (according to the survey) who are more likely to attend concerts and fancons than the fans of any other character, including the fans of Buffy and/or Angel. Still: many of his fans are not story-oriented, and do not seek out fan fiction to correct plot lines they do not like.

9. In his book, *Mail and Internet Surveys: The Tailored Design Method*, Dillman patiently explains that 'Net researchers only need a sample size of 100 to produce results that are both valid and reliable.

10. Many thanks extended to the moderator/host of Angel: Carpe Noctem. Her generosity in spreading the news about the goals of the fandom project's surveys reduced the projected time for all three surveys from eighteen months to three months.

11. These findings are combined with ethnographic impressions and notes that are the result of thirty-six months of studying Web blogging in the fandom. Previous research findings were presented at The Slayage, 2004 and 2006; Phauxcon, a fancon, in 2006, and in the International Journal of the Humanities.

12. Authorized fan fiction is authorized by a TV series' creators and executive production companies. They own the series, and they authorize writers to produce "novelizations," for sale in bookstores and on the 'Net. Such works produce (hopefully) a profit. Unauthorized fan fiction is the fan fiction produced by the fan for the enjoyment of oneself/other fans. Some creators, most notably J. K. Rowling and Anne Rice, deplore fan fiction and do whatever they can legally to prevent it. Others, like Joss Whedon, the creator of BtVS and AtS, encourage the fans to produce fan fiction. See Hellekson and Busse, in the References.

Works Cited

Bacon-Smith, Camille. *Enterprising Women: Television Fandom and the Creation of Popular Myth*. Philadelphia: University of Pennsylvania Press. 1992.

Dillman, Don. *Mail and Internet Surveys: The Tailored Design Method*. New York: John Wiley & Sons. 2nd ed. 2000.

Durkheim, Emile. *The Elementary Forms of the Religious Life*. New York: Oxford University Press, 1971.

Grollmus, Denise. "Buffy Brings Fans Together," *The Beacon Journal*, July 21, 2003.

Harris, Cheryl, and Alison Alexander, editors. *Theorizing Fandom: Fans, Subculture, and Identity*. Cresskill, NJ: Hampton Press, 1998.

Hellekson, Karen and Kristina Busse, editors. *Fan Fiction and Fan Communities in the Age of the Internet*. Jefferson, NC: McFarland, 2006.

Hills, Matt. *Fan Cultures*. London: Routledge. 1992

Jenkins, Henry. *Textual Poachers: Television Fans & Participatory Culture*. New York: Routledge, 1992.

Kaveney, Roz, editor. *Reading the Vampire Slayer: An Unofficial Critical Companion to Buffy and Angel*. London: Tauris Parke, 20012.

Kirby-Diaz, Mary. "The Fandom Project: What Makes a Fandom Run —'Ships, Fanfiction, Plot Devices, Favorite Characters, and FanCons." *International Journal of the Humanities*, Volume 3, Issue 4, pp. 257–266.

Lewis, Lisa, editor. *The Adoring Audience: Fan Culture and Popular Media*. New York: 1992.

Lindlof, Thomas R., Kelly Coyle, and Debra Grodin. "Is There a Text in This Audience? Science Fiction and Interpretive Schism." *Theorizing Fandom: Fans, Subculture, and Identity*. Cheryl Harris and Alison Alexander, eds. Cresskill, NJ: Hampton Press, 1998. 199-247.

Pauwels, Luc. "Websites as visual and multimodal cultural expressions: opportunities and issues of online hybrid media research." *Media, Culture & Society*, 27: 4. 604–613.

Princess Twilight, "Fandom Sociology: The Mechanics Behind the Beast," <http://www.octavesoftheheart.com/fandom.html>

Pugh, Sheenagh. *The Democratic Genre: Fan Fiction in a Literary Context*. Bridgend, Wales: Seren/Poetry Wales Press, 2005.

Shuttleworth, Ian, "Bite Me, Professor," FT.com, September 11, 2003. *http://news.ft.com/Content Server?pagename=FT.com/StoryFT/FullStory&c=Story*

Simmel, Georg. *On Individuality and Social Forms*. Chicago: University of Chicago Press, 1971.

Wellman, Barry, and Barry Leighton. 1979. "Networks, Neighborhoods, and Communities: Approaches to the Study of the Community Question." *Urban Affairs Quarterly* 14:363–390.

Wilcox, Rhonda V., and David Lavery. *Fighting the Forces: What's at Stake in Buffy the Vampire Slayer*. Lanham, MD: Rowman & Littlefield, 2002.

Yeffeth, Glenn. *Seven Seasons of Buffy: Science Fiction and Fantasy Writers Discuss Their Favorite Television Show*. Dallas: Benbella Books, 2003.

"In the World, But Not of It": An Ethnographic Analysis of an Online Buffy the Vampire Slayer Fan Community

Asim Ali

Introduction

Buffy the Vampire Slayer first aired in March 1997 on what was then the new Warner Brothers television network (The WB). As an adjunct to the show, The WB created an official *Buffy* website. This website included a section called the Bronze. The Bronze — named after the fictitious club on *Buffy* that served as the center of social life for the show's characters — included a chat room, a threaded posting board, and a linear posting board. Soon after the series premier of *Buffy the Vampire Slayer*, the Bronze became the locus of a cohesive fan community. This fan community, whose members are known as Bronzers, proved remarkably resilient, surviving numerous changes to its online home, the closure of the Bronze upon *Buffy*'s move from The WB to UPN, the end of *Buffy* and its spin-off series *Angel*, and even the demise of both television networks that aired *Buffy*.

This chapter presents the first part of an ethnographic analysis of the Internet fan community that formed at the linear posting board known as the Bronze. This chapter examines the connection between *Buffy the Vampire Slayer* and the Bronze, and the process by which a group of individual fans became a community. It also describes the process of becoming a Bronzer: as I attempted to understand what the Bronze community meant to its members, I followed a trajectory similar to that of other Bronzers, progressing from fan to community member. Furthermore, I twice shifted from being an observer to being a participant, as I progressed from being a guy watching TV, to a *Buffy* fan, to an observer of the Bronze, to a member of the Bronze community.

The first section of this chapter is on *Buffy the Vampire Slayer* (*BtVS*). It was the first two seasons of the show that led me to the Bronze, and then to conduct ethnographic research on the Bronze community. Since the Bronze would not exist without *Buffy*, this section provides general background information on the show. These were the formative years of the show, since they laid the foundation for the remainder of the series. The second section of this chapter is on the Bronze community, and focuses specifically on Bronzers who frequented the Bronze linear posting board. This section is based on my participant observation at the Bronze and on ethnographic interviews with Bronzers.

Buffy the Vampire Slayer

By the second or third episode of *Buffy*— around the end of March 1997 — I was completely hooked on the show. But for some reason, I was surprised that I would like a show like *Buffy*. It was about a Southern California high school girl who was secretly a slayer of vampires; the lack of *gravitas* in such a concept was almost unseemly, especially for an academic. Perhaps it was out of some embarrassing need to justify my new obsession that I started devoting serious thought to why I liked the series. Or, maybe there was something intuitively meaningful in it that my brain was struggling to verbalize. Whatever the reason, I found in it a great deal of relevance to life in general, and my life in particular, especially my life as an erstwhile high school student in Southern California. But I also found that not too many people were impressed by my new favorite pastime. So, aside from the perverse joy I felt in telling people that *Buffy* was the most profound thing I had ever seen and watching their reactions, I didn't get much positive feedback from my pronouncements that the solutions to most of life's problems could be found on Mondays at nine P.M. (8 central) on The WB. Incidentally, by its second season, the show had moved to Tuesdays at eight P.M. Seven central.

Initially it was the dialog in *Buffy* that captivated me. It was remarkably rich and incredibly funny. The characters — most of them high school students — were self-reflexive in the extreme, to the point that their conversations sounded almost like they were occurring in the third person, happening out "on the table" rather than emanating from their heads. I found myself wondering whether my own wretched teenage experience might have been less awkward had I been as communicative. Of course, even if I'd had the communication skills, I would still have had to use them, and I don't know if any amount of cajoling would have convinced me to let anyone into the private little hell that was my teenage life. Besides, if the characters in *BtVS* were any indication, there would have been plenty of awkwardness regardless of how communicative I had been. Nonetheless, because the simultaneity of self-reflection and teen angst was so fascinatingly believable, *Buffy* reminded me of just how many loose ends I had managed to leave untied as a teenager. I doubt that those ends will ever be tied, but at least I have a little closure by understanding my own past via *Buffy*.

While the dialog was what got me hooked, a second characteristic of *BtVS* emerged as I continued to watch: this show inverted everything at every possible opportunity, and somehow in the process, cut through the layers of socialization and assumptions that characterize life. Set in the fictional, ostensibly perfect, and largely homogeneous "one-Starbucks town" of Sunnydale, California, this show pierced the veneer of the vapid suburban American dream and laid bare the "nuts and bolts that hold the surface of reality together."[1]

Buffy is a very postmodern show. It's about shaking up standard notions and ideas, about slamming together a diversity of beliefs, and then waiting until the dust settles to see which of them are left standing. It's about the multiplicity and fluidity of ideas, meanings, and identities, and how mixing them up allows us to deconstruct our own hidden assumptions. In Sunnydale, life is figuratively but also literally an illusion: unbeknownst to all but a few of its (living) inhabitants, it's sitting on top of the mouth of hell. Indeed, the opening to the hellmouth is below Buffy's high school, Sunnydale High. Buffy and a few of her school friends see the world for what it really is, and because of this, they are ostracized and alienated. Worse, they are also constantly blamed for the violence and mayhem that they spend their nights trying to stop. Their efforts result in a constant string of detentions, bad grades, groundings by confused parents, dead bodies on school grounds, and even suspensions and arrests. Plus, they are almost killed on a regular basis.

According to series creator Joss Whedon (who also produced, directed, and wrote many episodes):

> the show's tone is [...] everything all at once. It has that sort of pop culture blender [...] that pomo thing. But, at the same time, the one thing we always stress is drama, and is the truth of things. [...] And we try and combine as many strange and often disparate elements as we can, but in a framework where they all make sense, and they all feel real [Whedon, "Marina Warner"].

Indeed, in *Buffy*, the heterogeneity that results from combining horror, humor, action, beauty, and drama — that "postmodern thing," as Whedon calls it — serves as a vehicle for uncovering truth and reality:

[T]he world is a scary and horrifying place, and everybody's going to get old and die, if they're that lucky, and [...] to set people up, to set children up to think that everything is, you know, sunshine and roses and Care Bears in the world I think is doing them a great disservice. Children need horror because there are things they don't understand [...]. If it scares them, if it shows them a little bit of the dark side of the world that is there and always will be, it's helping them out when they end up facing it as adults [Whedon, "Marina Warner"].

On a more personal level, Joss says of his interest in horror:

I've always been interested in vampires, I think, because of the isolation they feel.
They're in the world, but not of it. As a child I always felt the same way, and *Buffy* deals with that kind of alienation" [Whedon, "Angel"].

According to the official *Buffy* fan magazine, "If Joss Whedon had had one good day in high school, we wouldn't be here," says *Buffy* co-executive producer David Greenwalt:

"I went through rejection, alienation, frustration, and more," says *Buffy* creator Whedon of his high school years. "I experienced each and every one of those things. I wasn't abused, I was just miserable and whiny. I had a harsh time. A great deal of what I write about I experienced" [Springer 18].

Furthermore, Joss seems to have a poststructuralist bent: when asked about his intention regarding the final episode of 1998, he replied: "Trust the tale, not the teller" (Whedon, online).

In *BtVS*, social institutions create the very divisiveness and exclusion they are designed to prevent. For example, concepts like "family" and "religion" become suspect in the world of *Buffy*. Adults seem to have no trouble believing that their kids are in gangs, or on drugs. But they find it incomprehensible that their children roam the streets at night fighting the evil whose very existence belies their worldviews. Notions of identity and individuality are similarly complicated as characters cycle through different *personas* as they move between home, school, hellmouth, and hell.[2] Beliefs regarding acceptable levels of violence and coercion are repeatedly confused and challenged in a world of soulless demons in which politicians and the police are just as likely to hinder as to help in the fight against evil.

BtVS begins with Buffy Summers, a high school sophomore, about to attend her first day of school at Sunnydale High. She has just moved to Sunnydale, California from Los Angeles with her divorced mother. In the first three seasons Buffy and her friends were in high school, after which they graduated, and Buffy started attending the fictitious UC Sunnydale.

Buffy is the Slayer, the only human who is the physical equal of a vampire, a fact that she desperately — and unsuccessfully — attempts to keep secret.

Rupert Giles is the school librarian and Buffy's Watcher. He trains her to kill vampires and spends his spare time conducting research on demonic activity. Buffy's closest friends are Willow and Xander. These four characters — Buffy, Willow, Xander, and Giles — form the core of the cast throughout all seven seasons of *Buffy*.

Cordelia is the rich, beautiful, popular, and selfish person that Buffy once was. Cordelia and her gaggle of fawning girlfriends harass other, less popular, high school students with their barbs. Her connection to Buffy and her friends is somewhat karmic: she doesn't like them; they don't like her. But, Cordelia and Xander date for awhile — which they both find embarrassing. Willow's boyfriend in high school and into the first year of college was Oz, the werewolf guitarist of the band Dingoes Ate My Baby. Unfortunately, his lycanthropy became so problematic in his freshman year of college that he decided to leave Sunnydale for less populated parts.

Angel is a vampire. In the Buffyverse, when humans become vampires, the human soul is replaced with a demon's soul. The demon is inherently evil. However, Angel is not evil; a curse restored his human soul, forcing his demonic self to be submerged beneath his human soul. Unfortunately, the curse was broken in the second season, which caused him to revert to being Angelus, a sadistic demon. During that time, he murdered Jenny Calendar, the computer science teacher and Giles' girlfriend. After three seasons of *Buffy*, during most of which Angel was Buffy's boyfriend, Angel decided to leave Sunnydale and move to Los Angeles.

Joyce Summers is Buffy's mother. Buffy's mother is a fairly typical parent in the Buffyverse: she's a wonderful person, but she's also clueless, ineffectual, and conventional. Joyce manages to remain blissfully ignorant of Buffy's true nature for most of the first two seasons of the show.

Outcasts Who Save the World

In contrast to the thuggish behavior of jocks, cheerleaders, frat guys, and just about anyone with either money or looks, our heroes are decidedly individualistic. They are not nonconformists, and certainly not rugged individualists. They are not even particularly heroic, courageous, or articulate. But they have learned to question dominant paradigms. They are people who act without relying on the learned assumptions, or "recipe knowledge," that characterize group behaviors (Berger and Luckmann 41–43).

According to Xander, Giles is able to take care of himself when there's a killer on the loose ("Never Kill a Boy on the First Date," "Puppet Show"). Jenny, the computer science teacher, is a self-proclaimed techno-pagan ("I Robot ... You Jane"). Buffy's first date in Sunnydale is with Owen, an attractive, intelligent classmate who likes poetry. Willow is sufficiently computer literate that she becomes the computer science teacher when Jenny is killed. Oz, the unflappable, sensitive, and incisive guitarist, is brilliant but unmotivated. Willow refers to him as "the smartest person never to graduate" from high school ("Beauty and the Beasts").

Xander spends much of his time obsessing about what it takes to be cool, and why he's not. Xander does notice, however, that whatever it is that makes one cool is something that Oz has, and he doesn't have ("The Zeppo"). At first, Oz's coolness is a source of suspicion for Xander; when Willow and Oz begin dating, he says about Willow: "I just don't trust Oz with her. I mean, he's a senior, he's attractive—okay, maybe not to me, but—and he's in a band. And we know what kind of element that attracts" ("Phases" Transcript).

Ironically, Buffy would undoubtedly be cool were it not for the fact that she is associated with bizarre happenings at school, and spends much of her time hanging around the "creepy librarian in that creepy library" ("Out of Mind, Out of Sight"). But instead of being one of the cool kids, Buffy's calling makes her an outcast. Buffy is the brawn of the gang; the rest of the Scoobies are the brains, spending much of their spare time in the library researching the forces of evil.

Outcasts Who Save Each Other

The use of violence leads to several boundary crossings as well. It is within the context of violence between humans, however, that *Buffy* provided its most controversial cultural criticism. In "Earshot," Buffy became temporarily telepathic and learned that someone on campus was planning a mass murder. In searching for the murderer, she discovered a student attempting to commit suicide. The dialog that resulted from Buffy's attempts to prevent the suicide was remarkable for its incisive and dramatic explication of the factors that lead people to become suicidal.

Unfortunately, these scenes were overshadowed by the real-life drama surrounding the episode. Filmed months in advance and originally scheduled to air on Tuesday, April 27, 1999, the episode was pulled because of its depiction of high school violence (Ryan, 1999). The previous Tuesday, April 20, 1999, there was a mass murder at Columbine High School. The network pulled the episode. A Bronzer associated with the show told me that the offending material was the following dialog:

> XANDER: I'm still having trouble with the fact that one of us is just gonna gun everybody down for no reason.
> CORDELIA: Yeah, because *that* never happens in American high schools.
> OZ: It's bordering on trendy at this point.

The implication is that high school violence is an ongoing problem that mainstream American society refuses to acknowledge. Indeed, I believe that "Earshot" exemplifies exactly the kind of discourse that can help identify and prevent the anomie that results in teenage suicide and Columbine-type violence. Ironically, The WB did exactly what "Earshot" so elegantly criticized: in what seemed like a convoluted case of blaming the messenger, The WB, rather than acknowledge *BtVS*'s implication that teen violence has been a longtime problem worthy of discussion, instead refused to air "Earshot" until the following September, 1999.

The Bronze

The official WB Bronze existed from 1997 to 2001. The Bronze community, however, continues to exist through a variety of networks and websites that maintain the characteristics — the conventions, jargon, and members — of the original site. One of these sites, The Bronze Beta, is a fan-run site that looks almost identical to the WB's *Bronze*. Thus, the Bronze may be said to include more than just the official WB *Bronze* website. The Bronze community can be said to include the fan community that formed at the official WB *Bronze* linear posting board and has since migrated to other sites.

This study is based on participant observation and ethnographic interviews begun in 1998 that have continued after the closure of the official *Bronze*, and have involved Bronzers at the official WB *Bronze* as well as at other sites.

I chose to conduct ethnographic research on *Buffy* fans because I initially could not understand the connection between *Buffy* and the online community to which it gave rise. Being a *Buffy* fan, I visited the official WB fan site many times during the first two seasons of the show. I noticed the area of the site called The Bronze, and assumed that this was a virtual version of the club on *Buffy*. At the time, however, the idea of virtual communication was new to me; I had little interest in talking to people on line, so I avoided the Bronze. But one day in the summer of 1998, being curious and having explored the rest of the site, I clicked on the icon for entering The Bronze, and was greeted with the following message:

Welcome to the Bronze
PLEASE READ BEFORE ENTERING

The Bronze Posting Board is a highly developed community of "Buffy" fans from around the world. If you're new, it can seem confusing, or you may feel like it's difficult to be heard. Please read the following information to learn more about how to participate[3]

When I first saw this greeting, I was taken aback. As it turns out, I would eventually review the information on this page repeatedly, both in order to learn how to participate and to try to understand some of the rules and assumptions on which this community was based. My initial reaction, however, was to the excerpt above: I had no idea how a community, much less a "highly developed" and global community, could come into existence based on a website that was based on a TV show. What exactly did it mean to be a "community" of people who did not interact in person, and whose community was based on a website that was based on a TV show? How could there be a community of persons whose only common ground was twice-removed from real life?

As a *Buffy* fan I had given a fair amount of thought to the show, and had found it useful in understanding my own life. I welcomed every opportunity to talk with people about *Buffy*. And yet, it never occurred to me to go on line to do so; even after I found the Bronze, I had no desire to communicate online. Indeed, the idea that anyone would willingly sit at a computer in order to be a part of a community seemed bizarre to me.

I chose the Bronze as a subject for ethnographic study because I simply could not understand the link between *Buffy* and the Bronze community. As a *Buffy* fan, I was an insider; but as something of a technophobe, I was an outsider. Thus, studying the Bronze would allow me to study — from an outsider's perspective — a community that was quite different from anything I had previously experienced. But, the community was not so different that I would have to learn an entirely new language or become conversant in a new set of texts (or TV shows).

The first order of business was to "lurk," which is to observe an interactive Internet site without participating or announcing one's own presence. The greeting mentioned above, which suggested that the Bronze "can seem confusing," was something of an understatement. As an example, consider the following series of posts. These four posts were posted by Bronze regulars, and are a typical example of what one might see at the Bronze. This excerpt, however, would be but a small portion of a typical board, since each board was available for posting for four hours, and could receive hundreds of posts. As indicated by the second line of each post, the following took place over one minute and twenty-five seconds:[4]

Closet Buffyholic says:

(Mon Feb 22 08:01:25 1999 [...])

krypticon: Somehow I think that my pontificating about the mating habits of farm animals involved less slurring of words than yours did. But you probably had more fun than me. C'est la vie. woo, check out that furin' language! And I still liked your other pick up line: "I may not be the most good looking guy in here, but I'm the only one talking to you." hee hee hee. But I think it could get you assaulted.

FSMCDman: Hello! Wow, you picked up a siggy awful fast, didn't you? Welcome! How goes the band scene?

fenric hola: How was down south? Warmer than here, I'll bet.
Doc: I am NOT either slacking, slacker.
  CB
^

Megdalen says:
(Mon Feb 22 08:00:55 [...])
  Chrissy! Nice first!
  poof
  Megdalen
^

Peanut says:
(Mon Feb 22 08:00:23 1999 [...])
  nah...
^

Chrissy says:
(Mon Feb 22 08:00:19 1999 [...])

Hey all! Not on vacation anymore so I can't be here for too long, but I thought I'd stop by anyway 'cause otherwise I'd missers y'all..

TO PBers— Saturday night was a blast! Hope we can do it again sometime :)

SOs to all my Bronzer buds, including but not limited to: *AKA Becker, Angle Man, Angela, angelgazer, ANGELofMUSIC, Anya, Arcadia, Asanti-momlet, banana, belmont, Big Al, Buffy13, BuffyBrazil, Cate, CharlieX, CHRIS, Circe, Closet Buffyholic, Cosmic Bob, Doc, DeMoriel, devil, Erestor, Erika Amato, EverDawn, Mr. EverDawn, Fatima, fenric, Godeater, goldspike, greengirl, Gryphon, gypsyrat, Heliconia, IMMORTAL, Jade, Jan, Jeff Pruitt, Jennifer Lynn, KAM, Lena, Little Willow, Macho Macho Man, Manx, Margot, Medusa2306, MeeB, -mere- , Night Owl, OzFan, Pippin, Princesscloud, Raven, ~sara~, Sarah W., SarahNicole, Savannah, StGermain, Taster's Choice, Tisiphone, TouroGal, TV James, VT, Willa, Mr. Willa* and all the people my list is still missing 'cause I constructed it during one of my off-the-board-due-to-whup phases....

Chrissy

~~Slave to~~ Owner and creator of the Who's Who of the Bronze page
WPWP #313
XDC #243
JP Gang #43
B/F in '99 #44
Proud member of Buffy, Eh?
Black sheep of the BWGDC
UB *SbAM*
First Mate of the Shameless Hussy Boat
Asanti is my momlet
-mere- is my kickboxing (and evilty) guru (and I am her *willing* Scott Evil)
Night Owl is my Uber Bud
SarahNicole is my Psychic Wonder Twin
Non-slavish CHRIS devotee

This series of posts captures several unique aspects of the Bronze, the first of which is that the Bronze *is* confusing. Each post appears as it is submitted at the top of the page; the posts are therefore in backward chronological order from top to bottom, creating the sense of a never-ending stream of comments.[5] Second, there is nothing inherent in posts that indicate to what they refer. In live conversation there are physical clues that provide the context for the spoken word; at the Bronze, there is no such context. While the top two posts here are addressed to specific persons, the fourth (Chrissy's) is addressed to everyone, and the third (Peanut's) has no meaning except in the context of this particular poster's previous (over the course of many months) posts. Furthermore, of these four posts, only one (Megdalen's) addresses the other posts; the other three address something that's not on the screen, and may not even be on the posting board. Third, even posts addressed to specific persons may never be read in their intended context, because there's no way to know whether the addressee is still present. Thus, the Bronze has a postmodern-poststructuralist, in fact — quality: these signifiers are not printed on a physical medium, and their content depends as much on the reader as the author.[6]

There are two ways that communicating at the Bronze might be made less confusing. The first is to "chat" online instead of "post." In a chat room, one can enter the virtual space, and communicate directly with others in real time. Chat rooms may be seen as extensions of e- mail or instant messaging, rather than as bulletin boards. The official *Buffy* site did contain a chat room, but the fact that *Bronzers* at the linear posting board chose to frequent the posting board, and not the chat room, demonstrates their preference for the former.[7] In fact, *Bronzers* are constantly explaining to "newbies" — people who are new to the site — that this is not a chat room; people should not expect immediate replies to their posts. Also, the fact that every site for newbies — of which there are at least three in addition to the official site — mentions that the Bronze is *not* a chat room indicates Bronzers' strong preference for the posting board format.

The second possibility is also one that Bronzers roundly reject. Apparently, many posting boards are "threaded," meaning that posters can either join an existing "thread" of the conversation, or they can start their own thread. The thread thus mediates topics of conversation, keeping them focused and allowing posters to stay "on topic" without having to scroll through hours of posts. Just as there was an official *Buffy* chat room, there was also an official threaded posting board.[8] However, very few linear posting board regulars seemed to have any interest in the threaded board. In fact Warner Brothers met with such strong resistance when it announced plans to discontinue the linear posting board that it dropped those plans for fear of alienating its fan base.

It is not only the structure of the linear posting board that causes confusion. There are also a great many words and conventions that are specific to the Bronze. For example, it is common for people to write their posts in both the first person and third person. Often, an individual's post is punctuated with narration written in italic type, thus making it possible for the individual to describe actions, the (fictitious) physical environment, or any other aspect of the Bronze from an "objective" viewpoint. This has the effect of creating a context in which the posting Bronzer's actions or comments occur. Furthermore, some posts are written from the point of view of the Bronzer's online persona, and some are written from the point of view of the real life (RL) person. It is not unusual for both points of view to be present in a single post. Finally, there is a great deal of Bronzer-speak. Some of this, like most emoticons and many abbreviations, are common to the Internet. But a large amount is not. There are, in fact, several unofficial websites dedicated to defining Bronze terms, including the Bronze *Welcome Wagon*, *The Posting Board Lingo Page*, and the *Buffy the Vampire Slayer Posting Board— Frequently Asked Questions* site.

I lurked over the course of a few weeks, during which time I began to understand slightly more than I had when I first started lurking. I learned, for example, that many people (as in Chrissy's post above) sign their names at the end of their posts, and follow their name with a signature, or "siggy." The siggy contains a variety of information, such as a list of clubs in which one is a member, names of other posters to whom one is "slavishly" or "non-slavishly" devoted, relationships to other posters (a "momlet," for example, being the rough equivalent of a mom at the Bronze), and a variety of quotes (usually from *Buffy*) and references (often to past conversations) that are significant. It is not unlike a handwritten signature, or the signature that appears at the bottom of a personal e-mail. Its function is basically the same: to describe the identity of the writer. It simultaneously connotes individuality and conformity. Like a handwritten signature, everyone has one, but everyone's is different. Similarly, a Bronze siggy is unique, highlighting accomplishments and a specific set of identifications. But it is also a marker of membership, evidence that one is a Bronzer.

An "SO" is a shout out, a personal acknowledgement of other posters, often kept on one's "shout list," which enables posters to say "hi" without having to post to a large number of people individually by name. Anything that keeps people away from the Bronze, like work, is "whup. " Hence, in Chrissy's shout list above, the last line is simultaneously an anticipatory apology for forgetting to shout to certain people, and an explanation for why this list may be incomplete.

Posts appear one on top of another; in the excerpt above, the latest post is the one on top. The second and third posts are referring to the fact that the board changes every four hours: a new, blank board appears, and the old one is archived for a week. Many Bronzers will "try for first," meaning that they will submit their posts such that they are first on the new board. The second post refers to a try for first that Peanut thought would be unsuccessful. She was right; the previous poster beat her by four seconds. The third post serves two functions: to congratulate the first poster (Chrissy) on her "first," and to mark the poster's departure.

Asterisks denote action, as opposed to conversation; therefore, *poof* is a way of saying "I'm not just saying that I'm leaving, but I've really left." This is significant because a great many Bronzers have trouble leaving, despite their repeated assertions that they are doing so. This is not unlike standing up to leave at a party and then becoming engaged in conversation and staying for another hour. Since actions speak louder than words, *poofing* is a way of signaling that one really has left.

Despite the fact that lurking allowed me to figure out much of what was going on at the Bronze, most of the insider-speak was still bewildering enough that I found it unfathomable that anyone could actually be having a conversation in this way. In retrospect, it seems that I could have lurked indefinitely without completely understanding what was going on. Fortunately, I didn't have to.

Bronzers

I was scared to look for informants. Not only did I not know what people at the Bronze were talking about (or how they were doing so), I had no desire to draw the attention of these strangers to myself, and certainly not in writing. So, after procrastinating for several days — possibly weeks — I finally got around to finding the Webmaster of the Bronze. He was a webgod by the name of Apollo. I wrote to him, asking if I could post a message asking for informants. He responded almost immediately, saying he didn't mind as long as it didn't happen more than a few times. So I posted a message, and by the next day had gotten three responses, one from *Patrick* in California, one from *Sally* in New Jersey, and one from *Destiny* in Washington, DC.[9] This chapter focuses on my two online informants, Patrick and Sally. In the following chapter, I will focus on Destiny and other members of the DC Bronzer community.

The first response I received was from Patrick, which immediately threw me into a tizzy. Not only had I not yet figured out what I wanted to ask, but he had already begun to volunteer information that I didn't know what to do with. According to Spradley, this is to be expected (Spradley 1979).

The ethnographer should not elicit simple answers to questions, since doing so will likely lead informants to simply say what the ethnographer wants to hear. On the contrary, the ethnographer should fully expect and encourage — and be encouraged by — informants who respond not simply to the questions as posed, but by sharing information that they think is important to themselves and other community members. The ethnographic interview is not merely about getting *answers*, but about discerning the *questions* to which informants are responding based on the information that they volunteer.

Nonetheless, until receiving Patrick's e-mail, it hadn't even occurred to me to consider what to do if someone actually responded to my post. Perhaps some part of me assumed that nobody really would respond. Or perhaps it was one thing to submit an anonymous post asking for volunteers, but a completely other thing to actually conduct the interviews. Regardless, when I saw the e-mail from Patrick, I did the only reasonable thing I could think of: I panicked. After all, I had never done this before, and here I was, an interloper in the trendy online cult of *Buffy* fans, brazenly trying to use them for my own selfish purposes. I was sure that if Patrick didn't already think I was an enormous dork, he probably would soon enough. But, seeing as how I had committed myself to this ethnographic project, I wrote back to Patrick and thanked him for his e-mail, and asked him to respond to a few questions, which he did.

In retrospect, my panic was probably wholly unnecessary; indeed, it turned out that many ethnographers have similar concerns. In his e-mails, Patrick was gracious and helpful, giving me his home and office e-mail addresses, and even offering a phone number at which I could call him. Patrick's first email to me is as follows:

Hi Asim —
You can call or e-mail me. [...] I've been on this board since inception, been a Buffy fan from show 1, helped with the Posting Board party in February, attended it, just had dinner with shannah, Occido, Kinsey, Enikl138, TVJames and Ozfan last week. It's very unusual, the most genuine online community I've seen in seven years of Internet surfing. You may know that at least two engagements have resulted from people who've met on this board, and who knows how many relationships.

Patrick was clearly impressed with the Bronze. I had yet to even ask him any questions, but Patrick had already made it clear to me that the Bronze was a community. Indeed, it was a unique community, and a much more complicated community than I could have imagined.

Furthermore, without any prompting, Patrick had told me that this community was "genuine," and suggested that this was due to the face-to-face interaction of community members.

Since Patrick had already begun to volunteer helpful information, I tried in my first set of e-mail questions to follow up on some of the points he made. I was surprised at how quickly he responded — in all of our communications, he usually replied within a day — and how informed his responses were. I found the following responses particularly illuminating (My questions are italicized; otherwise, no changes have been made).

Please tell me a bit (or a lot, if you're up for it) about the following: What is it about the show (BtVS) that captures your interest?

Above all, the writing. The show is actually an allegory of the traumas, travails and emotional highs and lows of growing up and being a human. Except that the traumas, travails and emotions are literally demons, vampires and forces of evil. It's a nice, literary conceit for TV. A normal, 17-year-old girl thinks the world will end if her mother doesn't let her out of the house that evening. In "Buffy," the world literally will end. In real life, a young girl who has premature sex with her older boyfriend may discover that he's turned into a creep afterwards. In "Buffy," the boyfriend literally turns into a devil demon. In real life, a young person may feel like the world is on their shoulders. In "Buffy," it really is. In real life, a young runaway may feel like they're no one, and that they could disappear for years without anyone noticing. In "Buffy," young runaways literally become No One, and they literally disappear for years without anyone noticing. The strength of the writing is that the writers, Joss Whedon foremost, seem to recall with uncanny accuracy what it feels like to be 17, and are true to their characters without being condescending or smarmy.

But all of this is done very knowingly, and ironically, and with great wit. The jokes and one-liners, which are all character-based and situational, come fast and furious, and sometimes it's hard to keep up. The characters are quirky, yet sympathetic: they stand for the outcast and awkward in all of us. For anyone who recalls being awkward or out of it, it's nice to see such characters as the saviors of the world.

Lastly, the actors portraying these quirky characters are uniformly appealing and fresh. Sarah Michelle Gellar, who is a veteran of TV, shows the greatest range and depth, and captures every nuance of emotion that Buffy goes through, and conveys it with total honesty. Nicholas Brendon, Alyson Hannigan and Charisma Carpenter similarly invest their characters with many layers, sometimes giddy as teenagers, sometimes poignant as the most experienced adults. And Anthony Stewart Head surprises us by taking a stock, fuddy-duddy Englishman and turning him into a figure with a dark past and barely suppressed longing and rage.

All together, it makes "Buffy" completely original, often delightful, and always surprising. What other TV show can do that?

What drew you to the Bronze?

I wanted to share my enthusiasm for the show, but didn't know anyone who actually watched it (or, if they did, would admit to it). I loved the show from the first, but found myself embarrassed to bring it up in mixed company. Knowing that there was a place to discuss it with like minds was immensely attractive.

Also, you mentioned that it's the most genuine online community. Do you spend a lot of time in other online communities? Can you describe what it is that makes them less genuine?

Yes, I've met a lot of the original posters. WE had a party in February, and I helped organize some of the food activities. I don't keep in regular touch with any of them, but hear from them from time to time. Just this month, had dinner with a bunch of them on the occasion of a visit from Washington, DC, by Shannah and Occido. But I know they're much tighter back East, especially in the DC area; Shannah, Occido, Blade and others hang out a lot. As for the engagement, I know of at least two: one couple whom I don't recall, and ~mere~ with RD, who happens to be connected with the show (he's David Greenwald's assistant).

It's that connectedness that makes it seem like a real community — that, and the fact that many posters have been on the Bronze for years. Were you aware that a while back the minds at Warner Bros revamped their Buffy website? They were going to do away with the Bronze as it existed and substitute a different kind of posting board, threaded like many others. there was a mutiny! People complained; e-mail flew; someone created a dual posting board on a completely separate Web site to substitute for the official one; people threatened to boycott the Web site altogether (though not the show!). In the end, WB and Fox recognized that they had something special here, and acceded to demands that the Bronze remain exactly as it was. And so it is. They even kept the name "The Bronze" (they were going to rename it "The Lounge").

As for other groups, I'm a regular on an X-Files mailing list, and have dropped in on a couple of chat rooms and boards elsewhere. The connections on these seem much more tenuous and topic-related, and people drift in and out regularly. Not like the Bronze, where conversations can run for days or weeks.

While I tend to think of *Buffy* as deconstructive, Patrick provided me with an insightful analysis of *Buffy* as allegory. He also suggested that I wasn't alone in finding meaning in *Buffy* and not being taken seriously because of it. Furthermore, his answers indicated that, whatever it was that was meaningful about the Bronze, it was a unique phenomenon. And so in my next set of questions, I tried to narrow my focus from *BtVS* and online communities in general to the Bronze and the "tight" DC community in particular.

What was it that got you posting/chatting? What kinds of things were you wanting to talk about? Can you give me an example of what you usually say/do when you enter the PB?

Boredom, mostly, and a desire to talk about the show with like minds. Haven't posted much lately; when I do, it's mostly my thoughts about how the show worked, or didn't, character interactions, favorite stuff, etc.

I'm also still thinking about the "genuine community" you mentioned. What I find interesting is that there's a whole bunch of conversation that I wouldn't have a clue how to make sense of. A lot of it seems to have absolutely nothing to do with the show. There are all sorts of different script, words and abbreviations and titles I've never heard of. How did you end up getting so into these conversations? How are newbies usually received (or not)? The few times I've lurked it seems like newbies are really conscious of their newbie status.

Best way is to address your comments directly to a person. Respond to a question, amplify a comment, etc. As for the abbreviations, etc., you pick 'em up by just hanging out and lurking. Titles of the eps are listed on the home page. Newbies are welcomed except when they're violating the rules (which are also listed on the buffy site), such as posting, "Angel is a hottie!" or "Buffy Rocks!" or asking if anyone has the stars' addresses, etc. Best way to work your way into the community is to lurk for a while, follow the ebb and flow of the conversation, then jump in with relevant posts to actual people. You'll be surprised how accomodating people can be, especially if you have something to contribute. As for the lack of on-topic conversations, well, that's the nature of these things. The more poeple get to know each other, the more they have to talk about that doesn't have much to do with Buffy.

How do you conceive of the Bronze posting board? I mean, if people boycotted over a name change, it sounds like more than just a web site...? Plus, it seems like a totally different thing than the chat-room or threaded posting board, but I'm not really sure how....

It's less like a chat room because you can only post three times an hour. And it's not like a threaded board because the entire conversation can be scanned at once. The ebb and flow is more like that of a bunch of people sitting around a table; some talking to everyone, some talking to a few people at a time. Some just talking to the person sitting (metaphorically) next to them. But you can switch back and forth at any time. In a threaded board, you must be on topic and are forced to talk to a small group, not to the whole group at a time.

You also mentioned Buffy-as-allegory, which I hadn't really thought of. What about that allegory struck a chord with you? What do you relate to?

Allegory in the sense that the action reflects inner states, emotionally or intellectually. A demon isn't just a demon; it's the external manisfestation of some problem, or an emotion, or a personal crisis on the part of Buffy or her friends. How she deals with the demon is a metaphor or allegory for how she deals with her problem.

Apparently, the Bronze is unique because it is more like a community than other online communities. This begs the question: what makes it more like a community, and why? One answer to this lies in the fact that it's a linear posting board. The threaded board focuses conversation by *topic*; the linear board clusters them according to people who want to talk with each other. As stated above, a linear posting board can be more confusing than a threaded board. Consequently, it demands more commitment, effort, and forethought to become engaged with a linear community, in comparison to a threaded board. To talk with someone on a linear board, you have to want to talk to *them*. In a threaded board, you want to discuss a specific *topic*; the "person" doesn't matter so much in a threaded board — the discussion topic is paramount.

Linear board discussions are not regulated; nothing keeps people "on topic," which means that *all* of the rough edges of conversation circumscribed on the threaded board are allowed to seep in at the linear posting board. In other words, part of what makes this community genuine is the flexibility people have in conversing and interacting with one another.

My only other online informant was Sally in New Jersey. I conducted one online interview with her, in which Sally echoed much of what Patrick had said. Following are excerpts of our conversation:

What is it about the show (BtVS) that captures your interest?

It has lots of everything in it ... satisfying my desire for different types of entertainment all at once. The writing is so incredibly intelligent, too, so it's not a zone-out time for me. I'm pulled completely into this other world for an hour, but some of it stays with me afterwards ... for days and months.

How long have you been posting/lurking at the Bronze?

I first posted in mid–August '97. I was off for the month, living at home in between working in NYC and going to graduate school; thus, I was bored. I had finally started watching Buffy in July, and so came upon the site while I was developing an Internet addiction. During the next few weeks, I posted a lot and exchanged e-mails with a bunch of people. At this point, I posted a lot more on-topic, and often the e-mails were information (re: the show). School soon overwhelmed me, so I stopped posting mid–September. Then, a few months later, I was visiting home on my birthday and had some free time. I checked the board, and saw that all these people were wishing me a happy birthday! I haven't left since.

What drew you to the Bronze?

The tail end of my previous response started to address that. This is a place people come to and remain at by choice. Even in RL extracurricular activities, you usually have some sort of commitment for a certain amount of time, or, at least, know that others will see you around, so you can't bail too easily. So, here is a place where people stay because they really want to be there. Since we're not doing much together — like a project — there aren't too many political struggles and major conflicts. When they do occur, they are about clashes of opinions and personalities when those opinions have been expressed. We're still all united in our passion for Buffy.

The people are extremely supportive. Sure, it doesn't take much to write <<< good vibes>>> to someone when they say they have an exam or job interview, but somehow you don't think about that when you read the stuff like that when it's addressed to you ... or anyone. Things have gone beyond this one "gathering place." People send presents/goodies to one another. People e-mail and IM ... and meet in person. We don't, by any means, always talk about Buffy. We have a lot of other things in common, similar tastes. Solid friendships and romances have started here. Back to supportiveness. When Seth Green comes online (I'm a bit smitten with him), people post to him, asking him to post to me, people e-mail me, people CALL me to tell me he's there. This place simply rocks.

My interviews with Patrick and Sally, as well as many subsequent informants, indicate that Bronzers, like me, found something intensely meaningful in *Buffy* that we wanted to discuss with like-minded individuals.

Bronzers find *Buffy* both aesthetically and intellectually engaging. Indeed, the literary quality of the show seems to attract fans who — like Joss Whedon and several of his main characters — are well-read, well-versed in popular culture, and like to write. However, the Bronze seems to be defined by more than just the quality of the show and the intensity of the fans. Apparently, there's something unique about at the Bronze, which makes me wonder: what does it do for people that they get so hooked? This is the question to be addressed in the next chapter.

Notes

1. Much of my description of *Buffy* invokes social constructionism (Berger and Luckmann). The first quotation in this passage, referring to Sunnydale as a "one–Starbucks town," is from a comment made by Xander in "Welcome to the Hellmouth." The second quotation is from Stone (182). Stone uses the vampire's gaze as an intellectual exercise, using the example of the vampire Lestat of Anne Rice's Vampire Chronicles. Stone suggests that if Lestat were to become an anthropologist, he might see through the constructedness of everyday life. Similarly, Joss Whedon's vampires are liminal characters for which the social construction cannot account; hence, most Sunnydale residents rationalize away the town's supernatural occurrences. Furthermore, it is the vampire's gaze that sees through the social construction: Sunnydale seems like an idyllic version of small-town middle America, but it sits atop the mouth of hell, and so it is at its core, literally, evil. Stone (as does as Turkle) also focuses on technology as containing the potential to allow individuals to see beyond the constructions and assumptions of everyday life, thus connecting vampires, technology, and social constructionism. Similarly, the Bronze connects these three elements, but does so in a virtual space.

2. John Caughey, in both "Gina as Steven" and *Negotiating Cultures and Identities*, explains how individuals make meaning through the use of "imaginary social worlds," and may cycle between various such worlds (*Negotiating* 50). There is an interesting parallel between *Buffy*'s characters cycling between social worlds and Bronzers doing so as they cycle between the virtual and the real.

3. This text was at the Bronze Welcome page, the URL for which was <http://www.buffy.com/slow/index_bronze.html>.

4. This is copied directly from the Bronze linear posting board of February 22, 1999. The text is unaltered, except that IP addresses have been replaced with bracketed ellipses. The Bronze was <http://board.buffy.com/bronze/postingboard.shtml>.

5. The Bronze exemplifies a postmodern view of language. According to Rosaldo: "Burke's parable of the endless conversation with no known beginning or ending, departs from the monumentalist's preoccupation with permanence and puts the unchanging foundation of classic norms into perpetual motion. You arrive, and the conversation is already in progress; you depart, and it continues without you" (104).

6. See, for example, Hawkes' *Structuralism and Semiotics*, and Best and Kellner's *Postmodern Theory*.

7. The official Buffy chat room was at <http://chatsrv.warnerbros.com:4080/chat/world/html/loginbuffy.html>, accessible via <http://www.Buffy.com>.

8. The official threaded posting board was at <http://www.buffy.com/slow/index_bronzetpb.html>.

9. The names of all Bronzers used in this paper are used with their permission. In those situations in which persons preferred not to be identified by either their real names or their posting board names, I have used an alias.

Works Cited

"'Angel' and 'The Puppet Show.'" *Buffy the Vampire Slayer*. Videocassette. Fox, 1998.
"Beauty and the Beasts." *Buffy the Vampire Slayer*. The WB Television Network. WBDC, Washington. 19 Oct. 1998.

"Becoming, Part Two." *Buffy the Vampire Slayer*. The WB Television Network. WBDC, Washington. 19 May 1998.

Berger, Peter L., and Thomas Luckmann. *The Social Construction of Reality: A Treatise in the Sociology of Knowledge*. New York: Anchor, 1966.

Best, Steven, and Douglas Kellner. *Postmodern Theory: Critical Interrogations*. New York: Guilford, 1991.

The Bronze. <http://board.buffy.com/bronze/postingboard.shtml>.

The Bronze Beta. <http://www.bronzebeta.com>.

Bronze Welcome Wagon. 22 May 2006. <http://www.angelfire.com/in/btvsjade/newbie.html>.

Buffy the Vampire Slayer Posting Board—Frequently Asked Questions. 22 May 2006 *http://home. earthlink.net/~leathrjacket/stina_Faq.html*

Caughey, John L. "Gina as Steven: The Social and Cultural Dimensions of a Media Relationship. " *Visual Anthropology Review*, Spring 1994: 126–65.

_____. *Negotiating Cultures and Identities: Life History Issues, Methods, and Readings*. Lincoln: University of Nebraska Press, 2006.

"Earshot." *Buffy the Vampire Slayer*. The WB Television Network. WBDC, Washington. Originally scheduled for broadcast on 27 Apr. 1999. 21 Sep. 1999.

"Faith, Hope, and Trick." *Buffy the Vampire Slayer*. The WB Television Network. WBDC, Washington. 6 Oct. 1998.

"Faith, Hope, and Trick" Transcript. Alexander Thompson. 1998. Rev. 13 Oct. 1998. *BuffyWorld.com*. 19 July 2007. <http://www.buffyworld.com/buffy/season1/transcripts/02_tran.shtml>.

"Fear, Itself." *Buffy the Vampire Slayer*. The WB Television Network. WBDC, Washington. 26 Oct. 1999.

"Go Fish." *Buffy the Vampire Slayer*. The WB Television Network. WBDC, Washington. 5 May 1998.

Hawks, Terence. *Structuralism and Semiotics*. Berkeley: University of California Press, 1977.

"I Robot ... You Jane." *Buffy the Vampire Slayer*. The WB Television Network. WBDC, Washington. 28 Apr. 1997.

LJ's Helpful Hints for New Posters. 22 May 2006. <http://home.earthlink.net/~leathrjacket/new_posters.html>.

"Never Kill a Boy on the First Date." *Buffy the Vampire Slayer*. The WB Television Network. WBDC, Washington. 31 Mar. 1997.

The Newbie Welcoming Committee. Oct. 1998. <http://www.geocities.com/TelevisionCity/Studio/1788/index.html>.

"Out of Mind, Out of Sight" Transcript. Alexander Thompson. 1997. Rev. 24 Sep. 1998. *BuffyWorld.com*. 14 June 2007. <http://www.buffyworld.com/buffy/season1/transcripts/11_tran.shtml>.

"The Pack." *Buffy the Vampire Slayer*. The WB Television Network. WBDC, Washington. 7 Apr. 1997.

Pathetically Helpful Bronzers Anonymous. 4 July 1998. Oct. 1998 <http://www.angelfire.com/mo/LisaPage/phbapage.html>.

"Phases." *Buffy the Vampire Slayer*. The WB Television Network. WBDC, Washington. 27 Jan. 1998.

_____. Transcript. Alexander Thompson. 1998. *BuffyWorld.com*. 13 June 2007. <http://www.buffyworld.com/buffy/season2/transcripts/27_tran.shtml>.

The Posting Board Lingo Page. Oct. 1998. <http://www.angelfire.com/in/btvsjade/pblingo.html>.

"Puppet Show." *Buffy the Vampire Slayer*. The WB Television Network. WBDC, Washington. 5 May 1997.

"Puppet Show" Transcript. Alexander Thompson. 1997. Rev. 24 June 1999. *BuffyWorld.com*. 15 June 2007. <http://www.buffyworld.com/buffy/season1/transcripts/09_tran.shtml>.

"Reptile Boy." *Buffy the Vampire Slayer*. The WB Television Network. WBDC, Washington. 13 Oct. 1997.

Rosaldo, Renato. *Culture & Truth: The Remaking of Social Analysis*. Boston: Beacon Press, 1993.

Ryan, Joal. "'Buffy' Slayed by School Massacre." *E! Online*. 23 Apr. 1999. 11 Sep. 2007. <http://www.eonline.com/news/article/index.jsp?uuid=94c67d87-e031-4685-8073-a3725a91687c>.

Spradley, James P. *The Ethnographic Interview*. Fort Worth: Harcourt, 1979.

Springer, Matt. "High School Hell." *Buffy the Vampire Slayer Official Magazine* Winter 1998: 16–19.

Stone, Allucquere Rosanne. *The War of Desire and Technology at the Close of the Mechanical Age*. Cambridge, MA: MIT, 1995.

Turkle, Sherry. *Life on the Screen: Identity in the Age of the Internet*. New York: Simon and Schuster, 1995.

"Welcome to the Hellmouth." *Buffy the Vampire Slayer*. The WB Television Network. WBDC, Washington. 10 Mar. 1997.

Wells, H.G. *The Island of Dr. Moreau*. New York: Bantam, 1994.

Washington. 17 Nov. 1998.

Whedon, Joss. "'Angel' and 'The Puppet Show.'" Interview. *Buffy the Vampire Slayer*. Videocassette. Fox, 1998.

_____. "Marina Warner." Interview. *Bookworm*. KCRW. 29 Apr. 1999. <http://www.kcrw.org/cgi-bin/db/kcrw.pl?tmplt_type=program&show_code=bw:>.

_____. Online posting. The Bronze. 15 Dec. 1998. <http://board.buffy.com/bronze/postingboard.shtml>.

"Where the Wild Things Are." *Buffy the Vampire Slayer*. The WB Television Network. WBDC, Washington. 25 Apr. 2000.

_____. Transcript. Joan the English Chick. *Buffyworld.com*. 13 June 2007. <http://www.buffyworld.com/buffy/season4/transcripts/74_tran.shtml>.

"The Zeppo." *Buffy the Vampire Slayer*. The WB Television Network. WBDC, Washington. 26 Jan. 1999.

Community, Language, and Postmodernism at the Mouth of Hell

Asim Ali

Introduction: The Mayberry Bronzers

This chapter presents the second part of an ethnographic analysis of the *Buffy the Vampire Slayer* (BtVS) Internet fan community that formed at the linear posting board known as the Bronze. The focus of this chapter is on the factors that make the Bronze a dynamic and unique Internet community, and on what makes the Bronze meaningful to community members. This analysis is based on ethnographic interviews with members of the Bronze community — who are known as Bronzers — and on participant observation at the Bronze. Much of this chapter is based on my interviews with Bronzers in the Washington, DC metropolitan area; these Bronzers came to be known as the Mayberry Bronzers. In this chapter, I highlight three Mayberry Bronzers with whom I conducted in-person interviews, and also discuss my increasing participation in the Bronze community, both online and off.

Destiny

When I first met her, Destiny was a college graduate in her twenties. She was working full-time while taking classes in preparation for graduate study. The first time we met in person was in the Plant Biology building on campus. She had sent me an e-mail an hour prior, saying, "I'm wearing a sort of Sumatran batik-y long dress with no waist. And I've got my Drusilla hair on today." I had no idea what this meant. Fortunately, she was the only person in the building's lobby when I came in.

Unlike me, she was very down-to-business, which confused me a bit, because my conversational style tends to be indirect and slowly paced, especially by East Coast standards. I attribute this not just to my personality, but to cultural factors as well: I grew up in California, the son of Indian immigrants. Destiny, I would learn later, grew up in New York, and her conversational style reflected that. As Michael Agar brilliantly explicates, this can lead to, among other things, awkward conversations (172).

I suspect our first conversation was more awkward for me than for Destiny, since she might have assumed that I knew what I was doing, whereas I knew that I didn't. My first clue that this was the case was the expression on her face when we first met. She had the same look on her face that my students typically do on the first day of class: they look expectantly at me, like I'm supposed to know what's going on, which usually prompts me to stifle a laugh. Which I did.

After some chit-chat about the batik-y dress, during which I tried not to act like I had no idea what one was, I gave her a spiel about my project, and mentioned how most people didn't seem to recognize the brilliance of *Buffy*. This comment is what seems to have gotten us past the initial awkwardness of never having met.

Once we started talking about the Bronze, I found Destiny to be a font of information. She immediately started telling me what a great community this was. It was, in fact, clear from the way she spoke that she assumed that I knew it was a community. I don't think it occurred to her that I might have thought otherwise.

I greatly enjoyed our first conversation, so much so that I said something about gushing with enthusiasm like a big goober, at which point she said "quote!" She went on to explain that Bronzers, in real life (RL) gatherings, often write down amusing comments — especially if they're more amusing when taken out of context — and post them on the board. As it happens, this ritual would come back to haunt me. A lot.

In talking with Destiny, it became clear that she is comfortable with computers. Although her college education was decidedly humanistic — she attended an all-female liberal arts college, from which she has a degree in opera — she was at the time working in a tech-support/system-administrator capacity. Unlike me, she seemed comfortable with the idea that one can surf the 'net in search of information that's otherwise not readily available, or for like-minded individuals who one wouldn't be likely to meet in real life. Like many of my other informants, she had visited other sites, but the Bronze is where she got hooked. When I asked her how she started posting, she said that at first, "I was so afraid of ~mere~ that I wouldn't post." But, she eventually overcame her fear of posters, like ~mere~, who she felt intimidated by. One day, after she had been lurking for a while, a topic of conversation arose —

Indian food — that she felt she could respond to. So she stopped lurking and started posting: she "delurked."

She first started posting after graduating from college and then moving to the Washington, DC area — which DC-area Bronzers came to call Mayberry. She found herself feeling increasingly isolated as a result of her difficulty in keeping in touch with old friends. Since she was good with computers, and loved *BtVS*, she started posting. Ironically, what started out as a low-maintenance, quasi-cyber social life became a set of high-maintenance real life friendships.

One reason that Bronzers develop such friendships is that most of the members are not viewing the Bronze as a substitute for real life, but rather as a vehicle to enrich real life. Through the Bronze, one could meet people with common interests in an increasingly fragmented society in which geography, occupation, and even family ties may not be enough to keep people connected.

Destiny mentioned to me that it's not unusual for people to be intimidated by the Bronze. In fact, her sister, who actually knew some of the Bronze regulars in real life, was intimidated enough that she refused to post. I said I could relate, that I had a lot of trouble following what was happening on the board, and wouldn't have a clue as to how or why I might start posting. I didn't realize that this last statement would also come back to haunt me.

Destiny described Bronzers as a caring, sympathetic group of people, as in any close-knit community. She was quite clear, however, that this community, just like any other, had its problems, including a stalker and a few relationships that didn't translate — or translated badly — from the Bronze to real life. But, on the other hand, there were relationships at the Bronze that translated quite well to RL. Destiny told me that "Booky and Skull were the first to get married." I found this statement striking. The names "Booky" and "Skull" were, after all, shortened versions of board names. But marriage was something that was very much a real life phenomenon. Destiny's use of nicknames of board names to describe people's real life marriage indicated that there could be no denying that the Bronze was neither real nor virtual. It was firmly lodged somewhere in between; there could be no going back to the simplistic view of real life and virtual reality as distinct worlds.

* * *

A few days after the first interview with Destiny, at which I had expressed my confusion about the appeal of the Bronze and my trepidation at the thought of posting, she called me to tell me about an interesting argument occurring at the Bronze. During that conversation, she also told me she thought I should de-lurk. Feeling self-conscious, especially since I was studying this community, I said that I thought it best if I remained a lurker. Destiny persisted, asking me if I had a nickname in mind. I said I didn't — the only one I could think of was taken — but mentioned that if I ever did de-lurk, I might use the board name "Quidam," since I had just seen the Cirque du Soleil production of the same name. The next day, while I was at the library, Destiny called me both at home and at work to tell me that people were posting to me "all over the place." I had been de-lurked.

Apparently, Destiny felt I should face my fear of writing to a few hundred strangers who didn't know me from Adam and would probably think I was dumb. Also, as she was to tell me later, she knew that I was probably lurking, and she thought that I would fit right in at the Bronze. She was, of course, correct: by becoming an active participant in the community, not only did I learn much more than I would have otherwise, but developed several important friendships. At the time, however, the opportunity Destiny provided to me by convincing me to de-lurk seemed more like a challenge. I had intended to be an observer and an interviewer, not a Bronzer. And yet, I suddenly found myself not the observer but the observed, the newbie trying to learn the community rules to fit in. The ethnographer's gaze had been reflected back, and the (artificial) distinction between observer and observed irrevocably confused.[1]

Over the course of my interviews with Destiny, I discovered that her parents are highly educated, and that she's very close to them, especially her father, because her mother was in graduate school during her formative years. Also, for some reason, it came up that she's Unitarian, and identifies with minorities in America because her mother is Puerto Rican. I would later discover that as a result of her college education, and her exposure to the humanities through her professor mother, she's familiar with feminist theory. She's also familiar with the idea of borderlands as theorized by Gloria Anzaldúa. As one example, she said she's fascinated by — possibly obsessed with — lycanthropy. When I asked her why, she said she's very interested in "involuntary transformation." For her, the werewolf — an important element in *Buffy*'s second and third seasons — speaks to the margins, the borderlands, in which humans can find themselves because of their race, gender, and sexuality.

My first interview with Destiny that didn't take place in the Plant Biology building happened over lunch in a downtown Thai restaurant. The interview had a bit of a surreal quality, mainly because the hostess kept yelling at me to hurry up and decide what I wanted, which left me feeling quite distracted. I was doing my best to not be too non-linear in my interviewing, when, seemingly of out of the blue, Destiny asked me if I was going to be there tomorrow. I had no idea what she was talking about. Then she reminded me that the Mayberry Bronzers were going to dinner at Cafe Atlantico, and

I should join them, and bring Mrs. Quidam. I hesitated, saying I didn't want to intrude, at which point she said to me, "you're not getting how this works." She was right: I wasn't. As it turns out, Bronzers tend to assume that persons who watch *Buffy* are pretty cool until proven otherwise.

So I went to dinner not sure what to expect, but wondering if the other Bronzers would be dressed like goths, or punks, or vampires, or witches, or something else occultish or supernatural. People. That night, there were sixteen of us all together, three of whom were from out of town. It turns out they were a pretty normal-looking, sociable bunch. My sense was that this was a college-educated, middle class, left-of-center group of people. Interestingly, this real life gathering matched the description of the Bronze given to me by several informants: a bunch of people sitting around a huge table, with everybody fading in and out of everybody else's conversations.

There was, however, one thing that I was not at all prepared for: the "quote" ritual. Apparently, at the beginning of the gathering — or perhaps beforehand — there was a decision made about who would be the "quote girl" for the day. I wasn't privy to this process, and so knew not that I would be sitting next to someone who would manage to write down all the stupid things I said — and there were many — over the course of the evening. I did, however, feel dubiously honored to discover how many of my "quotes" would appear later at the Bronze.

Writing a Better World

As mentioned above, there are several RL relationships that originated at the Bronze. But what I find even more interesting is that several non–RL relationships originated there as well. One of these was a wedding, which marked the first time I had ever seen the Whedon Improvisational Theater Troupe (WITT) in action. A WITT is particular story collectively created by Bronzers on the board. Bronzers often agree ahead of time to write an event into existence at a certain time, and then, at the appointed time, post improvised pieces of narrative that contribute to that event. In this case, the agreed-upon event was a wedding at the Bronze.

Much to my amazement, virtually everyone who posted during this event contributed to its creation. Furthermore, there seemed to be no objection to the fact that three people got married (to each other). Writing mostly in italics to indicate third person narrative rather than the usual direct speech, Bronzers came in, sat down, and enjoyed the wedding. Destiny spent most of the afternoon frantically running around (in italics, of course), making sure the flowers were in place, the cake was ordered, and so on. For the better part of four hours, Bronzers posted as if a real time wedding was taking place, literally writing the wedding into existence. Posters described themselves entering the Bronze, and then proceeded to write detailed descriptions of their wedding attire, where they sat, what they drank, even how often they fell asleep during the ceremony. Their personas, their physical selves, and the physical space that they inhabited were all created in vivid, and generally humorous, detail.

The wedding serves to highlight several themes. First, Bronzers tend to be extremely imaginative and literate. Second, Bronzers are literally writing the Bronze into existence. Third, as alluded to above, the Bronze is a close-knit community brought together by a love of *Buffy*. Apparently, *Buffy*, boredom, or something else draws people to the Bronze, and once there, its regulars devote large blocks of time to events such as the WITT wedding.

In my experience, just keeping up with normal conversations requires a fair amount of time and attention. Indeed, Destiny said that her first post of the day typically took one hour of her morning; once I became a regular poster, I found the same to be true for me. I would estimate that being a regular Bronzer required a minimum two-hour daily time commitment from me. Since many Bronzers are posting from work, being a regular would seem to require extraordinary parallel processing and logical compartmentalization. It would also seem to require a certain willingness to use technology to subvert its own function as a productivity-enhancing, labor-saving device. In this sense, the computer, that symbol of white-collar alienation and atomization, is used much as the Sony Walkman is used in Rey Chow's description — as a technology used to partially offset, subvert, and resist the cultural and economic hegemony that it supports (145).

The second of these themes strikes me as being particularly relevant to understanding how it is that the Bronze has become such a "genuine" community. Bronzers are, in effect, using language to objectify themselves, to make subjective experiences more objective. Language is what allows them to think outside themselves, to make less subjective what's in their heads (Berger and Luckmann 61). Just as the characters in *Buffy* are self-reflexive, using language to think out loud, to think outside of themselves, so too are Bronzers. This is not to say that Bronzers are a self-selecting group of people who are actually similar to the characters in *Buffy*. But there is a connection: Bronzers use language in a fashion similar to that of *Buffy*'s Scooby Gang. Since much of this language is either adopted or adapted from the show, or is a result of discussing it, it is not surprising that there are similarities. The difference is one of intent, rather than outcome: whereas the Scooby Gang uses language to engage its audience, Bronzers do it to write their worlds. They also use this unique language to engage their audience — as some Bronzers did when they knew I was a lurking ethnographer — and to perform their identities, especially during WITT performances. But the identities that Bronzers perform are largely their own identities, although they may be stylized or idealized versions.

In social constructionist parlance, language is used to objectify knowledge, which can then become institutionalized. Institutions, once codified, then become taken for granted by individuals and become the common sense order of the universe that "coerces" individuals into behaving according to institutional norms. Language creates institutions that, once objectified, are external forces acting upon the individual. However, the Bronze is able to resist the reification of its constructs. One reason for this is that Bronzer language exists between written language and spoken language. In the Anglo-American cultural tradition, the written word is considered permanent, whereas the spoken word is considered fleeting, and it is in this tradition that both *Buffy* and the Bronze operate. But Bronzer language is neither as permanent as words on paper, nor as impermanent as vocal language. Words can be chosen more carefully than in real time conversations. But, they disappear after one week unless someone bothers to copy them. The Bronze is therefore characterized by change, but not by the pace of change in real time. It is stable but not permanent, flexible but not fleeting.

Because Bronzers don't interact face to face — at least not at the Bronze — there is also greater latitude in being true to oneself. At the Bronze, I needn't respond to anyone who I don't like. And, I can write in as evocative or sensual a manner as I want — within certain limits — because the thoughts that are conveyed are not easily backed up with actions. Hence, writing *smooch* at the end of a post is different than kissing the real person; it's a sign of affection, but without physical baggage. Furthermore, Bronzers can reinscribe themselves via their online personas. They can be any imaginable physical entity, or they can get married in threesomes, or wear clothes they would never wear in public (even though they might own them in real life). They can, in effect, be more like their idealized selves.

There are other ways in which the Bronze resists ossification. For example, even though Bronzers write themselves and their physical environments into existence, the Bronze is not a physical space. There can be as many doors, bars, tables, closets, or rooms as anyone cares to imagine. Many of these physical creations are eventually forgotten, but some — like the Font of Employment, in which Bronzers are ritually dunked for good luck in their job-search endeavors — are popular enough that they become a regular part of the imagined physicality of the Bronze. Since no individuals' construct need necessarily conflict with anyone else's, one source of conflict — that over physical space — is transformed into an encouragement of a changing imagined physical space.

As with all institutions, new blood shakes up the mix. While there are certainly people who do not pay much attention to newbies, there are many who do: there are at least four sites that provide information for newbies. Much to my surprise, I've rarely seen a "newbie drive-by" (a hastily prepared post by someone who is not a Bronzer and has not bothered to learn the posting rules) that did not result in helpful posts, usually with links to the "Bronze Welcome Wagon," an unofficial site with a great deal of information on how to become a Bronzer. While inconsiderate newbie posts will sometimes elicit angry responses from Bronze regulars, for the most part Bronzers welcome newbies as long as they are not malicious. Newbies who are malicious — "trolls" in Internet parlance — are called "bezoars," and are typically ignored. Bezoars, named after the demonic creature of the *Buffy* episode "Bad Eggs," usually go away on their own once they realize that nobody's paying attention to them. However, there have been cases in which bezoars have persistently disrupted the board, in which case someone will usually track down their location and report them to their Internet service provider.

Thus, newbies elicit a wide range of reactions, depending on who is at the Bronze and how crowded it is. But, in the case of newbies who carefully de-lurk and announce their newbie status, most Bronzers are downright warm and friendly. Indeed, the prevalence of sites with helpful hints for newbies indicates that a good number of Bronzers have continually devoted substantial effort to keeping the Bronze inclusive. These sites are usually maintained by subgroups ("clubs") of the Bronze, such as the Newbie Welcoming Committee and Pathetically Helpful Bronzers Anonymous. This is not to say that cliques don't form. In fact, at least one Bronze club has become an invitation-only club for which new members must be sponsored. But, the Bronze *per se* has resisted this type of stratification.

Finally, and most importantly, the very language that in many instances can lead to a degree of social control is used to disrupt institutional tendencies at the Bronze. This is accomplished through the use of slang. Language can objectify by providing a common basis for understanding meaning. But Bronzers use the process in reverse: slang is prevalent to the point where precise word choice seems more the exception than the rule. It allows Bronzers to create a richness and connotation that would not exist if they used precise, and hence strictly denotative, language. Similar to the manner in which an electric guitarist uses distortion, meaning is conveyed not only in the sound, but in the noise surrounding the sound. The result is a swirling mass of coded phrases, layered meanings, and double entendres. This becomes especially apparent in cases in which Bronzers are discussing topics that they deem inappropriate for this "family board." For example, rather than not talk about topics of a sexual nature, Bronzers instead do so with various degrees of opacity by "piggybacking" additional meanings onto standard words for the benefit of those in the know.

It is this slang that I initially found so bewildering about the Bronze. But in retrospect, it is this connotative use of language that simultaneously encourages creativity, encourages new posters to learn about the people they're posting to before jumping into a conversation, and allows for conversations that create a feeling of community. I believe that it is this messy, imprecise, and unstable language that makes the Bronze a community; without it, the Bronze would likely become just another sterile, topical, denotative, well-defined, and efficient medium of communication.

Blade—The Vampire Hunter

I had been posting for several months when I first interviewed Blade—The Vampire Hunter. We had met once before, briefly, but our first interview was really the first time I had talked with him. While I still felt like a relative newbie, I don't know if I was seen that way. I had, after all, by this time joined a couple of clubs: I was the 27th member of BAD (Bronzers Adoring Darla), and the 12th member of the PBPK (Posting Board Porch Kitties). I was also a member of MacWatchers, a group of Bronzers who used and shared information about Macintosh computers.

I had also by this time become a groupie. I so enjoyed one particular Bronzer's posts that she allowed me to become the seventh of her groupies. It was through groupie-dom that I got my first taste of firsthand WITT: several Bronzers, on the occasion of the birthday of she-to-whom-we-group, each took turns grabbing the microphone and praising the day that she was born. In retrospect, I'm not sure why we did this. But it was fun, and very funny, too, as we each took turns waxing melodramatic off the top of our heads. And from work, no less.

I had also witnessed some negative events at the Bronze. One of these involved a cyberstalker; the other, a suicide. Both of these events were interesting to me because of the confusion surrounding them. The suicide, for example, was an eloquent and elaborate description of a Bronzer entering the Bronze and killing herself. I don't why she did this; I can only speculate that she felt alienated enough to make it clear that her persona would not return. The frightening thing, however, was that nobody seemed to know at the time whether this online suicide would be accompanied by a real life suicide. Fortunately, that situation seems to have resolved itself with no loss of life.

The cyberstalker issue is similarly confusing. In my e-mail communications with the person accused of stalking, it became clear that he was unaware that he had crossed the boundary of what others considered appropriate electronic communication. Thus, at one extreme were Bronzers who supported this individual; they felt that there was a clique that was trying to control who could and couldn't post, and were looking for flimsy excuses to ostracize others. At the other extreme, however, were Bronzers who felt that persons who repeatedly violated another's personal (electronic) space should not be allowed to continue posting. I doubt that I will ever know exactly what happened, as every version of the stalking that I've heard has been different. But the situation points to one of the contradictions faced by Bronzers: their tolerant community, if it is to remain that way, must remain open to antithetical and even intolerant points of view.

Blade is what Destiny refers to as one of the "old guard," meaning that he has been posting pretty much from the beginning. He is a most atypical person. He's an Air Force Captain, and holds a B.A. in philosophy, a J.D., and a black belt in Tang Su Do. When I first interviewed him, he was a trial lawyer in the office of the Judge Advocate General, where his job title was "Chief of Military Justice." He is also the President of the Whole Wide World, a title that he acquired after he organized the first Posting Board Party in Los Angeles, at which someone commented that, judging by his ability to throw a gala event and graciously mingle with the guests, he would make a good politician. Apparently, as often happens at the Bronze, things got "out of hand," and the next thing he knew, he was President of the Whole Wide World.

Blade's an interesting, and interested, person. He negotiates several dramatically different worlds, and he does so very conscientiously, on a regular basis. Like the comic book character from whom he takes his name, he is an African-American man. He talks easily about racial issues, describing, for example, his less-than-ideal childhood in a stereotypical "black neighborhood," or arguments he would have with fellow African-American law students about what it meant to be a "race traitor." He says that he is often described as "a nice guy, but not what you'd expect."

He's definitely not what I expected, and I suspect Blade wouldn't want it any other way. He's a firm believer in the benefits of multiplicity, saying that if there's one thing he learned as a philosophy major, it's that there's never a single right answer. And so he consciously tries to take the best of whatever world he's in and leave the rest behind. He sees himself as a liminal individual; in fact, he rather seems to enjoy challenging other people's assumptions. He specifically mentioned how interesting the expressions on people's faces are when they walk into his office and see it decorated not with the trappings of military success, but with action figures.

Blade is much more optimistic than I am, particularly with regard to technology. Whereas I tend to view technology as another means by which capital and capitalists exert their hegemonic influence over individuals, Blade sees in technology the possibility that the next generation might inherit a more tolerant world than the one in which we grew up. [2] For Blade, the Bronze exemplifies this possibility: it bridges gaps between people, potentially allowing Bronzers to move beyond differences in race, gender, sexuality, geography, physical appearance, or whatever. Blade admits that it's not a perfect virtual world, but because it brings together people who would probably never communicate with each other in real life, it's a thoroughly enjoyable exercise in tolerance and diversity.

A few days after my first interview with Blade, he posted his first State of the Bronze address. Many of the issues he addressed humorously in that post were issues that we discussed quite seriously in our interview. Whether our conversation had anything to do with this address I don't know. However, when I thanked him for his inspirational words the next day at the Bronze, he mentioned that he hoped this gave me something more to work with.

It did. Not only was I glad to read the words of someone who had such high hopes for the future, but I was happy to know that someone else was thinking about issues that concern me, and was even of a like mind regarding some of them. His words also served as a reminder of just how artificial subject/object distinctions are: until my work on the Bronze is complete, I'll always feel at least a little like an outsider, a voyeur, turning my fellow Bronzers into a self-serving research project. But at the same time, I can't deny the possibility that the experimenter is affecting the experiment, or even that the experimenter is being experimented on himself.

What follows is excerpted from the first State of the Bronze address.

State of the Bronze Address says:
(Wed Jan 20 10:49:35 1999 [...])
Madame Vice President, members of the Cabinet, Apollo Interactive, the Honorable Joss Whedon, the Honorable RD, distinguished VIPs, honored guests, my fellow Bronzers. Today I have the honor of reporting to you the State of the Bronze. Today I stand before you to report that the Bronze is the single greatest, most diverse, open minded, forward thinking cyber community in history. For the first time in our history, people from all walks of life, social & economic backgrounds, ages, cultural backgrounds, religions, political views, and from every corner of the globe have come together in a community which has demonstrated these lines can be crossed and we as a community can unite for the good of all. My fellow Bronzers, I stand before you to report that the state of our Bronze is strong [...].

The Bronze must continue to build bridges which bring people together along racial, economic, cultural, religious gender, and political backgrounds. America's journey down this road, has been a long one. For the Bronze, we are the pioneers that will keep this truly free community alive. Free of hatred, bigotry, racism, sexism, and discrimination [...].

The Bronze may have begun as a fan based community, centered around genius writing, superb acting, excellent special effects, and incredible stunts, but now we are so much more. Although we can never forget the Sunnydale roots from which we sprung, let us now realize that it is not this which holds us together. For now the bond we share as a community is stronger than ever before, with a power not seen anywhere else on the Internet. It is time for us to see this is our time, we are on the cusp of a new dawn for America. Several seasons from now, another President of the Whole Wide World will post in this place and report on the State of the Bronze. She or he will look back on a 21st century bronze shaped in so many ways by the decisions we make here and now, by the promises we make. So let it be said of us then that we were thinking not only of our time, but of our future. Of continuing the forward thinking, high ideal, creative momentum, and the putting aside of divisions to find the true strength we know we are capable of [...].

Thank you and good afternoon.

Blade — The Vampire Hunter
President of the Whole Wide World

Taster's Choice

Like Blade, Taster's Choice (TC) has been a Bronzer since the board's inception. His board name is a reference to the Taster's Choice coffee commercials that aired in the early 1990s that featured Anthony Stewart Head, who would go on to play Giles on *Buffy*. In our first interview, he told me about the uproar that was caused by Warner Brothers' attempt to modify the Bronze linear posting board. In fact, he still has the letter he wrote to The WB urging it not to make changes to the board or eliminate it. His reasoning was twofold: not only had a remarkable fan community sprung up because of *Buffy*, but the WB would be wise to not discourage that fan base. TC told me the story of this first Bronzer rebellion without being asked about it. He was, in fact, the second person to do so; another informant, Patrick, had referred to it as a "mutiny." That this event was the first thing they mentioned suggests that it was a defining event for the community. Indeed, it was the event that guaranteed the transformation of the Bronze from a promotion for *Buffy* to a self-sustained community.

On the one hand, this rebellion was hardly subversive, since keeping the fans happy was of great benefit to The WB in promoting *Buffy*. But on the other hand, it indicated a radical change in popular culture: in effect, the fans extracted a *quid pro quo* from The WB by insisting that they have a voice in defining the fandom. In this sense, the Bronzer rebellion served as a founding myth because it guaranteed the existence of the community, because the fans stood up to the big corporation and won. But even more than that, the Bronzer rebellion solidified the democratization of fandom that began with the first letter-writing campaign to keep the original *Star Trek* series on the air. No longer could producers simply take for granted a passive audience. For better or for worse — or both — the audience insisted on being part of the cultural production process.

TC, like my other informants, is hardly a teen slacker. When I first met him, he had recently completed his master's degree in Early Christian Theology, after which he worked on a congressional campaign in Iowa. When the campaign was over, he came to Mayberry (DC) from Dubuque to look for a job. I met him through Destiny; he was staying with her while looking for a place to live in the area. His decision to move to Mayberry was based on two factors: his occupational background made the nation's capital a likely place for him to find a job; and he knew Bronzers here.

In many ways, TC is a typical old-fashioned Midwestern liberal. He grew up in a lower-middle class suburban environment, what he calls a "blue-collar ethnic" community. He's comfortable talking about his socialist leanings, his Irish Catholic roots, his strong Christian beliefs, and the fact that his mother was the first person in his family to go to college. About the only thing we haven't discussed in detail is his graduate school experience, which was certainly unpleasant, even by graduate student standards.

TC has two "wifettes"; the WITT wedding referred to above was his. When I asked him whether polygyny, even in virtual form, wasn't somewhat un–Christian, he seemed a bit surprised that I should ask the question. I don't actually recall whether he ever answered my question. But it did lead to a very lengthy discussion about Christianity, and how he went to graduate school to discover for himself what "real" Christianity was, and how unconvinced he is by the "postmodern turn." For TC, authorial intent is paramount; reader response theory is bogus; and the Self— his Christian self— inheres firmly in his body.

TC is hardly what I would call a cultural relativist. For example, where I saw cultural criticism in *Buffy*, TC saw the classical Greek hero's journey. And yet, as with most of the Bronzers I've met, he seems perfectly comfortable with the idea that his views are not shared by his fellow Mayberrians. Indeed, Destiny captured my view of religion quite well when she spoke of her own religious upbringing: "I associate religion with this hidebound Catholicism that my parents practice, or practiced, which was always kind of, you know, no partying, no carousing, no drinking." To which TC responded: "You hung out with the wrong bunch of Catholics!"

Postmodern Community: Who Did This?

I have been hesitant to identify strong links between *Buffy* and the Bronze lest I overstate those connections. Still, I believe that much of what makes the Bronze unique is the same thing that makes *Buffy* unique: a postmodern view of society that lends itself to a use of language that can simultaneously deconstruct assumptions about society and reconstruct new types of community. How much of the Bronze can be explained by this postmodern view, however, is beyond me, and I suspect it always will be. My explanation is undoubtedly one among many, but it does suggest the importance of alternative communities, not as communities of "others," but as communities built along non-traditional lines that coexist with traditional communities and that fill some important human need, what Howard Rheingold refers to as the "hunger for community" (xx).

The Bronze is a function of BtVS, and throughout its existence has exhibited a great deal of institutional flexibility. But the question remains: how did it get this way? The fact that the Bronze comprises *Buffy* fans suggests its current characteristics, but does not necessitate them. Similarly, the fact that the Bronze tends to exhibit tolerance and flexibility is not evidence that it cannot be otherwise. What is it that turns this possibility of a flexible, open, and "genuine" community into a reality?

When I first met Destiny, she had been posting for about six months. She posted from work, and it quickly became clear to me that her work environment was far from ideal. I was therefore thrilled when I read her post to the Bronze that she had found a new job. I was saddened, though, when she announced about two weeks later that this was her last day at the Bronze, because it wouldn't be possible for her to post from her new job.

I was overwhelmed by the posts she received in response, and found myself getting choked up as I read the heartfelt goodbyes and well-wishes of my fellow Bronzers. And I was surprised: even though we lived barely ten miles apart and keep in touch outside of the Bronze, I found myself already missing her.

It was at this point that I realized that in focusing on the structure of the Bronze, I had given insufficient attention to the importance of individual agency, and to the individuals who set the tone at the Bronze. I realized that the Bronze's potential as an open and tolerant community would not have been realized were it not for particular individuals. All of the individuals whose names appear in this ethnography are respected members of the community, people whose words defined the community in its early years, people who would go out of their way to welcome outsiders like me. This is not to say that everybody would find the Bronze as open as I do. But that's not for lack of trying on the part of a few key Bronzers.

These persons, like Destiny, are not merely members of the community; they are shapers of it. They are, basically, thoughtful people. They respond to people's posts in a positive manner, and they always respond, even if it takes a few days. They don't disrespect people, even obnoxious newbies (or clueless ethnographers). And, most importantly, they respond to posts *in kind*, always taking them seriously. Destiny, for example, has always comprehended the seriousness of certain posts, or the playfulness of other posts, and responded accordingly. Rather than merely post messages about herself for others to read, her messages also take into account what other people want to hear. She doesn't just talk about herself; she draws out others. She doesn't just put her thoughts out there; she interacts with other people's thoughts. Furthermore, she does what not everyone is willing to do: she talks to newbies, knowing full well that many of them may soon disappear for good.

When Destiny announced that she would be leaving the Bronze, I had been posting for less than a year. I no longer felt like a newbie, but rather like I had found a place where I belonged. That's why it gave me a bizarre sense of closure when Destiny disappeared. I knew she was still out there. And I knew that even though she wasn't posting, that huge conversation called the Bronze would seamlessly continue.

At that point I found myself compelled, more than ever, to welcome new people, to provide the sort of environment that others provided for me. Interestingly, it was an environment that I had never been in at work. At the Bronze, people actually noticed when I wasn't there, and I could talk to the same people every day, creating a sense of normalcy that didn't occur in my real life work environment, where students and faculty were constantly coming and going according the hours they set for themselves, and where the routines and familiar faces changed every semester.

Conclusions

In the course of my interviews with Bronzers, and of my increasing addiction to the Bronze, three themes emerged. The first of these is the concept of community. Is the Bronze a community? I think that it definitely is. In fact, I also believe that it's a unique community, because it resists stagnation. One reason for this is *BtVS* itself: because the show challenges the audience to question accepted norms, it encourages thoughtful, critical, and lengthy discussion. Indeed, if the posting board didn't allow for long conversations that could meander far from their starting point, it's doubtful the community would be as close-knit.

Another reason that the Bronze resists stagnation is that brings people together based on a very specific context —*Buffy*— but does not necessarily lend itself to any other contexts. This means that there is very little I can assume about persons with whom I'm speaking: categories such as age, nationality, gender, sexuality, race, or occupation become largely irrelevant until more information is provided. Bronzers are able to meet people who, in real life, they are separated from due to geographical or occupational barriers. Most of the Bronzers I have met live in parts of the world I would never visit, and have jobs that would otherwise never lead them to interact with me.

Furthermore, as Blade mentioned in his presidential address, many Bronzers feel they are freed from the constraints of bigotry, since bigotry tends to focus on physical characteristics, on the body. However, it is important not to overstate the relevance of interacting in the virtual world while leaving one's physical self in the real world. As Kolko, Nakamura, and Rodman show, people bring the same subjectivity, the same biases and assumptions, into cyberspace that they have in real life (1–4). In the case of the Bronze, a majority of members are white, and there is considerably less ethnic diversity than in real life. There are also very few regular members who can't afford a computer, Internet access, and the time to post.[3]

The second theme is the importance of language. What originally drew me to *Buffy* was the dialog. The unique discourse that characterizes *Buffy* is used by Bronzers to constitute the Bronze in a unique way, allowing Bronzers to push their Bronze reality into more meaningful and relevant (to themselves) directions. Furthermore, the reality that is the Bronze can be transformed to be applicable to RL much faster than real life institutions, and hence it's a safe haven, a place where the conflicts of real life can be dealt with by writing into existence a world that can handle them. In this sense, the Bronze is better than reality, because its institutional structure matches more closely the subjective lived experiences — the reality that people actually think and feel and experience internally — of its members. This is not to say that people are consciously constituting the Bronze, or that they're aware that it's being done, or even that they're not engaged in pure escapism. But, as both Turkle and Stone argue regarding virtual life generally, the Bronze can be extremely beneficial for persons who use it to engage real life more effectively. It allows them to retake control of the signifier and use it to make a community that's more in keeping with their ideal worlds.

Obviously, this wouldn't work if Bronzers weren't predisposed to being literary. But, like Joss Whedon, who is known for his liberal arts background and literary styling, Bronzers seem to relish the text — and the intertextual references — in *Buffy*, and this comes through at the Bronze. Indeed, among Bronzers, there appear to be an inordinate number of lawyers, editors, and members with degrees in the humanities. Furthermore, many Bronzers write fan fiction. But, even if this was not the case, a cursory examination of typical posts indicates a creative and literate group of people who are able to use the flexible linear structure of the Bronze to let loose their creative and community-building impulses.

The third theme is the particular (postmodern) use of language, especially slang. The Bronze use of slang is of interest in ways that relate to the concepts of language and community as mentioned above. Slang has the effect of denoting less precisely: inventive use of language can create a vagueness that in turn lends a depth of meaning to words. Use of slang and non-standard terms allows the speaker to connote more and denote less, thereby allowing the listener or reader to fill in more of the gaps with his or her own imagination, to understand the content in a more meaningful way. In a sense, this type of connotative language contains an implicit admission that language is at best an imperfect substitute for meaning. Therefore, rather than inflate the importance of language, which would merely be pretending that it's more useful than it is, many Bronzers write in a way that points to the limitations of language. Rather than focus on precision, Bronzers often focus instead on imagery, which, because it doesn't even try to convey specific meaning, conveys it better than precise and denotative verbiage.

One example of this can be seen in the mistakes people make in their posts. Typically, upon noticing a mistake, a Bronzer will post again with corrections, which will often be followed by a statement such as "eye=suck." This is as if to say, "I realize I messed up my last post and I'm sorry but there's nothing I can do about it now so I guess I suck." Such a statement is an enormous generalization to make based on a misspelling. But it indicates not only a certain reflexiveness, but also an unwillingness to argue semantics. To say "I suck" is to overstate one's apology to the degree that it leaves little room for discussion, as if to say "I admitted I suck for screwing up my post, so deal with it." Furthermore, it indicates a lack of attachment to the subject at hand. To say that something "sucks," is to have so unreasoned an opinion, that all debate on the issue is forestalled. It's an indication that I'm not willing to get into a big discussion to justify my views because I'm not too attached to them, and that I'm willing to open myself up to other people's unreasoned criticism. It's like admitting that "I hate this but you probably don't, so we've got our opinions and we'll never convince each other because language is too imperfect and maybe there's no absolute truth anyway, so let's agree to disagree."

As another example, consider three non-standard words that are frequently used — in my experience more so than any others — at the Bronze: "tag," "bezoar," and "whup. " A "tag" is an HTML tag, and is usually referred to in the context of a "dropped tag." Tags are used to change the style of posts, but when tags are "dropped" at the end — when someone forgets to use a closing tag — the whole post retains the special characteristic. So, for example, if I forget to put a closing italics tag at the end of a word, then the computer won't know to stop italicizing, and everything I type will be italicized. Tags have taken on mythical qualities at the Bronze: not only is there a club to save and feed them, but there is also one devoted to slaying runaway tags. Why devote so much energy to giving life to something that makes posts look funny? Dropped tags are the ultimate symbol of miscommunication. For example, a State of the Bronze address would probably be much less impressive if the whole thing alternated randomly between superscript and italics.

Similarly, bezoars and whup have also taken on mythic qualities. Many people actively fight them, ascribing to them fierce beast-like qualities. There is a club for bezoar killers, and a product called "whup-b-gone." What exactly are these creatures? Bezoars are people who flame, non-regular posters whose purpose is to antagonize. Whup is work. Interestingly, many Bronzers have "personalized" work, mean people, and miscommunication, ascribing to them free will and vile characteristics, which they then fight in their third-person Bronzer incarnations.

Generally, the Bronzer perspective is one of multiplicity. My informants, while obviously not a random sample, all focused on diversity, on difference, and on the importance of meeting new and interesting people. They vary greatly, at least ostensibly, in their beliefs. But, they all seem to accept the existence of a wide variety of beliefs, and this, I believe, is what enables them to maintain their community.

The Bronze, then, is unique because it takes a group of people who can identify with marginalization, and turns them into a community, allowing them to write into existence the world as it would be if it was a better place. *Buffy* speaks to the outcast in all of us, and this explains the attraction of the Bronze, as well as the ability of its members to be a community: if we're all outcasts, it behooves us to be inclusive. This is not to say that Bronzers are outcasts or loners; on the contrary, they generally seem to be both social and sociable. But they're also people who know what it's like to be on the margins, to not fully fit in, to not belong to cliques. Indeed, more than one Bronzer has speculated that the Bronze is a community of outsiders, a group of people who know how to fit into the real world, but who may not feel comfortable doing so. One Mayberrian, in relaying her high school experiences to me, exclaimed that she had made a recent discovery of which she was still incredulous: "I was one of the *cool* people in high school!" I can't help but wonder how she would've turned out had she known this as a teenager.

Notes

1. See, for example, both Rosaldo and Berkhofer on the problems and dangers of maintaining (constructed) boundaries between Self and Other, subject and object, us and them. Where

Rosaldo discusses these false binaries from an anthropological perspective, Berkhofer does so from a theoretical perspective. See also Desmond and Dominguez (477) on the ability of ethnographers, whether unwittingly or not, to maintain power imbalances.

2. Jameson (in Jameson and Miyoshi) discusses both of these views in some detail; Best and Kellner provide a cursory treatment in their first chapter.

3. To my knowledge, no demographic information on Bronzers has ever been generated. My estimates are based my own observations. For example, my "shout list" as of April 2000 listed the names of 102 Bronzers with whom I regularly conversed. Of that list, I know the gender of 85, of which 60 are women. Of the 36 people whose occupations I know, virtually all are either students or white-collar professionals, including several lawyers, editors, information technology specialists, and even four Bronzers with PhDs. As another example, as of March 2002, valMichael's birthday list, which has since been taken off line, indicates that 1,437 Bronzers sent him their birth dates. Of those, the youngest was 10 years old, the oldest was 61, the average age was 27.1, the median age was 25.6, and the mode was 20.

Based on my own observations, the comments of Bronzers, and the few magazine and newspaper articles written about the fandom, I think it's safe to say it consists disproportionately of white women. My impression is that most Bronzers tend to be white, female, heterosexual, middle- or upper-class (they have computers with Internet access from which they can post during the day), and perhaps politically liberal. Indeed, it seems that in general Bronzers tend to be older and more highly educated than the advertising and marketing of *Buffy* would suggest.

Works Cited

Agar, Michael. *Language Shock: Understanding the Culture of Conversation*. New York: Quill, 1994.

Anzaldua, Gloria. *Borderlands x La Frontera: The New Mestiza*. San Francisco: Aunt Lute, 1987.

"Bad Eggs." Buffy the Vampire Slayer. The WB Television Network. WBDC, Washington, DC. 19 Oct. 1998.

Berkhofer, Robert F. *Beyond the Great Story: History as Text and Discourse*. Cambridge, MA: Belknap Press of Harvard University Press, 1995.

Best, Steven, and Douglas Kellner. *Postmodern Theory: Critical Interrogations*. New York: Guilford, 1991.

Desmond, Jane C., and Virginia R. Dominguez. "Resituating American Studies in a Critical Internationalism." *American Quarterly* 48 (1996): 475–90.

Jameson, Fredric, and Masao Miyoshi, eds. *The Cultures of Globalization*. Durham: Duke University Press, 1998.

Kolko, Beth E., Lisa Nakamura, and Gilbert B. Rodman, eds. *Race in Cyberspace*. New York: Routledge, 2000.

Rheingold, Howard. *The Virtual Community: Homesteading on the Electronic Frontier*. Rev. ed. Cambridge, MA: MIT Press, 2000.

Rosaldo, Renato. *Culture & Truth: The Remaking of Social Analysis*. Boston: Beacon Press, 1993.

Stone, Allucquere Rosanne. *The War of Desire and Technology at the Close of the Mechanical Age*. Cambridge. MA: MIT, 1995.

Turkle, Sherry. *Life on the Screen: Identity in the Age of the Internet*. New York: Simon and Schuster, 1995.

"Fake It Till You Make It": *Understanding Media Addiction and* Buffy the Vampire Slayer

David Kociemba

"I've gone to two *Buffy* posting-board parties, which were intense. Some people just live, eat, breathe, and die this show. It's flattering and at times frightening. [laughs] But this is why we play, to reach people and affect people. At the end of the day, we want to thank people for being so enthusiastic and loyal. But my name is Eliza and I play a *character* named Faith!"—Eliza Dushku [Reiss 164]

"It's wonderful to get lost in a story, isn't it?"—Andrew, "Storyteller" [B7016]

Characters involved in crises, interventions, or recovery, litter the *Buffy the Vampire Slayer* and *Angel* television series. As part of the fantasy genre, however, the binges and withdrawal symptoms of addiction are linked to nontraditional substances and pursuits, such as black magicks, and the vampire's drinking of blood. Such narratives of the battle between compelled and chosen desires fit right in the foundational story of a girl fated to be different yet who fought to be normal. The two series give its fans the tools to identify a developing addiction through Willow's malignant dependency on black magicks in the sixth season of *BtVS* and the storylines of Faith and Angel. But what happens when fantasy television investigates fandom as an addiction? In the final two seasons of *BtVS*, fans are encouraged to turn that diagnostic gaze on their own lives, as the obsessions of Warren, Andrew, and Jonathan with mass media products mirror the fan's mastery of the Buffyverse. Yet, the recovery model the series uses to that point faces two troubling questions when applied to media addiction. How does the use of narrative in a 12-step recovery program change when a fascination with narrative and stories is part of the addiction? And can performing sobriety — or learning to "fake it till you make it" (Flynn 147) — work when imaginative role-playing is the addictive pursuit?[1] Andrew's experiences in *BtVS*'s seventh season give the troubled fan one possible solution.

> Neither this article nor these series claim that all or even most of fandom are media addicts. Writing fan fiction, attending conventions, doing cosplay, playing the series' role playing games, or posting to various fan community message boards are not proof of a media addiction.[2] Habitual use of or dependency on a substance or activity alone is not enough to define addiction. Addictions produce serious negative life consequences, such as the loss of relationships, jobs, or one's freedom. The life marked by addiction is damaged and damaging. Joss Whedon described the distinction between addiction and the devotion that the series creators sought to create when he said, "I have never had any particular life of my own, so I don't see any particular reason why anyone should run out to get one. Of course, if they're dressing up like Willow and staying in their basement for nine months at a time, that's not good. But the show's designed to foster slavish devotion; it has it from me, and I entirely respect it in others" [Havens 43–44].

Is there such a thing as media addiction? Treating habitual, compulsive, and, in extreme cases, pathological media use as an addiction is not uncontroversial. The model used here is the one LaRose, Lin, and Easton use to describe the general symptoms found in accounts of Internet addiction (228–9). Their description finds its source in a diagnostic model drawing from operational definitions built from popular accounts of television addiction (used in McIlwraith 1998; McIlwraith et al. 1991; Smith 1986), as well as definitions of television dependence drawn from diagnostic criteria for substance dependence (Kubey 1996). Nor are LaRose, Lin, and Easton alone in creating such links. They cite the fact that researchers have put the American Psychiatric Association's (A.P.A.) diagnostic criteria to various uses. One study defines addiction to video games using the A.P.A.'s criteria for addiction to gambling (Griffiths 1991). Several studies define television addiction (McIlwraith 1998) or Internet addiction (Brenner 1997; Scherer 1997) using its criteria for psychoactive substance abuse dependency. Another author synthesizes its criteria for both gambling and drug addiction to define Internet Addiction Disorder (Young 1998; 1999). Finally, several other authors equate media addiction to existing criteria for behavioral addictions (Griffiths 1999; 2000; Greenberg et al. 1999; and Rozin & Stoess 1993) or to Impulse Control Disorders (Cooper, Scherer, Boies, & Gordon 1999 and Shapira et al. 2000). The metaphor of a mental disease in which chemicals naturally produced in the brain are involved in the addiction process inspires all of these diagnostic criteria (LaRose, Lin, and Easton 226–228).

Television, Internet, and video game addictions show substantial correlations, according to Greenberg et al. (1999).[3] Three studies show a low but statistically significant correlation between personality traits, television addiction symptoms and amount of television use (Finn 1992; McIlwraith 1998; and McIlwraith et al. 1991). Some research shows a positive relationship between depression and Internet use (Kraut et al. 1998; Sanders 2000; Young and Rogers 1998), loneliness and time spent watching television (Canary and Spitzberg 1993), and attention deficits with television addiction (McIlwraith 1998). On the other hand, severe negative life consequences (like divorce or social isolation) are necessary to distinguish addiction from habit, but that requirement has not been observed in past studies (LaRose, Lin, and Easton 229–235). Still, these studies indicate a dialogue in the sciences on the existence and meaning of media addiction that just predates the final two seasons of *BtVS*.

The disordered or addictive personality, operant conditioning, and social-cognitive models are three prevalent views on the origins and development of media addiction. The addictive personality model suggests that a particular underlying personality type might explain all addictions. Viewers understand Warren and Andrew through this model. Due to their relative lack of screen time prior to the sixth season, it's simply who they are. The operant conditioning model sees consumption dependency progressing through four phases: initiation, transition to ongoing use, addiction, and behavior change. Willow's a classic example of the operant conditioning model. She uses black magicks as self-medication, which leads to negative life consequences, which leads to greater self-medication. Social-cognitive theory describes a process featuring a (lack of) self-control through (un)timely self-monitoring, evaluation against personal standards or group norms, and self-administered rewards, tangible or psychological in nature. Willow and Jonathan's extensive character histories allow the audience to experience their addictions through the social-cognitive model's much more complex understanding of the interplay of self and society.

No one theory fully explains media addiction and recovery. If underlying personality traits explain all addictions, it is still far from certain that the same trait predisposes someone to an addiction to media as well as to substances. In the operant conditioning model, depression and low self-esteem are both causes and consequences of media addiction, which is indicated by a cyclical pattern of using media products to self-medicate stress, loneliness, depression, or anxiety that results in severe negative life events (The addictive personality model would focus on what in the patient's personality led him to have that pain to self-medicate in the first place). The weakness of the classical conditioning model, according to LaRose, Lin, and Easton, is that recovery depends on abstinence from or habituation to the cues that trigger the conditioned response, followed by therapy and re-training in social skills.

That's highly unlikely in the face of modern media product's omnipresence and the social acceptability of media consumption. The average American watched 28.8 hours of television weekly in 2004, with at least one set in over 98 percent of all homes (Papazian 77). That figure may understate the average American's immersion in media culture, according to the recent "Middletown" studies of Papper, Holmes, and Popovich. The studies show that the figures for observed media consumption more than double the figures of self-reported media consumption: 4.8 hours daily were self-reported by phone, 9.5 hours daily by diary, and 11.7 hours daily by the direct observation of observers on eight hour shifts. The authors write, "The least media-active person we observed spent five and a quarter hours with the media; the most active person spent over 17 hours — essentially every waking moment — with the media" (Papper, Holmes, and Popovich 5). Observed use always exceeded perceived use. People use at least two media simultaneously almost one quarter of the time when observed; summing all directly observed media use would result in 15.4 hours per day instead of the 11.7 hours of time observed.[4] Why the discrepancy? The discrepancies between self-reports and the direct observation of media consumption can be explained by a variety of factors ranging from the nature of the research methods to the necessarily tentative conclusions that any single study must make.[5] But surely some other possible explanations should be considered. Perhaps the subjects report their intended rather than their actual media use. Perhaps the subjects' self-monitoring is deficient or not timely. Perhaps the external rewards of pleasurable media products provide more, better, or more consistent psychological rewards than the subjects can or do. For the study's authors, the extremely high "did not watch" and "did not listen" responses may make concealment "the key to the apparent underestimation of time spent with media, especially radio and television [...]" (Papper, Holmes, and Popovich 42n3).

The disordered or addictive personality model fails to explain the frequency of the average American's preoccupation with, high tolerance for, and concealment of media use. Learning theory fails to explain why more people are not addicted to the media or what kind of social skills recovering addicts could use successfully in such a media-saturated environment. Social-cognitive theory depends on a healthy personal standard or group norm for its feedback loop to work. It cannot describe adequately what a recovery might mean in such a social environment.

> In short, these theories fail to explain how all of us have not become some version of Andrew, Jonathan and Warren or how we can recover from such a dreadful fate if we discover that we have become them.

With season six's depiction of gun-toting villains, two attempted rapes, and a black magicks binge that nearly ends the world, life in the Buffyverse shown to be both dangerous and endangered. Through its depiction of failed and floundering relationships, dead-end jobs, and nerdy villainy, the series suggests that its fans' lives might be similarly damaged and damaging. Ripping away the safety of the screen offers fans the regular opportunity to undertake a personal inventory of their lives and encourages them to "admit, accept, and patiently correct [their] defects," as Alcoholics Anonymous' "Big Book" puts it (*Twelve Steps and Twelve Traditions* 8). To do so, audiences must navigate parallel narratives dealing with the threat of addiction. Willow descends into an addiction to black magicks, which is represented as a substance addiction. The season's ostensible villains, "The Trio"— Warren, Jonathan, and Andrew — reflect the fan's own addiction to fantasy and the Buffyverse in particular.

Willow provides the viewers with a model for identifying an addiction: preoccupation (excessive use, craving or feeling arousal or tension during use), increasing tolerance, relapses, withdrawal, loss of control, life consequences (disregard for the disruptions caused), concealment, and escapism as self-medication (LaRose, Lin, and Easton 228–9). She uses black magicks to escape from negative feelings. The season opening spell of resurrection helps her medicate her understandable depression at the death of her best friend. Her mid-season binge is just after the revelation that her spell ripped Buffy from Heaven ("Once More, with Feeling" B6007). Another binge occurs after her use leads to the end of her relationship with Tara. Use of black magicks generates arousal, as Willow incorporates spell casting into her sex life with Tara ("Once More, with Feeling"). Willow experiences a physical high while using on several occasions, most notably in a "head rush" which causes the image to blur and shimmer in "Grave" (B6022). She demonstrates excessive use by failing to reserve her power only to save lives. Willow casts a spell of forgetting on Tara after their first fight as a couple ("All the Way" B6006). Willow demonstrates an inability to control her use as well. She tries and fails to forgo using for a week ("Tabula Rasa" B6008). She fails to set limits on her use after losing her powers temporarily, visiting Rack (the black magicks dealer) later that same night ("Wrecked" B6010). After that visit, Willow is shown in the shower leaning into its spray, both hands against the tile wall, crying. She returns to the dealer. She confesses to Buffy in that same episode that she "won't miss the nosebleeds and the headaches and stuff." When Willow quits, she experiences withdrawal. As she lies in her bed at night, panting and staring at the ceiling, one hand is clenched into a fist on the pillow.[6]

While it's tempting to dismiss the significance of The Trio due to their comic nature, the series frequently uses comedy to investigate serious issues.[7] The Trio balances and deepens the series' investigation into the question of addictive pleasures because they will reach fans more attuned to comedy than melodrama. The pleasures The Trio's comedy generates makes them more powerful than they would be if they could only operate in one genre. They are more like Xander and the Mayor than Kendra or Adam. More generally, different genres reward different viewing postures. Comedy uses pleasure to encourage viewers to make connections between seemingly opposed concepts, to read against the grain of experience, and to better understand the arbitrary and political nature of social codes. The bittersweet pleasures of the relationship and addiction melodramas, on the other hand, train its viewers to deepen emotional commitments and to become more aware of the politics of social relationships. Both sets of skills would be necessary for an unhappy fan to investigate their lifestyle.

The Trio's decision to team up and take over Sunnydale represents their craving for an even more intimate connection to the narratives that they have so clearly mastered. One major signifier of the depths of their addiction is their complete lack of discernment and taste (After all, this series made a zombie a devoted fan of *Walker, Texas Ranger* in "The Zeppo" [B3013]). Their literature is exclusively composed of comic books. During heists, they reference *Ocean's Eleven, Mission: Impossible*, The Legion of Doom from *Challenge of the Super Friends* and the magicians Siegfried and Roy. The record "Frampton Comes Alive!" is a feature of their lair. Their one extended discussion of a media product is over which actor played the best James Bond, which results in fisticuffs towards the end of "Life Serial" (B6005). Whatever the merits of any one of these media products, when taken together they suggest the media addict's version of Wild Turkey or Ripple. They repetitively consume serial narratives that are repetitive themselves. They show no interest in the artistic tradition they come from. They don't cite Daniel Clowes, Art Spiegelman, Alan Moore or even R. Crumb. They don't watch Akira Kurosawa films, despite the latter's decisive influence on George Lucas. They don't care what their beloved media icons mean. They don't talk about male sexual fantasies of power and control or Cold War anxiety. They're not discussing the editing, cinematography, or score. They use these media products as an excuse to display their intellectual mastery. Their inappropriately vehement assertions during the Bond debate mirror the ones over whether *BtVS* peaked in its third season.

In "Superstar" (B4017), Jonathan reveals the limitations of mastery of media products when compared to genuine understanding of them. He casts a spell that enables him to rewrite the *BtVS* world in a manner more to his liking. As his carefully constructed imposter narrative falls apart, we learn more details about his act of appropriation. He's written himself to be the star of *The Matrix*, Michael Jordan, Hugh Hefner, a hard-boiled detective, a secret agent, a swimsuit model, coach of the U.S. Women's World Cup soccer team, and even Angel. This character — who grew from human scenery into something more than complex than any of the roles he steals — is seemingly powerless to create new narratives. He can only patch together parts of other ones. Similarly, in "Gone" (B6011), Andrew and Warren debate whether to kill Buffy based on what Lex Luthor would do in similar circumstances rather think it through themselves. A.A. provides an apt description of The Trio: "Perhaps the real trouble was our almost total inability to point imagination toward the right objectives. There's nothing the matter with constructive imagination; all sound achievement rests upon it." (*Twelve Steps and Twelve Traditions* 100)

Nor is this passion limited to quotation and representation. It extends to veneration of icons. In "Smashed" (B6009), Spike gets them all to do his bidding simply by threatening to pull the head off of their "limited edition, 1979, mint condition Boba Fett" figurine. All three of them are literally held hostage by their obsession with this mythic narrative. After this crisis has passed, Andrew clutches the unharmed collectible to his breast, rocking slightly. Almost as if it were a baby, he croons to it that "It's okay, it's okay. It'll be fine." Of course, *BtVS* action figures have been made by three different companies: 9" figures by Exclusive Premiere, 6" figures by Moore Action and 12" figures by Sideshow Toy, with the biggest wave of releases starting with an announcement at the American International Toy Fair 2000 (Toymania). In a moment that makes even more explicit the creators' critique of such collectors and the series' own culpability, Buffy later finds a shelf of scantily clad action heroine figurines, picks one up, and grimaces at its masturbatory nature ("Seeing Red" B6019). The Trio represent the kind of casual viewers that watch the series to ogle Sarah Michelle Gellar during the cool fight scenes. Their reverence is one manifestation of their preoccupation with and incredible tolerance for doses of media products.

It's evident that The Trio are more interested in what these media icons can do for them sexually and psychologically than in what they mean. What's more disturbing is what the obsessive consumption of this material does to them. The decision to turn to a life of crime — in a town where such a practice could hardly be less safe — itself is an indication that they've lost control over their media use. Having kidnapped Willow, The Trio meets Buffy for their showdown at a video arcade in "Gone" (B6011). While Warren's facing a threatening slayer, Andrew and Jonathan are playing an arcade game involving the kind of single combat they will soon face. Yet they are more interested in how to get a kick past their computer opponent's "drunken monkey fist" than in Buffy's actual fists. Classic signs of an addiction include engaging in the activity for longer than intended, an inability to stop once started, using it to calm anxiety, structuring other activities around the addictive pursuit, reductions in the time allotted to other activities, and disregard for the disruptions to work that result. For Andrew and Jonathan, one video game is too many, a hundred are not enough. That experience might have been eerily familiar to any Andrews and Jonathans in the viewing audience, for five video games inspired by *BtVS* were released on six different platforms.[8]

The Trio face two quintessential severe negative life consequences: two of them commit murder and two of them end up dead. Warren ends up being flayed alive by a vengeful Willow, who first punishes him by extending his obsession with merging fantasy and reality into learning what being hit by a bullet feels like. "It's not like it is in the comics," she sneers ("Villains" B6020). And Jonathan gets stabbed to death by his only surviving friend, Andrew ("Conversations with Dead People" B7007).

Another prominent negative life consequence is their social isolation. Some might argue that their media consumption is what binds these three friends together. It's what they talk about, argue with, and are inspired by. But they're not really friends. The first time we see the three of them together, they fall all over themselves trying to betray one another when the going gets rough, leading Jonathan to say, "I hate you guys" ("Flooded" B6004). They betray each other at the beginning and end of their time together on screen, and bicker their way through the middle. They are together, but ultimately they are alone. They embody this observation: "Almost without exception, alcoholics are tortured by loneliness. Even before our drinking got bad and people began to cut us off, nearly all of us suffered the feeling that we didn't quite belong [...]. There was always that mysterious barrier we could neither surmount nor understand" (*Twelve Steps and Twelve Traditions* 57).

Their media use is a consequence, cause, and manifestation of the addict's "total inability to form a true partnership with another human being" (*Twelve Steps and Twelve Traditions* 53). Their lair features a surveillance camera hooked up to a periscope that they then train on a woman sunbathing, a virtual reality headset, a flamethrower, a bank of networked computers, three bean bag chairs, a big-screen television set which uses the empty corridors from the videogame *Doom* as its screensaver, and comic books. It's a den of iniquity that features the best that modern media technology has to offer in aids to simulating physical intimacy, violence, and social connection.

The Trio are depicted as using their habitual media references in ways that they can't or shouldn't be used. With Spike, The Trio finally meet someone they can't designate as either a target or a flunky. Hearing Spike's English accent, Andrew tries to befriend him by observing, "I've seen every episode of *Doctor Who*. Not *Red Dwarf* though..." ("Smashed" B6009). While enduring more banter, Spike frowns, scowls, swears, yells, and at one point says, "Help me out here, Spock. I don't speak loser." It's as if "we were actors on a stage, suddenly realizing that we did not know a single line of our parts" (*Twelve Steps and Twelve Traditions* 57). Having been caught betraying Jonathan, Andrew tries restart their friendship on its old terms in "Villains" (B6020). Now that they share a jail cell, he encourages Jonathan to share his opinion on the relative merits of various stages of Matthew Broderick's career. It takes Jonathan a few moments to realize that they're both using their media knowledge to escape from the unpleasant reality that they find themselves in. For alcoholics, "escape via the bottle was always our solution." (*Twelve Steps and Twelve Traditions* 74)

It was through merging with the fantasy more completely that The Trio sought to transform their social isolation into the more positive attribute of standing apart from the crowd. Andrew seems to hoard media expertise to help him perform under pressure. He coolly references the traditional parting shot of B-movie villains just before activating his jet pack in "Seeing Red," saying, "Well played, Slayer.... This round to you. But the game is far from over." Of course, it was completely ineffective, as he flew immediately into an overhang, comically knocking himself unconscious. Rack, the black magic dealer, guesses that The Trio was the name of a failed rock band in "Villains." That episode twice shows Warren incredulous at their anonymity as villains. The imagined presence of an admiring audience seems to be as important to him as the pleasures of getting away with the crimes themselves. These three nerds clearly want to become star performers in genre entertainment. And since Jonathan already failed in writing himself into a narrative as the hero in "Superstar," they'll just have to play the part of the bad guys. They integrated their addictive pursuit into every part of their lives and still desire the more intense experience of becoming super-villains.

Finally, The Trio's addiction to media produces and reinforces their sexual isolation and erodes their ability to feel empathy. Warren makes physically life-like robotic replicas of Buffy and of his concept of the perfect girlfriend, although he refuses to make a Christina Ricci robot for Andrew. The Trio react with awe at the prospect of "free cable porn." Finally, they resort to using a "cerebral dampener" to make any woman they desire their "willing sex slave" ("Dead Things" B6013). Warren's ex-girlfriend, Katrina, is the first and only target of this device that grants the power to rewrite people. When the device shorts out, she storms into the next room to find Jonathan and Andrew working off their sexual aggression with a mock light saber duel while waiting for their "turn" with her. She yells, "Well, this is not some fantasy, it's not a game, you freaks! It's rape!" Warren kills her when she tries to leave.

One of the many things shocking about this scene is that it's actually familiar. At the end of "Superstar," when the effects of Jonathan's spell are rapidly fading from everyone's memories, he has this conversation with Buffy:

> JONATHAN: Hi. I wasn't sure you'd come over. Everyone's mostly forgetting. But, I think some people are kind of angry.
> BUFFY: Yeah!
> JONATHAN: Nobody's even talking to me. And ... the twins moved out.
> BUFFY: Why did you do it anyway? No. I get why. How?
> JONATHAN: After the thing with the bell tower and the gun, I went to counseling. You know other kids with problems a-and one of them had this spell. He glossed right over the monster. Well, anyway I just — I — I just wanted to apologize. Nobody was supposed to get hurt.
> BUFFY: Jonathan you get why everyone is angry though, right? It's not just the monster. People didn't like being the little actors in your sock puppet theater.
> JONATHAN: You weren't! You weren't socks! We were friends.
> BUFFY: Jonathan you can't keep trying to make everything work out with some big gesture all at once. Things are complicated. They take time and work.

Such exchanges are precisely why A.A.'s 12-step model requires people to admit their wrongs to another human being, for, "There are cases where our ancient enemy, rationalization, has stepped in and has justified conduct which was really wrong. The temptation here is to imagine that we had good motives and reasons when we really didn't" (*Twelve Steps and Twelve Traditions* 94). Counting the angry twins from his mansion, sweet Jonathan's sexual fantasy of control and power has twice triumphed over his allegedly good intentions. The addiction to fantasy is in charge, not him. Like the alcoholic, however, he is still the one responsible for what he's done while using.

Of this episode, Justine Larbalestier wrote, "Jonathan's desires to be a Buffylike superhero and to be publicly recognized as such (an acknowledgment that Buffy, with the exception of "The Prom," does not receive) are embarrassing and come dangerously close to caricaturing the relationship of fans to the show" (234). This episode should be considered as more in the nature of an opportunity rather than an insult or an in-joke. Consider this episode an especially direct instance of the series giving its most devoted viewers an opportunity to engage in a "searching and fearless moral inventory," as the fourth step of A.A. puts it.

The Trio are shown to be powerless over media consumption and their lives definitely became unmanageable. With Andrew in season seven, the series seems to be asking, "Where do we go from here?," a question that both Buffy and most A.A. newcomers ask (*Twelve Steps and Twelve Traditions* 25). As in season six's parallel addiction narratives, the final season encourages viewers to draw connections between Willow and Andrew's recoveries.

Previously, the series had used the redemptive arcs of Angel and Faith to initiate fans into the language, rituals, and uncertainties of the 12-step model for recovery (Consult the appendix for a full list of its steps and traditions). For both Willow and Andrew, the series must adapt the A.A. model to fit their particular addictions (In real life, it has been altered to accommodate addictions to gambling, sex, and over-eating). Given Willow's life in Sunnydale, abstinence likely won't work. Andrew's particular dependency raises two additional troubling questions: How does the use of narrative in a 12-step recovery program change when a fascination with narrative and stories is part of the addiction? And can performing sobriety — or learning to "fake it till you make it" (Flynn 147) — work when imaginative role-playing is the addictive pursuit?

The basic understanding of redemptive recovery was set with Angel. His story functions like a drunkalogue that describes "what it was like, what happened, and what it's like now," as one A.A. member described such performances (Flynn 151). He hits all of the classic steps. He undertakes the blood addict's version of the alcoholic's "beer experiment" by draining only criminals (Dye 292–293). Whistler, a demon who is "not a bad guy," functions as his sponsor, getting Angel to admit that his life has become unmanageable and introduces him to the A.A. concept of a "God as we understood Him" via the Powers That Be (*Twelve Steps and Twelve Traditions* 5). Through his discussions with Buffy about his life with Darla, Drusilla, and Spike, the series directly shows Angel's "searching and fearless moral inventory" that must be "admitted to God, to ourselves, and to another human being" (*Twelve Steps and Twelve Traditions* 6). The tone of his response to the "Christmas miracle" dawn snowstorm in "Amends" (B3010) evokes the alcoholic's subjective experience of the "miracle of being relieved from a compulsion to drink" (Marrus 310). With Angel's story, the audience was positioned rather like they would be at a drunkalogue delivered at an A.A. meeting. In both cases, the audience knows that the speaker must survive the harrowing experiences in order to testify to them.

That snowstorm sparks Angel to make direct amends to those he harmed. Angel's experience with the remaining steps — taking personal inventory, improving his connection with God as he understood him, and carrying this message to others — is one subject of *Angel*. The mission of Angel Investigations? "We help the hopeless," as his partner, Cordelia, put it ("I Fall to Pieces" A1004). One of the most notorious of the hopeless that Angel helps, is Faith. The series positions Faith's redemptive arc as a battle with a behavioral addiction to evil, expanding its investigation of compulsion and desire beyond Angel's battle. In the process, the use of A.A.'s 12-Step model becomes most explicit. In "Sanctuary," Faith incredulously observes, "I've got to be the first Slayer in history sponsored by a vampire" (A1018). That episode also references the A.A. saying of taking it "one day at a time." "Sanctuary" most clearly demonstrates Angel doing the 12th Step work of carrying this message of a spiritual awakening and giving the "gift which amounts to a new state of consciousness and being" (*Twelve Steps and Twelve Traditions* 107). Truly, it is here that the Buffyverse most embodies the third tradition of A.A.: "The only requirement for A.A. membership is a desire to stop drinking" (*Twelve Steps and Twelve Traditions* 10). It isn't as difficult to forgive Angel's blood binge in season two of *BtVS* as it is for viewers to understand Faith's murderous treachery and class resentments over seasons three and four. The emotional hardship of actually living A.A.'s principle of embracing genuine outsiders becomes most apparent through Faith's story.

The first difference that viewers might notice is with the beginning of Andrew's recovery. Typically, people in A.A. remain anonymous and free to leave. Andrew gets kidnapped when he runs into Willow while he's buying lots of blood at the butcher's shop for a dark ritual. He spends most of several episodes tied to a chair. This approach is also quite different from the recoveries of the others. Whistler taunts Angel, but persuades him to follow him. Faith starts her first "dry" day with pastries in "Sanctuary." When Faith asks if she's Angel's prisoner, he opens the door to allow her to walk out. At the start of her recovery at a coven in England, Willow comments, "When you brought me here, I thought it was to kill me or to lock me in some mystical dungeon for all eternity or — with the torture. Instead, you go all Dumbledore on me. I'm learning about magic. All about energy and Gaia and root systems" ("Lessons" B7001). Andrew, however, gets slapped around by Anya and Dawn. Buffy dangles Andrew over a pit and threatens him with a knife to encourage him to make a sincere admission of an unmanageable life.

Perhaps this house arrest phase might be best thought of as an involuntary committal or a drying-out period in a rehab program before a referral to an outpatient program or A.A. During this time period, Andrew tries to make connections through media references but is constantly rebuffed. Dawn responds to his attempt to strike up a conversation about Timothy Dalton or to play "Six Degrees of Kevin Bacon" by noting that, if he's lonely, "Then maybe you shouldn't've killed your only friend" ("Showtime" B7011). They never let him touch a computer. After five episodes, Andrew's reduced to reading the operator's manual for the new microwave.

The one person that he does bond with is Xander, as in this exchange in "Bring on the Night" (7010):

> ANDREW: Man, this place gives me the creeps. It's like in "Wonder Woman," issue 297/299 —
> XANDER: "Catacombs"— yeah with the skeletons.
> ANDREW & XANDER: (simultaneously, smiling and nodding) That was cool.
> XANDER: (suddenly frowns and pushes Andrew) Move it. This way.

There's some reason to think that Xander could have been Andrew, if things had turned out differently. Consider Xander's bedroom during high school, first seen in "Bewitched, Bothered and Bewildered" (B2016). It's littered with cultural artifacts. Xander recognizes his Klingon love poetry and gets Andrew's comic book references. Xander provides a positive role model for Andrew, however, because he stops himself from getting lost in talking about them (The gang's visible impatience with Xander's habit suggests the importance of community vigilance). Xander's also the one that points out to Andrew that they don't follow Buffy. They work together because they're friends. Through Xander especially, Andrew gets to see what's to be gained by recovery: "we saw them calmly accept impossible situations, seeking neither to run nor to recriminate. This was not only faith; it was faith that worked under all conditions" (*Twelve Steps and Twelve Traditions* 31).

Buffy's the one that understands that Andrew's addiction to fantasy and stories is the underlying problem. Some might be surprised that Buffy is the one to pick up on this. But consider her history. During the first two seasons, Buffy did frequently use pop culture references to tease Giles. After the first two seasons, however, she slowly decreases the frequency of such references. Her early media references have a use for her, but they're not an expression of her. A glance in Buffy's bedroom indicates the contrast with Xander. Buffy's bedroom only has a tasteful print of Psyche, by Susan Seddon Boulet, while media artifacts litter Xander's high school bedroom.[9] So she's the one that's most irritated by Andrew's hero worship, interrupting him and using references to *Misery* to threaten him. After one outburst, Buffy asks Xander to gag him. When he begins his video documentary project in "Storyteller," she's the one to call it "idiotic" and "a waste of time."

The many times that Buffy silences Andrew are an important early part of his recovery. That's because recovery starts with listening. As a storytelling culture, A.A. requires audiences. Their 12-step model emphasizes the need for an honest yet affirming audience to the confessions offered at meetings generally and for the fifth step particularly. "We sit in A.A. meetings and listen, not only to receive something ourselves, but to give the reassurance and support which our presence can bring" (*Twelve Steps and Twelve Traditions* 110). One listens intently at these meetings; watching them is not the center of the experience. A.A.'s oral nature presents a culture shock for a visual media addict. Note that all but one of Andrew's references has its base in visual media products: comic books, films, and television series. He never mentions a band or a radio station. Listening is hard for Andrew. He's too eager to talk. Tom Lenk often delivers Andrew's lines at a faster speed than those around him to suggest Andrew's eagerness to display his (intellectual, cultural) mastery. Before Andrew can learn how to talk the talk and before he can walk the walk, Andrew must undo a lifetime of spectatorship and learn active, engaged listening.

Andrew has to learn how to set aside comparison. Much of the interaction between The Trio consisted of bickering. They listened to each other only so that they could refute the other person. But, in 12-step recovery programs "new members are usually told 'don't compare, try to identify'" (Flynn 155). You can tell that the series creators regard this advice as important because the First Evil tries to undermine that behavior to subvert Andrew. In "First Date" (B7014), the First Evil suggests that it's unfair that they make Andrew seek redemption for murder and not Spike, Anya and Willow. Leota Dye suggests that A.A. presents new members with certain phrases, such as "live and let live," as "a way of changing beliefs and behaviors; they are part of the guidance offered by the HP" (241). Again, the series and the program emphasize how important listening is. For *BtVS*, it's not just how frequently one is in the audience that defines the nature of an addiction to media. What kind of audience you are matters.

"Storyteller" functions as Andrew's drunkalogue. As such, it reveals two last ways that the series changes the canonical 12-step model to adapt it to media addiction. The first change deals with the presentation and evolution of the drunkalogue, the basic narrative act of the oral culture of A.A. Media addiction unearths a complexity in how the drunkalogue functions as a repeated narrative. To suggest an authentic confession, practiced speakers adopt a certain style: "Rarely do they employ literary devices such as metaphor or allusion as fellow alcoholics know what the life of a drinker is like. Rather the stories contain a style of 'integrity, coherence, simplicity' with similar plot elements such as the speaker's introduction to alcohol, early drinking, a fall, and a recovery" (Dye 286). This style involves a stripping away of literary artifice, yet remains conventional and bound by rules to create a story that is "crude, dirty, full of miracles," as one A.A. member put it (Elpenore 46–47, as quoted in Dye 286). But newcomers to A.A. are expected to become better storytellers over time:

> Telling and retelling their stories, re-performing their primary performances, becomes the main communication practice of members in AA meetings. With new or especially untalented performers, this repetition can be boring and tedious to the audience. Continued practice, however, usually results in the development of a comfortable level of performance skill and artistry for most members [Flynn 149].

Thus, A.A. members are to deliver stories that are original, yet conventional in its narrative form and presentation. Still, they are expected to create rather than quote.

One of the goofiest episodes in the series, "Storyteller" begins with a spoof of *Masterpiece Theater*, clashing the classical violin scoring, a leather armchair set in front of a roaring fire, and his silk smoking jacket with a *Star Wars* poster, a comic book laid open on a pedestal, and a shelf of action figures. Later scenes include a sequence that can only be described as a soft core ad for cereal, a re-write of season six that makes Andrew the star in the worst fan fiction tradition, and two scenes of low-rent Greek tragedy on the dirt stage provided by a basement. These scenes are thoroughly a part of the camp tradition. Through extremely artificial performances and formal techniques that point to them as techniques and artistic decisions, camp creates the kind of critical distance necessary for an understanding of gender, sexuality, and identity as pure performance. Camp favors exaggeration, artifice, and extremity as a formal strategy of subversion designed to slip homosexual experience out of its cultural closet and into mainstream cultural products. For a character that describes Spike as "hot," Jonathan as "just the cutest thing," and sighs longingly at the mere mention of Scott Bakula, Andrew's use of this approach suggests his sexual proclivities ("Entropy" B6018, "Storyteller," and "First Date").

This camp aesthetic represents the section of the drunkalogue that depicts what the addiction was like. The episode highlights how inappropriate camp's techniques of quotation and appropriation are as a form of authentic confession. As a result, they're both uproariously funny and tedious at the same time. Anya accurately likens them to masturbation. The problem is that Andrew uses this technique to tell everyone's story but his own. For the purposes of this episode, the camp aesthetic isn't a covert form of authenticity. It's a mask that uses its amusing surface to distract its audience from the emotional vulnerabilities of its creator. More simply, a veteran of A.A. might label the camp sections of Andrew's testimony to be "stinkin' thinkin.'"

Nonetheless, "Storyteller" does model healthy uses of narrative for its audience. In the first, Andrew simply asks Xander to talk about leaving Anya at the altar one year ago. A productive discussion ensues between the pair, resulting in the break-up sex that allows them both to get some closure on a relationship that some suspected was based on sex in the first place. The second such sequence ends the episode. Andrew sits on the closed toilet seat in the bathroom, looks into the video camera (and thus at the viewing audience of the series), and confesses, "Here's the thing. I killed my best friend. There's a big fight coming, and I don't know what's going to happen. I don't even think I'm going to live through it. That's, uh, probably the way it should be. I guess I'm..." Then he sighs and abruptly shuts off the camera, sending the episode into its credit sequence. These two sequences are used to communicate directly and promote conversation, rather than to create spectacles that encourage escape.

Since the episode ends with his admission of powerlessness over his fantasies and a declaration of his sincere desire to stop, the drunkalogue is the entire episode, not just its last few seconds. The camp sequences suggest "what it was like." The narrative scenes setting up his confrontation with Buffy in the school basement show "what happened." And the final confession states "what it's like now" (Flynn 151). A strategic use of camp's insincerity is shown to be a valid part of the media addict's drunkalogue, provided that they do not use it as a means of avoiding "a searching and fearless moral inventory of ourselves." A drunkalogue is shown to be a story, with one crucial difference from the camp fairy tales Andrew's been spinning: no script or compulsion can change the fact everybody's responsible.

After this episode, Andrew does the "unspectacular but important tasks that make good Twelfth Step work possible" for the others (*Twelve Steps and Twelve Traditions* 110). In the last two episodes of *BtVS*, Andrew demonstrates his own brand of heroism by keeping up morale, providing first aid, and even looting an abandoned hospital for needed medical supplies. Convinced he'll die during this final battle, Andrew's forced to live "one day at a time." He's beginning to make the kind of connections that could end the loneliness that had caused and been the cause of his media consumption. He makes a tentative, but real, connection with Spike over the delightful nature of "those onion blossom things" they serve at restaurants ("Empty Places" B7019). He teases Anya for her love of humanity and they take a break from the business of averting disaster long enough to have a wheelchair fight ("End of Days" B7021). Next, he uses his imagination to bond with Amanda, Giles, and Xander over a game of *Dungeons and Dragons*, in which the players have to actively create and negotiate the heroic tale together (Eden Studios premiered the role playing games based on the Buffyverse at GenCon the prior year). With Anya and the gang, he's learning the distinction between the use of fantasy as escapism and as a playful and interactive act of imagination. And he bears witness to Anya's death, a healthy form of spectatorship very much related to the kind of listening skills required of the audiences at A.A. meetings.

The Buffyverse ends with Andrew's recovery as a work-in-progress. He gives an acceptance speech thanking various people in his life for his impending heroic death ("Chosen" B7022). He shows that he's still working the steps by the fact that he never tries to make direct amends to Willow for his part in what happened to her and to Tara. He's not perfect. He's faking his way through it. Yet there's some indication that he's making progress too. This recovery remains a provisional one, as they must be.

Andrew's character serves a catalyst for starting an indirect dialogue with the most intense and loyal part of *Buffy the Vampire Slayer*'s audience. Through witnessing other characters' addictions, the fandom develops the tools to identify a developing addiction. Through The Trio, the series' creators ask whether their fandom's lives might be damaged and damaging, but also suggest that their narratives and products might bear some responsibility for those problems too. Through Andrew, the series offers fans some tentative suggestions for how to "fake it till you make it": be abstinent, identify rather than compare, listen actively, find a vigilant community and a role model, and be wary of the practices of quotation and appropriation while living a life of (media) sobriety.

It had been easy for viewers to deny a similarity to the misogynist Warren and too easy to accept Jonathan without thinking hard about the implications of "Superstar." But Andrew strips away the safety of the screen at the end of "Storyteller." Talking directly to the fans as a fan is a technique that makes it hard for viewers to deny any recognition they might experience. Andrew's acknowledgement of the presence of the audience testifies to their involvement in his redemption. Like all audiences of drunkalogues, however, the identification and recognition inherent in active listening leaves us thinking about how we've lived our lives too. We find ourselves in such a story, rather than getting lost in it.

Appendix A: Twelve Steps

1. We admitted we were powerless over alcohol — that our lives had become unmanageable.

2. Came to believe that a Power greater than ourselves could restore us to sanity.

3. Made a decision to turn our will and our lives over to the care of God as we understood Him.

4. Made a searching and fearless moral inventory of ourselves.

5. Admitted to God, to ourselves and to another human being the exact nature of our wrongs.

6. Were entirely ready to have God remove all these defects of character.

7. Humbly asked Him to remove our shortcomings.

8. Made a list of all persons we had harmed, and became willing to make amends to them all.

9. Made direct amends to such people wherever possible, except when to do so would injure them or others.

10. Continued to take personal inventory and when we were wrong promptly admitted it.

11. Sought through prayer and meditation to improve our conscious contact with God, as we understood Him, praying only for knowledge of His will for us and the power to carry that out.

12. Having had a spiritual awakening as the result of these steps, we tried to carry this message to alcoholics, and to practice these principles in all our affairs.

Notes

1. Although the term "addiction" has been replaced by "dependence" in the field of clinical psychology (American Psychiatric Association 1994), this article uses the former term because of the series' heavy use of the 12-Step models of recovery, its prevalence in clinical literature (Larose, Lin, and Easton 227), and the likelihood that a popular audience would associate these problems with such a term.

2. In fact, the series creators themselves were participants and lurkers on various internet fan

boards. The writers used these forums as a form of quality control and wrote lines and scenes referencing fan debates, and created entire episodes in light of fan response.

3. The correlation, according to Greenberg et al. (1999) is r=.43 to .72.

4. Self-reports significantly understated multi-tasking in all media. The authors write: "The telephone survey results on media multitasking generally bore little similarity to observed results. While the data from the diary study are much closer to that observed, they pale in depth and texture compared to observation. For example, the total media multitasking in the diary study (12.4 percent) was half as much as the observation study (23.7 percent)." Furthermore, "As far as media multitasking is concerned, diary research appears to have produced results most similar to observation results for music, computer programs and magazines; it is farthest off on TV, Internet, game boxes and books. Telephone survey research appears fully capable of determining whether people possess various media technologies, but their accuracy in even the simple task of determining whether they used a particular medium appears suspect" (Papper, Holmes, and Popovich, 19).

5. Papper, Holmes, and Popovich note the limitations of their survey, listing the mid-summer timing; some difficulties aligning the diary and observation methods to the telephone survey results; a low response rate for one-day diaries that was not a difficulty for the one-week diaries; presence of the observers changing the nature of the observed, especially given the total lack of observed pornography consumption; the relatively small size and non-random quality of the sample for direct observation, although 16,000 hours were observed; and inter-rater reliability was not measured, due to the time and resource constraints involved in doing so for the 37 observers used (Papper, Holmes, and Popovich 39–41).

6. The series suggests a parallel between Willow's withdrawal and Buffy's decision to end her relationship with Spike by cutting to a shot of Buffy's sleepless night in her garlic-strewn bedroom. Having been ripped from heaven by Willow's resurrection spell, Buffy spends much of that season trying to escape "this strange estrangement" that she sings about in the musical episode, "Once More, with Feeling" (B6007). She uses sex to self-medicate her understandable numbness. Before her first kiss with Spike, Buffy sings in that same episode that "I just want to feel." In "Dead Things" (B6013), Buffy admits to Tara that the only time she feels anything is when she has sexual intercourse with a partner who's "everything I hate." Buffy laments her loss of control, saying, "Why can't I stop? Why do I keep letting him in?" Her sexual activities nearly end her friendship with Xander, while her secrecy promotes the very emotional distance the activity was to salve. Despite these similarities, the series has Buffy white-knuckle her way through the recovery process. That makes it difficult to definitively state whether this is the representation of a dangerous habit or an addiction.

7. Consider Anya and Cordelia's status as comic truth-tellers, Xander's evolution from comedian to comic hero, and the Mayor's insight into Buffy and Angel's relationship. In addition, think about how the good humor in "The Witch" (B1003), "Bewitched, Bothered, and Bewildered" (B2016), "The Zeppo" (B3013), "Gingerbread" (B3011), "Doppelgangland" (B3016), "Who Are You?" (B4016), "Once More, with Feeling" (B6007) and "Doublemeat Palace" (B6012) make their serious inquiries into the nature of gender performance, the difficulty of personal transformation and the critique of corporate exploitation palatable for a mass audience.

8. They are: "Buffy the Vampire Slayer" (for Nintendo's Game Boy Color), "Buffy the Vampire Slayer" (for Xbox/PC), "Buffy the Vampire Slayer: Wrath of the Darkhul King" (for Game Boy Advance), "Buffy the Vampire Slayer: Chaos Bleeds" (for Xbox, PS2, and Nintendo GameCube), and "Buffy the Vampire Slayer: The Quest for Oz" (for Mobile).

9. A tip of the pen for this observation goes to a student formerly in my *Buffy* seminar at Emerson College, Laura Kessenich.

Works Cited

Brenner, V. "Psychology of Computer Use XLVII: Parameters of Internet Use, Abuse, and Addiction: The First 90 Days of the Internet Usage Study." *Psychology Reports* 80 (1997): 879–882.

Bryant, J., and D. Anderson, eds. *Perspectives on Media Effects*. Hillsdale, NJ: Lawrence Erlbaum Associates, 1986.

Canary, D. J. and B. H. Spitzberg. "Loneliness and Media Gratification." *Communication Research* 20 (1993): 800–821.

Cooper, A., C. Scherer, S. C. Boies, and B. Gordon. "Sexuality on the Internet: From Sexual Exploration to Pathological Expression." *Professional Psychology: Research and Practice* 30 (1999): 154–164.

Dye, Leota E. "A Dramatistic Analysis of Key Words in Alcoholics Anonymous." Eastland, Herndon, and Barr 233–243.

_____. "Narrative in Alcoholics Anonymous: A Typology of Functions." Eastland, Herndon, and Barr 285–299.

Eastland, Lynette S., Sandra L Herndon, and Jeanine R. Barr, eds. *Communication in Recovery: Perspective on Twelve Step Groups*. Cresskill, NJ: Hampton Press, 1999.

Elpenore (pseudo.). "A Drunkard's Progress: AA and the Sobering Strength of Myth." *Harper's Magazine*. Oct. 1986: 42–48.

Finn, S. "Television Addiction — An Evaluation of Four Competing Media-Use Models." *Journalism Quarterly* 69 (1992): 422–435.

Flynn, Kathleen A. "Performing Sobriety: Story Living and Storytelling in Alcoholics Anonymous." Eastland, Herndon, and Barr 145–170.

Greenberg, J. L., S. E. Lewis, and D. K. Dodd. "Overlapping Addictions and Self-esteem among College Men and Women." *Addictive Behaviors* 24 (2000): 565–571.

Griffiths, M. "Amusement Machine Playing in Childhood and Adolescence: A Comparative Analysis of Video Games and Fruit Machines." *Journal of Adolescence* 14 (1991): 53–73.

_____. "Excessive Internet Use: Implications for Sexual Behavior." *CyberPsychology and Behavior* 3 (1999): 211–218.

_____. "Internet Addiction: Fact or Fiction?" *Psychologist* 12 (1999): 246–250.

Havens, Candace. *Joss Whedon: The Genius Behind Buffy*. Dallas: BenBella Books, 2003.

Kraut, R., M. Patterson, V. Lundmark, S. Kiesler, T. Mukophadhyay, and W. Scherlis. "Internet Paradox: A Social Technology that Reduces Social Involvement and Psychological Well-Being?" *American Psychologist* 53 (1998): 1017–1031.

Kubey, R. "Television Dependence, Diagnosis and Prevention: With Commentary on Video Games, Pornography, and Media Education." MacBeth 221–260.

Larbalestier, Justine. "*Buffy*'s Mary Sue Is Jonathan: *Buffy* Acknowledges the Fans." Wilcox and Lavery 227–238.

LaRose, Robert A., Carolyn A. Lin, and Matthew S. Eastin. "Unregulated Internet Usage: Addiction, Habit, or Deficient Self-Regulation?" *Media Psychology* 5 (2003): 225–253.

MacBeth, T. *Tuning In to Young Viewers: Social Science Perspectives on Television*. Newbury Park, CA: Sage, 1996.

Marrus, Francine E. "Living in the Light: Transformational Myths in Alcoholics Anonymous." Eastland, Herndon, and Barr 301–316.

McIlwraith, R. D. "'I'm Addicted to Television': The Personality, Imagination and TV watching pattern of Self-identified TV addicts." *Journal of Broadcasting and Electronic Media* 42: 371–386.

McIlwraith, R., R. S. Jacobvitz, R. Kubey, and A. Alexander. "Television Addiction — Theories and Data behind the Ubiquitous Metaphor." *American Behavioral Scientist* 35: 104–121.

Papper, Robert A., Michael E. Holmes, and Mark N. Popovich. "Middletown Media Studies." *The International Digital Media & Arts Association Journal* 1.1 (Spring 2004).

Riess, Jana. *What Would Buffy Do?: The Vampire Slayer as Spiritual Guide*. Hoboken: John Wiley & Sons, 2004.

Rozin, P., and C. Stoess. "Is There a General Tendency to Become Addicted?" *Addictive Behaviors* 18 (1993): 81–87.

Russell, Howard, Mark Connelly, George Bischel and Tracy Vaughn. *Buffyworld*. 2 Aug. 2007. *<www.buffyworld.com>*.

Sanders, C. E. "The Relationship of Internet Use to Depression and Social Isolation among Adolescents." *Adolescence* 35 (2000): 237–242.

Scherer, K. "College Life Online: Healthy and Unhealthy Internet Use." *Journal of College Student Development* 38 (1997): 655–664.

Shapira, N. A., T. D. Goldsmith, P. E. Keck, U. M. Khosla, and S. L. McElroy. "Psychiatric Features of Individuals with Problematic Internet Use." *Journal of Affective Disorders* 57 (2000): 267–272.

Smith, R. "Television Addiction." Bryant and Anderson 109–128.

"Toymania." *toymania.com.* 9 April 2006. <*http://www.toymania.com/toyfair2000/sideshow/twelveinchers.shtml* >

Twelve Steps and Twelve Traditions. 20th. New York: Alcoholics Anonymous World Services, Inc., 1980.

VandeCreek, L. ,and T. Jackson, eds. *Innovations in Clinical Practice: A Sourcebook.* Volume 17. Sarasota, FL: Professional Resource Press, 1999.

Wilcox, Rhonda V., and David Lavery, eds. *Fighting the Forces.* Lanham, MD: Rowman & Littlefield, 2002.

Young, K.S. *Caught in the Net.* New York: Wiley, 1998.

_____. "Evaluation and Treatment of Internet Addiction." VandeCreek and Jackson. 19–31.

_____, and R. C. Rogers. "The Relationship between Depression and Internet Addiction." *CyberPsychology and Behavior* 1 (1998): 25–36.

The Problematic Definition of "Fan": A Survey of Fannish Involvement in the Buffyverse

Claudia Rebaza

While the concepts of "fan" and "fandom" have been around for some time, agreement on what constitutes either term is not a settled matter. Certainly one goal for fan studies must be to better define the topic of study, or at least provide classifications so that different models of "fandom" and "fan" can be identified and discussed with some common ground. Different strands of study have focused on "fan" as a communal participant (Tulloch and Jenkins 1995; Lewis 1992), as well as "fan" as an individual interacting idiosyncratically with a fannish text (Hills 2002; Sandvoss 2005). The definition of "fan" or "fandom" varies among fans as well as academics. Just as with other social groups, questions such as who is a member, what constitutes a community, and how people signal membership to one another, are matters of continual negotiation (Cusack and Cavanagh 2001).

One definition of fandom is "All the fans of a sport, an activity, or a famous person," and of fan, "An ardent devotee; an enthusiast" (American Heritage Dictionary 2007). These are problematic definitions for those in media studies. Are media fans actually fans of an activity such as watching television or reading a book? Or are they fans of a particular text? If you look at fan groups and the continual negotiations regarding what is considered "canon," it would seem that the text is the central issue. However a text may appear in various media incarnations such as books, films, comics, animation, or theater performances. New content delivery channels such as the Internet may create new mediums for study. An individual may be a fan of only one of these media incarnations or many. Therefore the medium of the *text* and the fan's resulting interaction with it — *the activity* — may indeed be the central focus of fannish involvement. As this article is being written, debate is underway in different areas of the overlapping "Buffy the Vampire Slayer" and "Angel" fandoms regarding the canonical status of the Buffy Season Eight comic series. While to some fans it seems beyond dispute that anything created by Joss Whedon is automatically "canon" and thus part of the fannish text, to others different issues prevail. These issues include physical representation, the size of the text's audience, and the level of acceptance by an individual's fannish peers. A person may thus consider *community interpretations of a text* to be a part of their fannish focus.

The dictionary definition of "fan" is vague and incomplete. It focuses on emotional reaction — a fan is defined as being "ardent" and "enthusiastic" — rather than conscious activities. However, in daily life recognizing a fan based only on their emotional response alone may be difficult. Visible enthusiasm is something often minimized for the sake of others who do not share that interest, especially in certain venues. Enthusiasm also varies greatly among individuals, regardless of the source. Practically, when defining who is or isn't the object of study, a person's level of emotion is a difficult marker for those engaged in fandom studies. A person's activities, on the other hand, *can* be measured, compared, and used as a foundation upon which to build definitions of the multiplicity of fans and their communities. For a person to take action, a certain level of interest and commitment is implied, which allows others to sketch out the emotional attachments likely to be present.

The dictionary definition also falls short in that it fails to suggest distinctions that separate the "ardent devotee" from someone who, for example, merely enjoys watching certain shows on TV. It's not likely to be merely enthusiasm that distinguishes the ardent devotee from the viewer, but *knowledge* of the fandom object. A person's in-depth knowledge allows for certain avenues of conversation with others who share a similar level of interest, whether they are fans or fellow professionals. Fandom knowledge is also something that is generally actively acquired, not passively absorbed.

Many readers may be familiar with the Comic Book Guy who appears on *The Simpsons*. His dry, disdainful pronouncements on the merits of his fannish object show only a minimal level of vocal enthusiasm compared to Bart's glee at finding a new comic title he longs to read. The amount of knowledge Comic Book Guy displays (and perhaps his feeling of superiority in its acquisition) is what actually marks him as a fan.

Knowledge, and the sharing of knowledge, is not the only form of active response to a text. In addition to seeking information, fans have been known to collect ancillary material about a fannish object (e.g., t-shirts, cards, collectibles), or create new material derived from the fannish object. This creative activity can have many avenues such as model building, the design of websites and databases, the writing of songs, the writing of fan fiction, or the painting of art. These differing responses to a fannish text may result in different factions within a fandom, since they focus not only on the text, but on a certain type of interaction with the text.

While discussion about a text is the central hallmark of any fandom, the format of that discussion can vary. This is particularly true now that many fandoms exist largely online, where written response is the common form of exchange. Fannish discussion may range from brief one-line exchanges to complex (and footnoted) essays. Discussion may also take place visually in the creation of fan films or music videos, which recontextualize texts to reflect certain interpretations; aurally in podcasts which provide audio commentary to the text or musical fanmixes; or in multimedia formats such as fan fiction which may include illustrations and soundtracks. A fan may use one or all of these to discuss views of the text with a community of other fans. It is also easy for a solitary individual to use these same formats to explore their own response to the text in isolation. In either case, the fan is either creating a response or seeking out and reacting to someone else's response.

One of the better-explored forms of fannish response has been fan fiction (fanfic). Numerous academic works have investigated aspects of fanfic writing or fanfic communities (Bacon-Smith 1991; Harris and Alexander 1998; Hellekson and Busse 2006) as well as the literary aspects of fanfic itself (Pugh 2005). Given the extensive reach of current Internet search tools, an increasing number of media outlets and members of the general public are becoming aware of this form of fannish response. Even so, in any fandom there are those who are completely unaware of other fans whose form of fannish response differs from their own. Can a fandom be defined as, "*All* the fans of a sport, an activity, or a famous person," if many of these fans do not even recognize one another as being fans? Is one possible definition of "fan" simply "a person who has knowledge of the fandom"?

This article will examine the issue of fan behavior and fannish involvement through the use of a survey conducted in November 2006. The survey responses will be reported in three parts: (1) Demographically, who it is that calls themselves a fan of the Buffyverse? (2) What are their fannish activities? (3) How do the demographics and activities of fans connect to the experiences they have within the fandom? By looking at how individual characteristics, activities, and personal reporting of fannish involvement intersect, it should be possible to determine if personal action can be used as a baseline for defining fans and fan groups.

Methodology

A comprehensive survey of fans for any series would be difficult — if not impossible — to conduct. The first problem is the issue of who qualifies as a fan. Since the terms "fan" and "fandom" are contested as to inclusion, one starting point must be for the survey takers to provide their own definitions. If an individual self-identifies as a fan of something (and is interested enough to respond to a survey request) then this response should set the baseline validity. A continuum of "fannish interest" is part of what this survey has been designed to explore so that, through a diversity of participants, definitions of "fan" and "fandom" can be brought into focus.

A diversity of fannish participants is difficult to achieve, however, in that isolated fans who do not share their fannish interests with others are not easily located and surveyed. Studies of "fans" often become studies of "social fans," or those who make their presence known in some way. The survey problem then, is how to target the many different groups who may make up a fandom. The most obvious locations to conduct surveys would result in clear demographic skews, rather than clear definitions of "fan" and "fandom." At conventions, for example, a survey would likely have both geographic and economic skews, favoring residents from the immediate area as well as those with the time and finances to travel. An online survey is also likely to produce an economic and educational skew. Recent surveys indicate Internet users are more likely to be from households with higher education or above-average household income (Pew Internet..., 2006). Neither location for fan gatherings is likely to include the more casual fans that do not interact with the larger fandom, but pursue their interests alone or with a few members of their family and friends. Lastly, any survey (or series of interviews) includes only those eligible who wish to take the time and trouble to respond. So, any profile of the "typical fan" is necessarily going to be incomplete and to favor certain characteristics. Knowing that any data gathered is incomplete does not mean that the study cannot reflect the true circumstances of many individuals, or present at least a partial portrait of the group as a whole. It is important to keep in mind, though, that the results of *this* survey reflect fans who have pursued their fannish interest online and who have at least *some* awareness of their online fandom.

The fandom survey detailed here was conducted online over the period of four weeks. Announcements of the survey were posted at several online fansites for *Buffy the Vampire Slayer* and *Angel* (the "Buffyverse"). The announcements explained that the survey data was for a doctoral thesis; once the survey closed, a link was posted to the completed results.

There were 1541 completed surveys and 122 partially completed surveys, for a total of 1663 responses. The survey software was designed to block multiple responses from the same IP address. The survey was in four parts with a total of sixty-five questions. Depending on their answers to earlier questions, not all survey takers were given all four parts. Seventy-five percent of the questions were multiple-choice; the remaining questions were open-ended. Survey takers were also given the opportunity to add comments at the end of the survey. Basic survey results were available online for six weeks after the survey closed, and discussion of the results was invited at some of the forums where the survey had been announced.

The four parts of the survey focused on (1) Demographic information, (2) Questions about writing fanfic, (3) Questions about reading fanfic, and (4) The individual's experience in fandom. Questions for Parts 1 and 4 were intermixed throughout the survey and answered by all survey takers. Parts 2 and 3 were offered only to those who had experience writing or reading fanfic. The overall results were cross-tabulated to identify a variety of demographic factors in behavior and filtered to contrast particular groups of respondents. All survey takers were anonymous; no identifying data was available. Respondents were directed to a form verifying that they were eighteen or older, and consented to the use of the data for research purposes.

Survey Report— Part 1. Who Call Themselves Fans of the Buffyverse? (Demographics)

This section presents key demographic characteristics of the online Buffyverse fans, as well as those of Buffyverse fanfic writers, identified by this survey. A profile of the online Buffyverse fan will be developed looking at factors such as education, income, location, geographic mobility, sex and age. These same factors will then be looked at again to see how fanfic writers compare with the larger fandom in terms of the (larger) demographic profile. As stated previously, the data reflect the overall characteristics of individuals who responded to *this* survey, and can not be extrapolated to represent *all* fans of this or other fandoms, nor can it be used to predict the characteristics of any given fan.

1. The Online Buffyverse Fan

Young, white, heterosexual, middle-class, college-educated American women

While there were notable exceptions to the above phrase, overall the survey respondents fit this description. The majority of the respondents were from the United States (67 percent). Although Buffyverse fans exist in all parts of the world, it is also likely that *BtVS* and *AtS* are the most popular in English-speaking countries. Other English-speaking areas represented were the U.K. (11 percent), Canada (7 percent), and Australia and New Zealand (5 percent). The U.K.'s population is 80 percent less than that of the U.S. and Canada's population is 89 percent of the United States,' consequently there was a skew toward U.S. responses (Statistical Abstract ... 2003). Although the fan forums where the survey was advertised were international in membership, language barriers are a likely factor for the minimal response of non–English speaking areas. Europe (other than the U.K.) represented 8 percent of the participants, and other global regions were represented by less than 1 percent of the respondents. Thus, both Europe and other global regions were thus underrepresented in the overall survey.

Younger people were over-represented, as 52 percent of respondents were under thirty, mostly college-aged. Only 20 percent of participants were over forty. It's not known is how many in the fandom are actually under eighteen. This is because, due to regulations for the protection of human research subjects, the survey consent form specified only those eighteen and older were to take the survey, and there was no option given for those under eighteen. The mean age might have dropped, had that option been included. However, with *BtVS* reaching its ten-year anniversary at the time of the survey, most of the "18–24" respondents were likely at least eighteen.

The education level for the group as a whole was quite high. While 32 percent of the American population report high school but no college, only 7 percent of the survey respondents reported the same. In contrast, 27 percent of the overall fan group reported having a graduate degree or higher. Given that in 2003, the U.S. census reported 9.3 percent of the U.S. population as holding at least a master's degree, the fan portrait is that of an educational elite. Although this statistic refers only to *American* participants, this statistic is comparison is still valuable in that the international respondents were substantially outweighed by U.S. respondents (and from multiple countries, making a true comparison quite difficult) and even if the U.S respondents were broken out separately, their education level would still be higher than the U.S. population as a whole.

Additionally, given survey takers' comments to the survey, at least some of the 34 percent who have completed an undergraduate degree are in or planning to pursue a master's degree at the present time.

The responses were more diverse in terms of economics. When asked about employment, 12 percent identified themselves as full-time students, the largest "occupation" response. Students were followed closely by those working in the educational field (11 percent); in IT, web design or programming (9 percent); in the writing/publishing fields (7 percent); and those in arts and entertainment (6 percent). Some typical student occupations such as clerical, retail and food service occupations (13 percent) were also well represented. Another survey question asked whether the respondent's current job was the one for which they had sought and trained. A majority (54 percent) said yes. It seems likely given these answers that many respondents over thirty are in their desired field of work. A good number are in the legal and health fields (9 percent), librarianship (5 percent) and other occupations that would account for the high number of graduate degree holders.

Therefore, when the income statistics for the group show that 52 percent of respondents fall below the U.S. national average in income ($35,000), this is likely due to the currently diminished earning capacities of the many college students who appear in the survey (U.S. Census Bureau, 2003). As one survey taker noted in comments, "I have negative income due to student loans." Overall though, the reported income in the survey peaked at $50–75,000 with 10 percent reporting over $100,000 a year.

The young age of respondents is also reflected in the marital and parenting status of most survey takers. Only 33 percent of respondents were sharing their home with a spouse, partner or children. Fifty-one percent of respondents reported they were not currently in a long-term relationship; 80 percent were childless.

Twenty-three percent of respondents considered themselves a member of a minority group. Of this 23 percent, over half (15 percent) considered themselves minorities due to sexual orientation. While estimates of GLBT individuals have varied, the more recent estimates in both the U.S. and Canada have ranged between 2–4 percent of the population (Black et al, 1999; Carpenter, in press). The 15 percent of such respondents is thus a significantly higher number than would likely be found in a general population sample.

By contrast, the survey has a comparatively low figure for combined racial (5 percent) or ethnic (7 percent) minorities among the respondents, as compared to the general U.S. population; African-Americans and Hispanics each make up over 12 percent of the population; Asians and other racial groups are an additional 10 percent (Grieco and Cassidy, 2001). Although the international response may have affected the interpretation of this question, two-thirds of the respondents were from the U.S. At least one comment to the survey noted that fans from non–Anglo nations share the feeling of being minorities within the fandom. An insignificant number of respondents also declared themselves as being a religious minority, disabled, or in more than one minority group.

Geographic mobility for online fans was somewhat high; 85 percent of respondents lived in at least two different populated areas and 17 percent having lived in more than seven, which is somewhat higher when compared to mobility in the U.S. population as a whole (Hansen, 2001)

The mobility statistic becomes even more interesting when looking at international results. According to U.S. estimates, slightly under 2 percent of Americans live abroad, many of them in military service (Statistical Abstract, 2003). Although this is 2 percent at any given time, 27 percent of survey respondents have lived in another country at some point, with more European survey takers (22–26 percent) having done so than American survey takers (18 percent).

When this survey's results were released for discussion (to the groups who taken it) three issues accounted for virtually all the comments. Two of them — voting statistics and reading rates — will be discussed later. The survey result that engendered the most discussion had to do with the number of male and female respondents. Seventy-four percent of respondents were women; 26 percent were men. A gender bias in survey responses is not uncommon, with women often being more likely to answer survey requests than men (Braunsbergera et al, 2003; Cull et al, 2005). However, where the bias exists it's been shown to vary results by less than 5 percent (Dixon, 2002). Therefore, if the online Buffyverse fandom was made up of a majority of men, or gender balanced, it's very unlikely that the total over a four-week survey period would show this much of a difference.

2. The Buffyverse Fanfic Writer

Younger and more female than the overall survey group

This article's focus is on identifying types of fannish involvement within the online Buffyverse fandom. Fanfic writing has been a recurring object of academic study and — apart from discussion and analysis — is also the most visible online fan activity. Fanfic writing/reading is one of the dominant forms of creative fan activity and one of the clearest in terms of tracking fan interest. For example, the largest current multifandom *fanfic* archive, Fanfiction.net, attracts four times the number of visitors to its site per month as the multifandom *discussion* site, *Television Without Pity* and 20 percent more than the popular multiplayer *game* site *World of Warcraft* Fanfiction.net also ranks among the top 2000 sites on the web in overall use, unlike either of the other two (Compete.com, 2007).

Demographically, in answering many questions throughout the survey, fanfic writers differed little from the overall respondents. Fanfic writers were — as in the overall fandom — mostly young white women. The most significant contrast comes when one looks at Buffyverse *fanfic writers* compared to those in the fandom *who have never written or even read fanfic* (non-ficreaders).

Fanfic writers do, however, skew younger and more female than the rest of the fandom. In confirmation of early ethnographic studies of fanfic writers, it is largely a female practice (83 percent women, 16 percent men) (Bacon-Smith 1991; Lewis, 1998). The gender split among non-ficreaders is much smaller, but still noticeable. If one is a female in this fandom, there is only a 7 percent chance that she has *never* tried reading any fanfic; for a male, it is 25 percent. Similarly, there is a 39 percent chance that a female has written fanfic, and only a 7 percent chance that a male Buffyverse fan has ever written fanfic for *any* fandom.

A different survey question addressed the frequency of fanfic writing. Most fanfic writers (68 percent) had written fanfic in the past year. Most of the female writers had written in the past year, whereas less than half of the male writers had. Therefore the non-current writers were more likely to be male than female. In other words, the female writers were more likely to be consistently engaged and the men more likely to dabble.

However, the third who had not were more likely to be male since only 44 percent of male writers had written in the past year, compared to 73 percent of women. In response to the question "have you ever written fanfic?" one respondent noted that the answer was "yes" only because he/she had written one story ever. Most likely other respondents who had not written fanfic recently are also not habitual writers of fan fiction. Given their lower writing frequency, these occasional writers were more likely to be male.

Fanfic writers tend to be young. Although all age groups were represented, more of the young respondents had written fanfic than older respondents, with 34 percent of the writers falling into the 18–24 year-old bracket. Only 7 percent of those over 50 had written fanfic. However, the youngest and oldest respondents were the most likely to have read fanfic, with over 90 percent in both the 18–24 and over-50 group having done so.

Asked how often the survey takers read fanfic, older readers were the most likely to read fanfic daily. Those 25–35 were the most likely to read fanfic infrequently. Leisure time thus seems to be a possible factor in fanfic reading frequency. However, when asked about *commercial* fiction reading habits, a different picture emerges. Fans 25–35 were the *most* likely to read fiction daily and those 18–24 the least likely. Why would this be the case?

There are two possible explanations. One is that younger college-age readers are already utilizing free reading time for fanfic, in addition to reading school assignments. This group still reads frequently, just on a weekly rather than daily basis. The second issue has to do with portability. Most fanfic is thus read online. Whether short or long, many fanfics are not well formatted for easy printing, particularly those posted and archived on blog sites such as LiveJournal. Printing is time-consuming and costly. Commercial fiction, on the other hand, is portable, making it easier to fit in reading time during an otherwise busy and mobile day. In summation, the more leisure time respondents have to use a computer, the more likely they are to be reading fanfic.

Fanfic writers are, as a group, less likely to be highly educated than the average Buffyverse fan. The young skew for fanfic writers accounts for part of this difference. Age and education level are closely correlated in the survey — the older the respondent, the more likely they are to be highly educated. With one-third of fanfic writers in this survey being 18–24, the likelihood that they have completed college is lower than among overall survey takers.

However, when the fanfic writers are compared to other survey takers in their *same* age bracket, fanfic writers are actually more likely to hold *graduate* degrees. Of fanfic writers 18–24, *8.3 percent* are likely to already hold graduate degrees compared to only 2.9 percent of non-ficreaders. Similarly, among those 25–30, 36 percent of fanfic writers hold graduate degrees, compared to 24 percent of non-ficreaders. Thus, while the typical Buffyverse fan is likely to be a college-educated young woman, the typical fanfic writer is even more likely to have completed at least some college. This suggests that people who are interested leisure writing also have a greater interest in higher education.

It also appears that fans who are GLBT may be more attracted to reading or writing fanfic. Those writing/reading fanfic were twice as likely to list themselves as being a sexual minority than those who did not. It should be clarified that although sexual minorities are more likely to be fanfic writers, a given fanfic writer is not more likely to be a member of a minority group. Regardless of category, 77 percent of the survey respondents did not consider themselves to be part of *any* minority group, no matter how broad the definition.

Fanfic writers are significantly less likely to be married or living with a partner than non-ficreaders and slightly more likely to be divorced, widowed, or in a long-distance relationship. Writing is often absorbing and most easily done with blocks of uninterrupted time. However, when breaking down the figures by relationship status and writing frequency, those who were married or living with a partner were actually slightly more likely to have written fanfic in the past year than those who were single, in a long-distance relationship, or in a long-term relationship. Also those who had children living at home were distinctly more likely to have written in the past year than those who did not have children. Time constraints within the household then would not seem to be a strong factor in terms of who writes and who doesn't. In other words, relationship status may be related to the amount of leisure time one has (because one's partner is not present, or because of divorce or widowhood, or age of children), therefore influencing fanfic writing. Thus, fanfic writing may be related to leisure time.

Another potential time factor influencing writing may be employment. Those with demanding careers may have less writing time than those who are in more temporary types of jobs. Because of the open-ended question used for employment information, it was not possible to correlate type of employment with whether or not the respondent wrote fanfic. Yet, the question asking whether survey takers had the job they wanted and trained for indicated that fanfic writers are less likely to be satisfied with their jobs (49 percent) than non-ficreaders (63 percent). Again, this is probably due in part to the fact that most college students have jobs of a temporary nature. In a correlation of education and job desirability, those with graduate degrees or higher had an 80 percent *positive* response to this question compared to high school graduates who had a 77 percent *negative* response. So fanfic writers may simply have more time on the job to write or may simply be working fewer hours than those who don't.

Income and education tend to be closely correlated factors in demographic surveys. Given that fanfic writers are younger and more likely to still be in school, training for their future careers, their income is also lower. Although income peaked at the $50–75,000 levels for fanfic writers, just as it did with the overall survey group, *fanfic writers were over-represented in lower income categories and non-ficreaders were over-represented in higher income categories.* A cross-tabulation of sex and income resulted in negligible differences, but age and income proved significant. A cross-tabulation showed that those in the 18–24 age bracket are dramatically over-represented in the lowest income bracket.

Survey Report—Part 2. Activities Within and Outside of the Fandom

In Part 1, a basic demographic profile was made of the online Buffyverse fan. This profile was then examined more closely in terms of two groups within the fandom — those who wrote fanfic and those who neither wrote nor read fanfic.

Some distinct differences were found centering on sex, age, and income. The income differences were largely due to respondents' age, consequently, only age and sex were included herein because they were the most dramatic differences, and age led to other effects noted below. The lower skewing age group of fanfic writers influenced other differences in terms of educational achievement, income, and marital and parental status.

In this section activities will be examined, first for the overall group, and then again between fanfic writers and non-ficreaders. It seems likely that the demographic factors seen in Part 1 will have an influence on individual behavior.

Tastes in Entertainment. Given that this is a fandom that centers on a media text, some of the survey questions focused on the respondent's interest in reading, television viewing, and entertainment genres.

1. The Online Buffyverse Fan

One of the most discussed questions from the survey was the one asking whether or not the survey taker preferred reading a book to watching television. This question was actually drawn from a 2004 "Angel Magazine" online reader survey, which found that 60 percent of readers preferred watching television to reading (*Angel* Magazine, 2004). In this 2006 survey however, the reverse was true — 57 percent of respondents chose reading — perhaps because the overall age and education of the respondents was higher. In cross-tabulating by age, the older the respondent, the more likely they chose books, with 71 percent of those over 50 doing so compared to 50 percent of those 18–24. Another factor in the response was gender: 63 percent of ***women*** preferred books compared to 41 percent of ***men***. These two factors bear out larger trends in the U.S. The 2004 *Reading at Risk* report found the average rate of fiction reading in the U.S. declining most steeply among young people and men (xi, NEA, 2004). Overall though, Buffyverse fandom is made up of heavy readers, regardless of age or sex.

The developing statistical picture of an educated, middle-class female group is not unlike that of the typical reader or library user. Asked how often they read fiction, nearly a third of all respondents said they did so daily, with only 6 percent doing so once a year or less. Female respondents were slightly more likely to read fiction frequently. According to "Reading at Risk," 75 percent of the survey respondents would be classified as "frequent" or "avid" readers, putting them in the top 16 percent of the overall reading public (4, NEA, 2004).

A gender split was apparent when it came to library use. Although 98 percent of all survey respondents had first used a library before the age of twelve, males were 10 percent less likely to use a library regularly than females, and the most likely not to have used one at all in the past year (Given the relatively small number of parents in the survey, children's use of the library is not a factor in this discrepancy). Overall 76 percent of respondents had used a library's materials or services at least once in the past year. Age is also a factor in library use, with those 18–24 being the heaviest library users, perhaps because they are in school. Cross-tabulations of education levels with reading rates and library use show a close correlation. A cross-tabulation of age and sex of all survey takers shows that there are virtually equal percentages of male and female respondents in all six of the survey's age brackets. Therefore, age and gender seem to be independent factors in library use among the fans surveyed here.

Respondents showed clear preferences in certain genres of entertainment, regardless of medium. Most respondents chose fantasy (74 percent) and science fiction (86 percent) as favorites. Least popular were romances (31 percent) and westerns (10 percent). Both males and females enjoyed suspense/thrillers in relatively equal proportions, but otherwise, tastes tended to fall in line with historically gendered preferences. Males were distinctly more interested in horror and westerns, and dramatically less interested in romances (12 percent). Females were least interested in westerns (7 percent), slightly more interested than males in mysteries, and slightly less interested in science fiction. Age seemed a factor in only two genres: romances were markedly preferred by those under thirty-five, and the oldest respondents had the most interest in mysteries — the youngest had the least.

2. The Buffyverse Fanfic Writer

Not surprisingly, people who enjoy writing are much more likely to prefer a book to television (65 to 35 percent) than are other respondents. Those who are not fanfic readers are the least likely to opt first for a book, indicating that at least part of the reason they do not read fanfic is because they do less reading in general. The difference however, is mostly by comparison, since non-ficreaders are almost evenly split between books and TV. Responses to questions about reading fanfic and reading published fiction indicate that fanfic writers are most likely to read either daily; non-ficreaders are least likely to read either daily. Nearly 20 percent of non-ficreaders indicate they either never read fiction or read it once a year. The same is true for only 7 percent of fanfic writers.

There is no difference between the groups in terms of library use, although there is a difference in behavior by age. Older non-ficreaders were more likely to be using the library than older fanfic writers. However 18–24 year old fanfic writers were more likely to be using the library than 18–24 year old non-ficreaders. As suggested previously, this heavier library use by young fanfic writers may be due to their being students, thus using a library for a variety of purposes other than leisure reading.

Sociability

Having looked at some of the entertainment habits and interests of Buffyverse fans, some traditional elements of media fandom emerged, such as an interest in science fiction and fantasy texts, over other popular genres. In addition, both the group as a whole and the fanfic writers are frequent readers.

Having these tastes in commonalities, we now look at the frequency and range of social interaction by those participating in online fandom.

1. The Online Buffyverse Fan

The first survey question asked respondents to rate their own fannishness. Survey takers chose how many different things they felt they had been a fan of during their lifetime. The answers showed that survey takers were very "fannish" people; that is, people who were likely to become quite taken with particular activities or forms of entertainment. The general concept of a fandom and its activities were not likely to be new to them. Sixty-seven percent had had five or more fannish interests during their lifetime. Only 2 percent of respondents had never become fans of anything before encountering the Buffyverse. Since the definition of "fan" was left up to the respondent, it's possible that some survey takers' listings might be considerably higher than self-reported. Part of what we will look at is how the definition of "fan" gets defined through interaction and activities. Are the survey takers primarily lurkers or active in the fandom? Are they new to fannish practices or experienced? How often do they participate?

Being social in offline fan groups was not particularly common. Seventy-two percent had either never done so, or done so only once or twice. A minority had done so over ten times (9 percent). However, 3 percent of respondents had never shared their fan interests with *anyone* offline, even though some of these individuals had been fans of various things.

Meeting in person is a more difficult thing than meeting online; many factors are involved in attending group events. Time and cost can be a deterrent, and meeting a large group of fans may be intimidating if one is attending alone. By comparison, meeting others online is cheap, convenient, and easier to abandon if one is uncomfortable. Most of the respondents found online interactions easier in some way. Only 10 percent of all survey takers were chronic lurkers, stating that they never interacted with other fans online.

Conversely, 19 percent of respondents were quite experienced in navigating online fandom, having been involved with five or more different fan interest groups. Fifty-one percent of respondents had been involved in 2–4 online fandoms.

Easy access to a computer and Internet service would have an effect on the frequency of online interaction. Asked how many hours survey takers spent online engaged in recreational pursuits, 81 percent spent at least an hour a day doing so. While it seemed two hours a day was common for most participants, 16 percent of respondents spent over thirty hours a week online for entertainment purposes. This is nearly as much time as they might expect to be working. Students, IT workers, and the self-employed, along with the four percent of the respondents who were unemployed, retired or disabled, were examples of occupations with more flexible schedules and lack of administrative oversight which might allow for such a high amount of recreational time online. Of the 2 percent of respondents who spent only an hour or two a week online for entertainment, either fan activities or discussions were their sole recreational use of the Internet, or they didn't interact due to lack of opportunity.

A different survey question sought to determine how important fan activities were to online use. Fifty-seven percent had already been online prior to taking part in a fandom. However, for 43 percent of the survey takers, one of the first things they used the Internet for was fan interests. The majority (77 percent) also visited several Buffyverse sites regularly, most choosing "2 to 4" sites, but 12 percent choosing "9 or more." The question asked respondents to identify large multi-site domains such as LiveJournal as one site. Thus the 23 percent of respondents who cited "Only 1" may actually be interacting a great deal, but just in one place. Additionally, *visits* are not equal to *interaction*. For example, someone looking for news or desktop wallpapers may visit numerous sites without actually talking to anyone. The question then becomes, what sorts of sites are being used by the fandom for all these activities? Are they primarily discussion sites or static informational sites? The answer is most of them *are* websites, but a lot of them are discussion- oriented sites as well.

A number of technologies were in current use: 69 percent listed weblogs; 56 percent named posting boards; 28 percent named mailing lists; 11 percent named newsgroups. Also in frequent use were technologies used to communicate directly with individuals, such as email (48 percent), chat and instant messaging (20 percent) and text messaging (3 percent). Since respondents could add their own categories, a few formats such as "Podcasts" and "RSS feeds" were included.

Given that two of the most active sites for the fandom, *Whedonesque* and LiveJournal, are blogs, one would have expected nearly 100 percent of respondents to have identified blogs as a visited site. Instead 97 percent responded they used *websites*. There has been some notable confusion demonstrated among *Whedonesque* users regarding what type of site it is, as many seem not to realize that a community blog is still a blog (Whedonesque, 2006). There is often a similar reaction to sites like LiveJournal, which are not classified as blogs by some academics or online users because they are considered "journals" or online diaries (Herring, 2004). Thus the 97 percent who replied they used "Websites" regularly may be confounding the two mediums. This confusion would also seem to be borne out by many of the respondents (5 percent) who named LiveJournal specifically, or named specific websites in answer to the question.

What this diverse group of responses indicates is that survey takers are visiting numerous online sites. A sizable number are also engaging in discussion at a number of locations, using everything from the oldest to the newest Internet tools and formats.

Two final questions were included in the survey to gauge the respondent's tendency to get involved in issues of importance to them. The first question asked whether or not the survey taker had voted in either of their last two national elections. As the survey was launched on the heels of the 2006 U.S. midterm elections, this was a recent issue. The reported voting response of 85 percent is quite high compared to the typical U.S. election turnout. Although party affiliation or candidate preference was not asked, observations of the Buffyverse fandom show a liberal slant, especially as regards social policy. This is supported by the overall educational status of the respondents (Gill, 2005).

In countries where voting is compulsory however, this statistic would not be meaningful. A second question asked whether the survey taker had taken part in an organization focused on political or social issues. While 51 percent of the respondents answered "yes," both of these political activity questions had a clear age bias in the response. Although 85 percent of respondents claimed to have voted, this ranged from 49 percent for those 18–24 to a high of 92 percent for those "Over 50." Given that all respondents were of voting age and the question asked about *either* of the two most recent elections, age restrictions were not a factor in the voting difference. Similarly, when asking about organizational activity, those 18–24 showed the lowest participation at 44 percent and those over fifty the highest, at 70 percent. This age bias is reflected in other voting surveys such as those reported by the U.S. Census (Cassata, 2007).

When looking at *fandom* participation however, age seems to have no bearing on who has or has not taken on community roles in the fandom. Asked about a range of positions (and offered the chance to add their own), 67 percent had not taken on any community roles. The most common volunteer activity was moderating an online community (20 percent). Other responses ranged from the 12 percent who reported being website designers or maintainers to the 1 percent who listed convention volunteer or website contributor.

Taking on community roles has relevance not only to a fan's level of interest in the fandom but also in their opportunities to socialize within the fandom. Although the people who take on such roles are not necessarily more sociable than other fans, their roles do give them an opportunity to be better *known* by other fans, even if this is due solely to username recognition. Overall, about a third of the respondents had volunteered in some way. What about the rest of the respondents? Aside from merely interacting with one another, do they make friends? Is fandom something respondents share with others offline?

The answer is yes, but it seems there is often a divide between having fannish interests and sharing those with the people closest to them. Most respondents have someone in their life who also shares fannish interests. These people are, however, more likely to be close (51 percent) or casual friends (37 percent), not *family*. At least 20 percent of the respondents didn't know *any other fans*. These 20 percent explain why some individuals may go online for fannish interaction. The relative lack of family members who are fannish (25 percent of siblings, 14 percent of parents) means that many individuals have had no one at home with whom to share those interests. When asked whether or not respondents felt closer to those friends or family members who shared this part of their lives, most survey takers said no, but a 44 percent said "Yes." Fortunately for most participants at least someone they knew, whether spouse or partner (20 percent), or other relative (12 percent), was also a fan. The smallest response was for children (7 percent) but considering the small number of parents in the survey, this could be expected.

How successful are online interactions in generating new friendships? Although it's not the majority, 46 percent have made friends through online fandom. A final question explored whether or not feeling comfortable with others online affected the development of friendships. Asked "Do you feel that your fandom is a safe place in which to express yourself?" 41 percent said "Yes," 4 percent said "No"; the majority responded that it depended on the online site (56 percent). These figures will be looked at in more detail when discussing the responses of fanfic writers.

2. The Buffyverse Fanfic Writer

Although there is a slight tendency for fanfic writers to have more fannish interests than non-ficreaders, overall differences between fanfic writers and non-fanfic readers were minimal. In general, fanfic writers are not markedly more "fannish" about things than other fans. They are, however, distinctly more *social* in their fan behavior. While 52 percent of non-ficreaders had never gone to fan gatherings, the same was true for only 37 percent of fanfic writers. Fanfic writers were also the most likely to have gone to ten or more fan-related events. This same sociability translated to online behavior. Although equal numbers of fanfic writers and non-ficreaders called the Buffyverse their first online fandom, fanfic writers were the most likely to have interacted with other fans online in seven or more fandoms. Given that involvement, they were also three times more likely to be spending over thirty hours a week online than were non-ficreaders. It should be mentioned again that this question asked about *all* recreational uses of the Internet, not merely fan activities. Fanfic writers were clearly comfortable online; they spent a lot of their leisure time there; and Internet access would not seem to be a significant problem for most of them.

When asked what first brought them online, fanfic writers were more than twice as likely as non-ficreaders to say it was a fan interest. When this question was analyzed by age, younger respondents were much more likely to have cited fan interests than older survey takers. The overall youth of fanfic writers may be influencing this statistic. Having been in college or in the workforce during the growth of the Internet, older respondents are more likely than younger ones to have first encountered the Internet for work or research purposes.

Fanfic writers clearly get around in the fandom. Most fanfic writers and non-ficreaders (47 percent of each) visited 2–4 sites. Non-ficreaders, on the other hand, are more likely to visit only one fandom site, and hardly any such respondents claimed to visit nine or more sites. Fanfic writers are also more likely to use all technologies than non-ficreaders — sometimes dramatically so. For example, fanfic writers are 30 percent more likely to use blogs than non-ficreaders, 34 percent more likely to use e-mail, and 26 percent more likely to use IM in their fan-related activities. Although "Websites/Archives" use is relatively identical between the two groups, the reasons may be different. Fanfic writers are more likely to visit "nine or more" sites, and it's possible many of these are fanfic archives. As the content of each archive varies, it's quite likely that fanfic writers (and readers) visit a variety of archives from time to time to see what has been added.

The only technology in which fanfic writers do not exceed average use is with newsgroups, where they are 2 percent lesss than non-ficreaders. This statistic seems to bear out claims about the early migration of fanfic writers away from newsgroups back in the early 1990's (Bury, 2005). In general, the more personal commitment and involvement required for a technology, the more likely fanfic writers are to use it compared to other fans.

When it came to the political activity questions there was almost no difference between fanfic writers and non-ficreaders. When it came to *fan activities* however, the difference was dramatic. Eighty-nine percent of non-ficreaders have never served in any kind of fandom support position. By comparison, 50 percent of fanfic writers have done so. One might expect fanfic writers (and readers) to take on support positions — which they do. They are in fact, the group *most* likely to have done support work, most notably as community moderators, but also significantly as website designers and maintainers, and event organizers. Some activities are biased towards fanfic work, like awards sites, fanfic archives or fandom newsletters. Still, within any given fandom there are numerous websites and communities that are not fanfic related. Respondents were also free to add their own categories to this question. Fanfic writers were the most likely to add categories, and the most likely to do website and community work.

At least part of the reason for fanfic writers' level of volunteer activity may have to do with their interest in connecting with others. A study of friendship in the U.S. showed an increase in married individuals who claim their spouse as their sole friend (McPherson et al, 2006). Thus, the survey results here may have as much to do with a respondent's marital status as to their fan connections offline.

The two areas that showed the greatest difference between fanfic writers and non-ficreaders were between fannish spouses and close friends. Since fewer fanfic writers are married or living with someone, it's not surprising that non-ficreaders were almost twice as likely to have a fannish spouse (32 percent to 18 percent). Fanfic writers had more close friends who were also fans (56 percent to 43 percent). The significance of these differences is difficult to interpret. The survey results here may have as much to do with marital status as to offline fan connections.

Fanfic writers do seem to value fannish connections among their family and friends more than non-ficreaders by a 10 percent margin. It is possible that fan interests are closely related to emotional bonds for this group. This interpretation is also supported by the finding that fanfic writers are nearly four *times* as likely to say they have made "a good friend" online than non-ficreaders. Although 32 percent of fanfic writers do not claim a close online friend, *82 percent* of non-ficreaders don't. Clearly many fanfic writers are finding not just social contact, but positive relations in their fannish activities. When asked "Do you feel that your fandom is a safe place in which to express yourself?" fanfic writers were more likely to say yes (44 percent) than non-ficreaders (35 percent), with only 2 percent saying "No," compared to 11 percent of non-ficreaders. Along with the gender gap, this gap in terms of fannish friendships is one of the most dramatic differences between fanfic writers and non-ficreaders.

Given the responses to these varied questions, it can be said that fanfic writers are more actively involved online in part because they are interested in making connections with other people. There are two possible factors involved. The first is that they have a dearth of social connections offline and are thus attempting to find them online. However, the question about family and friends who are fans seems to diminish this possibility. A second explanation is that fanfic writers simply have a greater level of fannish interest and this leads to more activities with others. The next section will look at this possibility.

Survey Report Part 3 — Fandom Involvement

In the previous section questions pertaining to sociability and fandom involvement produced different levels of activity for different groups. While it would seem likely that sociable people would be more involved in a fandom, this does not mean that less sociable people would automatically be lurkers. Those who don't interact much with others have numerous ways of contributing to a fandom. Websites, technical support, or creative works are just a few examples. What this section will focus on is whether it is generally the *same* groups who are both socially active as well as contributors of fandom resources.

1. The Online Buffyverse Fan

Besides fanfic writing, two other questions addressed creative fan works. The first asked if they had ever made a fan video and the second asked whether they had ever created graphics. Only 9 percent had ever made a video, while 45 percent had created graphics. Although fan vids have been made since the introduction of the VCR, computer software has simplified the work enormously, allowing a boom in fan video making. Vids are now found in large public video archives such as YouTube and iMeem. Vids demand a great deal of time and effort, often with very little feedback. Legally, they are also the riskiest sort of fan production with their use of copyrighted clips and music. Although the majority of U.S. Internet users now have high-speed access, for many others downloading is still slow and vid storage can add up quickly (Pew Internet...2006). The number of people making vids may be growing, but as of this survey, they were still a minority in the fandom. What is interesting about vid making is that it is not as gender-skewed as fanfic, with only 10 percent of women and 6 percent of men reporting they had made one. These numbers continue to show a strong gender skew.

Graphics are most often made to decorate and personalize online spaces, whether they are story banners, user icons, or photo manipulations and they can be found on even the plainest of websites. A fairly high number of respondents — 45 percent — have tinkered with visuals at some time. Interestingly, they have not been creating website banners (18 percent) or computer wallpapers (21 percent) as often as icons (35 percent). A gender skew is evident when it comes to graphics, with 49 percent of women and 32 percent of men having made some. This is still a small difference compared to the 80/20 split in fanfic writing. It also may have something to do with the value of graphics to the two genders. Men were slightly more likely than women to say that the visual appeal of an online location was "not very important" although a minority of both sexes said it was "very important" (20 percent).

Survey takers were also asked if they felt they were collectors of anything.

Sixty-six percent responded admitted to being collectors. The result had a distinct gender skew in that 71 percent of men, but only 63 percent of women considered themselves collectors.

A final question about fandom involvement asked the survey taker if participating in fandom had "broadened your horizons in some way." Seven options were given as well as a write-in option to add a response in their own words. Only 15 percent of respondents said "No." Most respondents replied that they had different views of the "Buffy" and "Angel" series (48 percent) or claimed to have met a wider spectrum of people than they had known before (43 percent). Other responses had to do with learning more about different topics (39 percent), gaining different views of other fans (37 percent), or changing their views on issues (28 percent). Central to the question of fannish involvement was "taking on new roles/activities" (22 percent) and feeling less inhibited in having "discussions with strangers" (25 percent).

2. The Buffyverse Fanfic Writer

Fanfic writers were, the most likely to have also created fan videos and graphics. Fourteen percent of fanfic writers had done so, whereas only 3 percent of non-ficreaders had created a fan video. Thirty-three percent of non-ficreaders had created graphics, compared to 62 percent of fanfic writers. Fanfic writers had, in fact, created more of every kind of graphic, with 50 percent having made icons. Although fewer had created photo manipulations, which take a high level of skill to do well, virtually no non-ficreaders had done so. In short, it appears that writers do not simply write, they create a variety of works and, as a group, they are "doer" in the fandom.

What is also interesting about the vid statistic is that it sheds light on the graphics results. Many fanfic writers like having icons, banners and other graphics to advertise and illustrate their stories. It would not be unexpected to see writers creating visual works as a means of self-promotion. However, vids do not serve as advertising, yet fanfic writers are still more likely to have created them. This seems to indicate that the graphics results (as well as the fandom support positions result) are not due solely to writers' efforts at "marketing" themselves and their work. Rather, fanfic writers are interested in becoming involved, and are motivated to be creative. There was no significant difference between fanfic writers and non-ficreaders in terms of being collectors — a non-creative form of fan activity.

A final question was asked of all respondents: how involved in the Buffyverse fandom did they consider themselves to be? Only 18 percent considered themselves to be "Very Involved." The majority was equally split between "Somewhat Involved" and "Occasionally Involved" (35 percent each). A minority (12 percent) said it was a fan interest that was mostly in the past for them; they were no longer active.

While this "middle range" of responses is to be expected, what is interesting is the split between fanfic writers and non-ficreaders. Twenty-two percent of fanfic writers consider themselves to be "very" involved in the fandom, compared to 9 percent of non-ficreaders. As a group, non-ficreaders are the most likely (52 percent) to say they are only occasionally involved in the fandom. It is impossible to determine what any individual survey taker means when they say "Very involved" as opposed to "Occasionally involved." However, other questions in this survey that focused on fannish activities, roles, interactions, etc., have all shed light on the self-reporting in this question. All along, responses have indicated that *as a group,* fanfic writers are very active and non-ficreaders are among the least active in the fandom. When asked to report on their own involvement, the two groups would seem to agree with this assessment. The question discussed earlier that asked about "broadened horizons" tied together involvement and personal benefits. Only 7 percent of fanfic writers say that their fandom involvement has not stretched them in some way. Thirty-three percent of non-ficreaders claim no benefits to being involved in the fandom. Fanfic writers are also nearly twice as likely to have provided a write-in response citing additional personal benefits.

Looking at the different choices in the "broadened horizons" question, only 5 percent of non-ficreaders said they had taken on new roles, and 9 percent said they felt less inhibited in having discussions with strangers. By comparison, 33 percent of fanfic writers had taken on new roles, and 33 percent also reported feeling less inhibited about chats with strangers. Also of note were responses to "I have contact with a broader spectrum of people"; 55 percent of fanfic readers agreed; only 16 percent of non-ficreaders agreed. Indeed, fanfic writers were twice as likely to say they had benefited from the fandom as non-ficreaders.

Summary

Part Two of this article focused on the survey takers' involvement in online fandom. It compared specific responses between groups identifying as fanfic writers and non-readers of fanfic, and demonstrated what individuals may mean when they describe their own fandom involvement as "occasional" or "very involved." When it comes to tastes in their entertainment, fannish sociability on and offline, and participation and contributions to the fandom, there are skews in the behavior of the two groups. There are also differences between the two groups in benefits they believe they have received from taking part in the fandom. Compared to non-ficreaders, fanfic writers seem to be more emotionally committed to participating online and interacting with others, whereas non-ficreaders seemed to be more infrequent participants with a lower level of commitment and less interest in emotional or social aspects of the fandom.

It must be restated that these conclusions can only be drawn based on the responses by these particular survey takers, and for the two groups as a whole. There are undoubtedly individuals who contradict these results. It is also impossible to tell from this survey how many people are now or have been involved in online Buffyverse fandom, and how many fans do or don't take part in fanfic writing.

Conclusion

At the beginning of this article the problematic definitions of "fan" and "fandom" were examined in terms of isolated versus interacting fans; fannish interest that centered on a text versus an activity; and how enthusiasm, knowledge or active response to the text may be markers of a "fan." By looking at the results of this survey of the online Buffyverse fandom, a few clues may arise as to how a sizable group of individuals may find some connection between activities and interaction and what it means to be a participant in a fandom. By asking about specific commitments of time and creativity, habits such as interaction and site visits, and benefits such as friendship or learning new things, a group of 1600 individuals provided data that showed a surprising amount of correlation between these factors and how involved they felt themselves to be in the Buffyverse fandom. While these results do not give us a "one-size-fits-all" definition of a "fan," they do give us a continuum of fannish involvement that can be used in future studies to classify fan participants. This study may also provide some insight into the differences between fans that are text-centered versus those who are activity centered, in terms of both demographics and level of involvement with others.

These results may also support an argument for moving away from the broad umbrella definition of fandom as "*All* the fans of a sport, an activity, or a famous person" to one that encompasses only those who are at least aware of and interested in the behavior and exchanges of other fans. The terms "fan" and "fandom" would thus more closely reflect a fannish continuum, where a given person might be a "fan" of some things in isolation or to a less involved degree, and would be a member of a "fandom" when involved in a deeper or more communal manner to a fannish object.

Works Cited

The Adoring Audience, ed. Lisa A. Lewis, London: Routledge, 1992.
American Heritage Dictionary of the English Language. <*http://education.yahoo.com/reference/
dictionary/*>.

Bacon-Smith, Camille. *Enterprising Women: Television Fandom and the Creation of Popular Myth.* Philadelphia: University of Pennsylvania Press, 1991.

Black, Dan, Gary Gates, Seth Sanders, and Lowell Taylor "Demographics of the Gay and Lesbian Population in the United States: Evidence from Available Systematic Data Sources." Center for Policy Research, Maxwell School of Citizenship and Public Affairs. Syracuse Universtiy, October 1999. *<http://cprweb.maxwell.syr.edu/cprwps/pdf/wp12.pdf>.*

Braunsbergera, Karin, Roger Gates, David J. Ortinau. "Prospective Respondent Integrity Behavior in Replying to Direct Mail Questionnaires: A Contributor in Overestimating Nonresponse Rates." *Journal of Business Research,* 2003. <http://www.dssresearch.com/PDFs/Mail%20Response%20Rates.pdf>.

Bury, Rhiannon. *Cyberspaces of their Own: Female Fandoms Online.* New York: Peter Lang Publishing, 2005.

Carpenter, Christopher S. "Sexual Orientation and Economic Well-Being in Canada." *Canadian Journal of Economics,* Article in Press. *<http://web.gsm.uci.edu/~kittc/CarpenterCanada GLB.pdf>.*

Cassata. Donna. "Voter Turnout Among the Young Still Lags." *USA Today.* March 4, 2007. <http://www.usatoday.com/news/elections/2007-03-04-787496319_x.htm >.

Compete.Com "6/2006 to 6/2007 Profile for TWoP, Fanfiction.net and World of Warcraft." 2007. <http://siteanalytics.compete.com/televisionwithoutpity.com+worldofwarcraft.com+fanfiction.net?metric=att>.

Cull, William L., Karen G. O'Connor, Sanford Sharp, Sanford, Suk-fong S. Tang. "Response Rates and Response Bias for 50 Surveys of Pediatricians." *Health Services Research.* February 1, 2005.<http://www.encyclopedia.com/doc/1G1-130649175.html>.

Cusack, Maurice, and Donucha Kavanagh. "The Organization of Stigma and the Stigma of Organizing." Standing Conference on Organizational Symbolism, 19th Conference Dublin, 2001. *<http://www.ucc.ie/ucc/depts/mgt/dk/cv/stigma.pdf>.*

Dixon. John. "Nonresponse Bias in the Consumer Expenditure Quarterly Survey." Proceedings of the Survey Research Methods Section, American Statistical Association, 2002. <http://www.amstat.org/sections/srms/proceedings/y2002/Files/JSM2002-000410.pdf>.

Fan Fiction and Fan Communities in the Age of the Internet: New Essays. Ed. Karen Hellekson and Kristina Busse,. Jefferson, NC: McFarland, 2006.

Gill, Kathy. "Educational Attainment and 2004 Vote." About.com, 2005. <http://uspolitics.about.com/library/bl_education_vote.htm>.

Grieco, Elizabeth M., and Rachel C. Cassidy. *Overview of Race and Hispanic Origin: Census 2000 Brief.,* U.S. Department of Commerce. Census Bureau. March 2001. *<http://www.census.gov/prod/2001pubs/c2kbr01-1.pdf>.*

Hansen, Kristin A. "Geographical Mobility" U.S. Department of Commerce. Census Bureau. January 2001. *<http://www.census.gov/population/www/pop-profile/geomob.html>.*

Herring, S. C., et al. "Women and Children Last: The Discursive Construction of Weblogs." *Into the Blogosphere: Rhetoric, Community, and Culture of Weblogs.* Ed. L. Gurak, et al. Minneapolis: University of Minnesota, 2004.

Hills, Matt. *Fan Cultures.* London: Routledge, 2002.

McPherson, Miller, Lynn Smith-Lovin, Matthew E. Brashears. "Social Isolation in America: Changes in Core Discussion Networks Over Two Decades." American Sociological Association, June 2006. <http://www.asanet.org/galleries/default-file/June06ASRFeature.pdf>.

National Endowment for the Arts. *Reading at Risk: A Survey of Literary Reading in America.* Washington, D.C., June 2004. xi–4. <http://www.nea.gov/pub/ReadingAtRisk.pdf>.

Pew Internet and American Life Project, "Demographics of Internet Users." December 2006 *<http://www.pewinternet.org/trends/User_Demo_1.11.07.htm>.*

Pugh, Sheenagh. *The Democratic Genre: Fan Fiction in a Literary Context.* Bridgend, Wales: Seren Books, 2005.

Sandvoss, Cornel. *Fans: The Mirror of Consumption.* Cambridge, UK: Polity Press, 2005.

Theorizing Fandom: Fans, Subculture and Identity. Ed. Cheryl Harris, and Alison Alexander. Cresskill, NJ: Hampton Press, 1998.

Tulloch, John, and Henry Jenkins. *Science Fiction Audiences: Watching Doctor Who and Star Trek.* New York: Routledge, 1995.

U.S. Department of Commerce. Census Bureau. *Current Population Survey,* March 2003. <http://nces.ed.gov/pubs2005/nativetrends/ShowTable.asp?table=tables/table_8_1.asp&indicator=8.1>.

_____. _____. *Statistical Abstract of the United States.* 2003. *<http://www.census.gov/prod/2003 pubs/02statab/statistical-abstract-02.html>.*

"Whedonesque Is Blog of the Week in the (UK) Times." Whedonesque. March 4, 2006. <http://whedonesque.com/comments/9718>.

"Easy to Associate Angsty Lyrics with Buffy": An Introduction to a Participatory Fan Culture: Buffy the Vampire Slayer *Vidders, Popular Music and the Internet*

Kathryn Hill

Buffy the Vampire Slayer (1997–2003), hereafter referred to as *BtVS*, is not only a television program it is also an example, in semiotic terms, of the "writerly text" (Barthes, 1974). The "writerly text" is a text that is open to creative contributions by those who encounter it, in this case media fandom. As discussed by Bacon-Smith (1992); Jenkins (1992, 2006a and 2006b); Harris and Alexander (1998); Bury (2005) and Hellekson and Busse (2006), since the emergence of a cult following surrounding Gene Roddenberry's *Star Trek* in the 1970s, media fandom in general has become increasingly participatory. This participation has been aided over the past ten years by the growing accessibility of the Internet. Fan involvement on the Internet is more than homage to the films and television shows they celebrate. Fans use their favorite shows to explore infinite possibilities suggested by the primary text: they appropriate it, break it up and then reassemble the pieces to suit their own desires. Drawing on De Certeau (1984), Jenkins (1992, pp. 23–24) describes this fan process as "textual poaching":

> Because popular narratives often fail to satisfy, fans must struggle with them, to try to articulate to themselves and others unrealized possibilities within the original works.... Far from sycophantic, fans actively assert their mastery over the mass-produced texts which provide the raw materials for their own cultural

productions and the basis for their social interactions. In the process, fans cease to be simply an audience for popular texts; instead, they become active participants in the construction and circulation of textual meanings.

In other words, not unlike a traditional folk process of transmission (see Lord, 1960; Ong, 1982 and Peabody, 1975), media fandom not only disseminates but constantly reinterprets popular culture.[1] The early Star Trek fanzine community called this process "The Joy of Infinite Diversity in Infinite Combinations" (Bacon-Smith, 1992, p. 219 and p. 284) or IDIC. The term IDIC is itself an example of textural poaching. The idea originated in Gene Roddenberry's contribution for the Star Trek episode *Is There in Truth No Beauty?* (Ep. 62) in which Mr. Spock, wearing a pendant symbolizing IDIC — a circle and intersecting triangle — explains that it represents the Vulcan belief that beauty, growth, and progress all result from the union of the unlike: "The glory of creation is in its infinite diversity ... and in the way our differences combine to create meaning and beauty." This idea suggests analogies to Barthes' (1974, p. 5) concept of the writerly text: "within the field of infinite difference ... the writerly text is ourselves writing, before the infinite play of the world ... the opening of networks, the infinity of languages.... To rewrite the writerly text would consist only in disseminating it, in dispersing it within the field of infinite difference."[2] The origin of IDIC in the science fiction world of Star Trek may explain why the pre–Internet fanzine community were the first to describe the sites of textual poaching as "universes" (Bacon-Smith, 1992, p. 57). The creation of a "universe" is a defining attribute of every cult text — a process Hills calls "hyperdiegesis": "the creation of a vast and detailed narrative space, only a fraction of which is ever directly seen or encountered within the text" (Hills, 2002, p. 137). Adapting the term, the alternate universe that has evolved around *BtVS* has come to be known as the "Buffyverse." Within this "Buffyverse" fans come together at everywhere from spoiler chatrooms to blogger sites to discuss the meanings and implications of the show. Since the transmission of the final episode[3] many fans have continued to explore and extend the original text of Buffy in fan fictions or "fanfics" — stories exploring implied and alternate storylines — and in the creation of music videos known as "vids." The latter — the fan activity known as "vidding" — is the focus of this paper.

Buffy "vidders" are fans of *BtVS* who make their own music videos. Using the latest computer technology and resources of the Internet, they splice together moments from the show, utilizing special effects such as altering film speed, color and lighting manipulations, cross-fades and double-exposures. Topics for vidding are limited only by the imagination of the fans, but tend to fall within certain themes: serious and/or humorous commentaries on storyline; action vids; character portraits; romantic relationship studies or "shipper" vids; "recruiter" vids designed in the style of television promotions to attract new fans; and alternate reality or "experimental" vids. Arguably the most common type of vids are "slash" vids — romantic and/or pornographic explorations of same sex pairings. The colorful term "slash" originated in the convention of employing a stroke or slash between the characters' names first employed by the Star Trek fanzine community in the early 1970s (for example Kirk/Spock or K/S).[4] These visual montages are co-ordinated to music and appropriate lyrics. Requiring often many hundreds of hours of work, the resulting creations are then placed on the Internet for feedback from other vidders and fans.

Because they are using copyright materials, *BtVS* vidders are a tight-knit private community that does not like to advertise their existence. To quote one vidder: "Due to the nature of our fannish pursuits, vidders tend to be a fairly conservative bunch and we try not to push our work out too far for fear of getting a cease and desist letter" (Vidder A, 5 January 2004). This illustrates an important contradiction: despite repeated claims for privacy and confidentiality, vidders accept the small risk of prosecution for the pleasure of sharing and discussing their work via the Internet. To this end they have their own Internet chat-rooms and websites that present monthly commendations for the best vids. Awards from these competition sites are proudly displayed on the vidders' personal web pages. As vidders are breaking copyright laws, none of the individuals whose work is discussed in this paper can be identified by name, or even pseudonym. This is a great shame. Within the hyper-reality of the Internet vidders' pseudonyms, what one vidder called their "default nom de net" (Vidder X, 29 February 2004) can function as *lexias* — intertextual doorways to many subtexts.[5] Such pseudonyms often mimic the creative wordplay associated with naming in the primary text. For example, the names of ancient goddesses are common pseudonyms just as the name of Willow's girlfriend, Tara, is that of the Indian goddess of Mercy, venerated in Tibetan Buddhism. This is one example of the ways that, despite its illegality, vidding, as a form of "textual poaching," is arguably keeping alive our own cultural mythologies. As Jenkins notes in his essay "Digital Land Grab": "this [folk] process of circulation and retelling improved the fit between story and culture, making these stories central to the way a people thought of themselves ... contemporary web culture is the traditional folk process working at lightning speed on a global scale" (Jenkins, 2000, p. 3). Unfortunately, because these cultural myths are now the intellectual property of corporate interests, this natural folk process is being disrupted. In other words, the fan vids discussed in this paper are examples of this now illegal folk process in action.

Taking their cue from the way *BtVS* is itself a postmodernist text — a *bricolage* of pop culture references[6] — vidders often cross-reference *BtVS* with other pop culture texts such as films and popular music — a process Jenkin's refers to as hetroglossia "the evocation and inflection of previously circulate materials" (Jenkins, 1992, p. 253). Examples include the use of the theme from *Friends* (1994–2004) — The Rembrandts' *I'll be there for you* (1994) — to create an opening television sequence for *BtVS* in the style of this NBC network series, the vidder (Vidder B) posing the question: "what if BtVS was a sitcom like FRIENDS? The opening could look like this," or the use of the theme from Tarantino's film *Pulp Fiction* (1994) — Dick Dales' surf classic *Misirlou* (1963) — to create a comedic study of the "geek" Andrew. To quote the vidder's (Vidder C) summary: "[this is] a preview for the ... episode *Storyteller* which had a focus on Andrew and what he sees through his camcorder fantasies." Such cross-referencing — in which a few musical notes can trigger many associations — recalls Barthes' (1974, p. 13) "lexias." Lexias are small units of meaning within a given text that generate multiple intertextual meanings with lexias in other texts. Because of the postmodernist nature of so much contemporary film and music, a lot of fan enjoyment comes from learning to recognize such "lexias" or intertextual references.[7] Take for example the following comments by one vidder praising another's work (Vidder E):

> When you came out with your first version of *The Longest Day* using the song *L'Arena* I had not seen the movie *Kill Bill II* so I didn't have any preconceived ideas about the song. When I watched the vid I thought it was outstanding, but the thing that I seemed to like the most about it was that it reminded me of the movie *The Magnificent Seven*. The way you presented the Angel characters into the vid and with the flow of the music, it paralleled *TMS* all the way to the climactic ending. Excellent Vid!! [Vidder D, 26 September 2004].

By utilizing such "lexias" vidders are enriching the fandom experience.[8] To quote a vidder from Florida:

> One of the things I love most about vidding is the idea that even after a show is over, or a movie has already been shot, and there seems no way to continue the series, you can always see a new vid of the film that completely changes how you thought of it or presents it in such a new and different way.... There may be a song you have always loved that you hear in a vid and suddenly it's shiny and new. Or maybe it can get you to like a song you never liked. The possibilities are practically endless [Vidder C, 17 July 2003].

"Textual poaching" of popular culture has been in existence long before *BtVS* but in the *Buffyverse* it has developed perhaps unique characteristics. Ambiguity within the primary text — "the endlessly deferred narrative," to quote Hills (2002, p. 35) — is a defining feature of all cult texts. Successful cult texts are those that "leave enough space for subjective 'creation'" (Hills, 2002, p. 136). In fact the very existence of fan fiction and vidding supports Eco's observation:

> That in order to transform a work into a cult object one must be able to break, dislocate, unhinge it so that one can remember only parts of it, irrespective of their original relationship with the whole (1987, p. 198).

Understanding this *BtVS's* creator, executive producer and principal scriptwriter, Joss Whedon, deliberately places ambiguities within the storyline to encourage fan involvement. As Whedon explains in relation to a cryptic scene between Buffy and her erstwhile vampire boyfriend, Spike, in the series' finale, *Chosen* (7.22):

> And that's one where I wanted the audience to fill in the blanks. I wanted whatever you want to have happened, to have happened ... it's up to the viewer. I think the viewer has earned that and I love that elliptical nature of their last night together. I think there should be work for the viewer to do in that sense emotionally, because I think that makes it more textured [Whedon, 2004b].

Not only does Whedon gives fans permission to explore their own explorations of subtext, he also encourages them to step beyond the primary television text into alternate realities in order to explore hypothetical events and relationships, a process Jenkins (1992, p. 162) terms "recontextualisation." As evident by the episodes "The Wish" (3.09) and "Superstar" (4.17), such "recontextualisation" is often incorporated into the show itself. As Larbalestier (2002, p. 228) observes:

> *Buffy* is a show that runs on subtext so that it frequently becomes text. This makes the kind of "poaching" activities that Henry Jenkins discusses even more complex. How do you poach a show that poaches itself, i.e. that has stand-alone episodes that appear to ignore the general arc of the show and play on the "what if" scenarios beloved of fan fiction?

The following vid summaries illustrate typical examples of constructed reality — what fandom call alternate universe or "AU" vids: "No heroines. No vampires. Just a story of a plain girl, and a psycho-stalker who'll do anything to get what he wants," (Vidder F, 11 September, 2004) or "After being fooled back into the relationship once, and into a marriage, Buffy finally finds the courage to leave her abusive and cheating boyfriend" (Canadian Vidder G, no date). When creating such alternate universe vids, vidders may utilize the subtext to create personal commentaries on real life experiences. In other words, it could be said that vidders use *BtVS* to express their personal views about their own lives and their society.

Before Jenkin's book *Textual Poachers* (1992), fandoms were generally maligned within both cultural studies and sociology. As Hills notes, Bourdieu's theory that a bourgeois education grants cultural capital to an social elite, meant that "good taste" functions as "a filter to block out whole entire areas of experience judged — and damned — as unworthy of investigation"

(Hills, 2002, p. 58). Bourdieu's elitist views of culture fail to take into consideration that "trash cultures"—everything defined by the ruling patriarchal hegemony as "bad taste" including genre products such as *BtVS*—can provide individuals disempowered by that ruling hegemony with their own unique cultural capital. Acknowledging the unique symbolic value[9] such "trash cultures" may have, recent reappraisals of fandom have started to view fans "as active collaborators in the research process" (Jenkins, 1992, p. 7). To quote Lowe:

> Taking cues from literary criticism, academic writers about film, comic books, literature, soap operas, professional wrestling—in short, nearly any and all artifacts of popular culture—increasingly understand meaning not as something intrinsic to a text but rather realized and performed by an audience. Meaning is constantly negotiated and highly dependent on context of consumption and identity of consumer [2003, p. 123].

In contrast to "the media-fostered stereotypes of fans as cultural dupes, social misfits and mindless consumers" (Jenkins, 1992, p. 23), online fan cultures are not only very participatory, they are also becoming increasingly assertive and critical of their favorite shows. To quote Nussbaum: "[fans gather] on [Internet] sites like *Television Without Pity*, to debate like snarky doctoral candidates, or propose alternate plots in the form of fan fiction" (2003, para.5). In relation to the vidding community, this has meant that the best vids, like the best fan fiction, not only offer various thoughtful explorations of complexities suggested by the primary text perhaps, but also suggest possible readings—commentaries upon pop culture itself.

One reason for *BtVS's* popularity is it is a metaphorical reflection of youth culture from 1997 to 2003. Using humor and metaphor, *BtVS* poses many questions concerning teenage relationships and identity, teenage sexuality, drug abuse and deviant behavior, social and peer group pressures, teenage alienation, religion, censorship and politics. Accepting the fact that many vidders are no longer teenagers,[10] they are still fans of popular music, and popular music is one of the most important means of defining youth culture at any time (see Hall and Jefferson, 1975; Hebdige, 1979; Kelly and McDonnell, 1999). By using current popular music, *BtVS* vidders are perhaps unintentionally creating commentaries on that youth culture and society in general. In his essay "Why Do Songs Have Words?" Frith (1988) writes an overview of "content analysis": the study of lyrical meaning in relation to American popular song. Frith starts by surveying the work of H.F. Mooney (Mooney, 1954), the first researcher to argue for a "reflection theory" in popular song analysis. As Frith notes (1988, p. 107):

> The theoretical assumption here is that the words of pop songs express general social attitudes.... Mooney's argument was that pop song lyrics reflected the emo-

tional needs of their time. The history of the American "mood" could thus be traced through the shifting themes of popular songs....[11]

The application of "content analysis" of popular song lyrics to analysis of changing social attitudes, has been used by many theorists since Mooney[12] and, as Frith notes (1996, p. 159), "is still faithfully followed in the pages of [the journal] *Popular Music and Society*."[13] This is despite conflicting sociological research into teenagers' response to song words (see Lazarsfeld, and Merton, 1948; Denisoff and Levine, 1972 and Robinson and Hirsch, 1972) that has proven "either they [teenagers] don't understand them [song lyrics] or they "don't really notice them" (semantically, that is)" (Frith, 1996, p. 164). More recent research (see Arnett, 1991; Frith, 1981; Gantz et al., 1978; Prinsky and Rosenbaum, 1987; Roe, 1985 and Rouner, 1990) has found different popular music subcultures and adolescent gender and age divisions have different levels of lyric comprehension. For example, Prinsky and Rosenbaum (1987, p. 85) found that: "17 percent of male adolescents (12 to 18 years old) and nearly 25 percent of females said they liked their favorite song because the words express how I feel." Frith (1981, p. 205) has found college-bound, middle-class English rock fans took the words of their favorite music considerably more seriously than did working-class youth, and Arnett (1991, p. 93) claims that: "today's heavy metal fans are also deeply involved with the messages in the lyrics [because they] ... resonate with the 'dismal condition of the world as they (see) it.'"[14] Arguably *BtVS* vidders could be interpreted as another subcultural group that places a high level of importance on song lyrics. Lazarsfeld and Merton (in Denisoff and Levine, 1972, p. 214) observe that in order for lyrics to be understood: "(1) the material must be significant to the listener; (2) it must be intelligible; and (3) it must be supplemented by personal acts of involvement." Lyrics are significant to *BtVS* vidders because they are a very important component of vidding process — the making of a music video involves the careful combing of carefully selected lyrics, music and visuals. Not only does this take many hours of painstaking work, but often reflects an acutely emotional involvement with the primary text. In addition, many vidders have a high level of familiarity with a great many song lyrics because they are constantly on the look out for that "special" lyric to give voice to a specific vidding endeavor. This may not mean *BtVS* vidders have a greater objective understanding of popular music, but if one combines the social and cultural values associated with specific musical styles with the personal views of *BtVS* vidders, it can been seen that music vids may contain a wealth of cultural and social information. By choosing certain pieces of music, vidders are offering their personal views on everything from current trends within contemporary pop culture to psychological profiles of contemporary teenagers and young adults. Everything and anything suggested by the primary text becomes an implicit subtext and open for manipulation.

One reason this approach offers insights into society is because between 2000 and 2004, *BtVS* vidders were a very active and tight-knit online community. And as Bacon-Smith (1992) notes in relation to her study of fanzine writers in the 1970s and 1980s, the members of fandom communities are motivated to create in response to the needs of that community: "creativity lies not in how a writer breaks with the tradition of the community's work but in how she uses the language of the group to shed a brighter light on the truth they work to communicate" (Bacon-Smith, 1992, p. 57). One delight of the *BtVS* vidding community is the vid challenge. Competition sites will post vid challenges in relation to specific topics. Alternatively a subscriber to an internet discussion group may request the use of a particular song for a particular subject, or, on personal web pages vidders ask fellow fans to suggest songs to be used in vids. Vidders engage in such activity because they enjoy the feedback it will generate. As one vidder notes:

> I've found that the most interesting thing about vidding is that I get more feedback when I use a song that was suggested to me than when I come up with a vid idea of my own. I haven't quite figured this phenomenon out yet.... [Perhaps its] because the suggesters tell their friends to watch it and word gets out [Vidder H, 17 July 2003].

The popularity of requested vids may also be because these are more likely to explore universal themes of interest to other fans. The following is one such example of a request posted on a *BtVS* vidding community internet board in September 2004:

> Since I have absolutely no time for vidding (I just started High School! Yay me!), I figured maybe someone would like to do this vid. It's a Wes Tribute with the song "45." At first I thought it would fit cuz a gun seems to be his weapon of choice. But the more I heard the song, the more it seemed to fit him. I'll probably take a break from making videos for a while, at least until my first big vacation. Happy vidding! [Vidder I, 11 September 2004].

The lyrics of this song, by alternate, "angsty"[15] metal band Shinedown, are a good fit for a study of this character's mental disintegration in the final season of the *BtVS* spin-off series *Angel*: *What ... happened to the young man's heart....* Arguably, in requesting a vid to this song, this young man could also be addressing his own uncertainties, albeit be it melodramatically, concerning a new page in his own life — that of starting high school. In other words, this vid request is a reflection of *BtVS*'s primary text — a melodramatic, over-the-top exploration of real adolescent fears.

It is perhaps no coincidence that vids that have generated the most feedback from other fans often explore sociological themes such as the use of alternate music to represent Buffy as an icon of youth culture; "girl power" and riot grrrl music in order to explore female empowerment; post-grunge and "emo" music for vids about teenage identity issues; the use of heavy metal and goth music to explore teenage delinquency and related moral panic themes; and the deliberate mixing of discordant styles in slash vids in order to challenge gender stereotypes.

Popular Music and the Gender of the "Voice"

Before any discussion of specific vidding examples can be attempted, the issue of the gender of the voice in popular music must be addressed. When it comes to choosing the "voice" for fan vids, the singer's gender raises many questions. Writing about the first vidders in the 1970s, Jenkins notes: "the videomakers are indifferent to the identity of the original singer, with male voices speaking thoughts of female characters and vice versa" (1992, pp. 235). And, as one of Jenkins' sources explains: "It isn't disturbing to someone necessarily because you are listening to the words. You don't pay attention to whose voice it is.... Mentally, you are just putting words together with the pictures" (in Jenkins, 1992, p. 235–36). This explains why early *Star Trek* vidders saw no contradiction in using a female voice, such as Bette Midler singing *The Wind Beneath My Wings*, to explore the friendship between Kirk and Spock. Jenkins therefore surmises: "the performer's personality must be effaced so that the singer may speak more effectively on behalf of the fictional character" (Jenkins, 1992, p. 236). Older vidders accept this, but younger vidders often find such gender reversals unsettling. What Jenkins describes may reflect how predominantly female vidders in the 1970s, as consumers of popular music, were subconsciously responding to the conventions that dictated what was then considered the dominant "voice" in popular music.

In the late 1960s and early 1970s rock was the predominant form of popular music. In its appropriation of black vocal styles associated with the blues, rock music granted greater authenticity to the young white male voice. As Frith (1996, p. 191), adapting Barthes' "grain of the voice," notes, the young male voice acquired a "voluptuous pleasure ... [in] the materiality of the body speaking its mother tongue." Combined with a stylistic emulation of 1960s girl groups by the "boy" groups The Beach Boys and The Beatles, this also meant greater authenticity was granted to the high male voice or falsetto. At the same time, as women were reduced to the role of back-up singers, the female voice in rock music lost its authenticity, becoming what Frith describes as an "ungrained" voice: "[a voice] concealing its own means of physical production" (Frith, 1996, p. 91).[16] It was not until the punk era in the late 1970s, and then the riot grrrl movement in the 1990s, that strong female voices re-emerged in rock. This explains why the older generation of vidders Jenkins was writing about in 1992 do not acknowledge gender when selecting songs for their vids — they are selecting songs that reflect conventions associated with popular music when they were themselves teenagers. This gender mixing may contain coded meanings the video makers themselves are unaware of, or, alternately, do not wish to acknowledge. Discussions on this topic with a *BtVS* vidder who has been making music vids since the early days of *Star Trek* fandom, raises interesting questions. For example, this vidder uses a "macho" male voice, Dave Gilmour's *There's No Way Out of Here,* for a vid about three strong female characters: "Buffy, Scully and Nikita — on their descent into hell" (splicing together scenes from *BtVS, The X Files* and *La Femme Nikita*) and female performers for vids exploring the personal feelings of male characters such as Sarah McLachlan's *Do What You Have to Do* for a vid about Angel's conflicting emotional relationships with Buffy and his own misogynist dark side, or Sheryl Crow's *I Shall Believe* to explore: "What Spike may have believed about his relationship with Buffy in season 7 and about himself." When I commented on these gender reversals, the vidder replied I had made her think about her vids in a new way:

> It's a funny thing in that I don't really think about the female voice thing much. It's only ever other people who point it out. I was halfway through "I shall believe" when I realized that people might gripe about Sheryl Crow's voice (which I've never liked much, but the song hit me hard). I think some people just really don't like women's voices much and so this becomes a larger issue. I've rarely met people who object to female voices for male vids who actually like any female artists — the people who object almost uniformly eschew female artists of any kind. They might make exceptions for ass-kickers like Chrissie Hynde, but otherwise, they don't use female artists ever. I wouldn't go so far as to say misogynistic, but I think there's a really strong streak of this in fandom. They will never, oddly, object to male voices for women, like David Gilmour. I can't figure it out — I think it's cultural.... I think some characters are just too macho to ever really successfully use female voices unless they're the rocking chick types — *Fast and the Furious* , for instance, I have an excellent song I'd love to do but the singer's voice is so babygirly that people would abreact no matter how good the vid. I know I could make them forget it, but ... I'm not willing to waste the time. Instead I found a Depeche Mode song and everyone's happy [Vidder J, 9 August 2004].

It never occurs to this vidder that rather than neutral narratives, reversing the gender of the singing voice "masculinizes" female characters and "feminizes" the male characters. Her comment that others objected to female artists of any kind but "oddly, never object to male voices for women" suggests that many people still accept the long established popular music convention that the male voice is the only authentic voice. The idea that the male voice is the only authentic voice may also offer support for one sociological interpretation of the original slash fiction. According to Penley (1992, p. 490), the reason why "slashers write their romances about two men, is that we still live in a patriarchal culture, and it is thus still not possible to imagine two women passionately in love with one another who go out and save the galaxy once a week." In other words denied their own voice by a conservative misogynist culture, the original female slashers and vidders needed male characters as surrogates to express their own identity and desires. Vidders are no longer tied to such gendered conventions but many within the vidding community still have fun playing with them.

This brings us to another important topic: *BtVS* is a text that encourages subversive readings. An important subtext of *Buffy the Vampire Slayer* is the questioning of gender stereotypes — the roles men and women play in society are constantly being tested within the primary text.[17] This has meant that unlike earlier vidders who had to create their own subtextual interpretations of their favorite genre shows, *BtVS* vidders need only respond to Whedon's own subversive subtexts. Fans sometimes have a lot of fun with such subtexts. For example, one vidder uses Clay Aiken's song *Measure of a Man* against carefully chosen scenes from both *BtVS* and its spin-off show *Angel* in order to create a humorous exploration of the gay subtexts between all the male characters on these two shows. As this vidder's website modestly states: "I think of this vid as my proof of how slashy these shows are. I didn't get every pairing I've read/written in the vid, but I got a goodly number" (Vidder K, no date). Other examples include a vidder's use of rap artist Coolio's *Gangsta's Paradise* (Vidder L) to characterize renegade Slayer Faith, as a masculinized female; various vidders use of White Town's *Your Woman* for comedic studies of Andrew, coding him as feminized male (such as the example by Vidder A); or the use of *Tired of Sex*, a song dismantling many macho stereotypes by alternate band Weezer, to portray the vampire Spike as a worn-out sex object (Vidder M).

When it comes to challenging gender stereotypes, slash vids need careful appraisal. "Slash" can be interpreted in many different ways. The following discussion of one slash vid suggests an interpretation very close to Bacon-Smith's (1992) original appraisal of slash fan fiction from the 1970s. It is very common for vidders and fan fic writers to influence each others' work or sometimes even work together. One vidder (Vidder N) finds inspiration for many of her vids in the fanfic of a friend and fellow *BtVS* fan (Fanfic writer A). This vidder's slash vid *Circle of Light*, pairing the vampires Spike/Angel, was not only inspired by her friend's slash fic but also by both ladies' mutual love of the music of Ani DiFranco.[18] *Circle of Light* illustrates how the best vids, like the best fan fiction, can explore subtexts suggested by the primary text. In this case, using the homoerotic relationship between the vampires

Angel and Spike — as a means to explore deeper coded readings of potentially dangerous subjects. As Bacon-Smith explains in terms of what she calls the "conservation of risk":

> In fiction, the women of the fan community construct a safe discourse with which to explore the dangerous subject of their own lives.... In the fan community, risk is often displaced onto the theme of the genre. An example is a fan who may want to talk about sexual relationships. She must choose the potential revelation present at the low level of abstraction in the genres about women in relationships with men or other women, or opt instead for the high-level abstraction of male homoerotic fiction, which carries a high-risk theme — male homosexuality — while providing a correspondingly greater literary distance from the author's own life [1992, pp. 203–4].

In both *BtVS* and its companion television series *Angel,* the vampires Angel and Spike provide fans with a relationship characterized by domination games and occasional violence and torture. Angel, as Spike's sire, is the father figure against whom Spike, the petulant child, must rebel to assert his individuality. Angel/Spike slash extends this violence and torture to stories often exploring sadomasochism — Angel as the alpha male and Spike as the submissive feminized partner. A very large percentage of fanfics written by women explore this topic area. As Bacon-Smith suggests (1992, pp. 203–304), it is possible such homoerotic stories and their accompanying, but highly disturbing, genre of hurt/comfort[19] provide a means for women fans to safely confront male sexual violence. Spike, as a feminized male but with superhuman powers, provides sufficient "distancing" or "conservation of risk" to discuss such a dangerous topic as female sexual submission and violence against women. It is no coincidence that Spike fan groups have raised monies for charities with names such as "Taking Back the Night,"[20] One reason Spike is often coded as female is because, unlike the typically uncommunicative male, in the primary text he constantly offers insights into the emotional makeup of the people around him — a talent which gives him the upper-hand in many fanfics. The song, *Circle of Light* (written by Ani DiFranco), used to accompany scenes of hurt/comfort presented in this slash vid, could be Spike's emotional attack upon the stoic unemotional Angel. Di Franco's song *Circle of Light* could be interpreted in many different ways (see Feigenbaum, 2005) including a lesbianism subtext. Unlike the openly loving, caring relationship of *BtVS* lesbian couple, Willow and Tara, Spike/Angel slash could provide a means of exploring any relationships perceived by those involved in them as too dangerous to bring out into the open. When it comes to slash the layers of coding are limitless.

Deep Play and Explorations of Female Sexuality

The way vidders offer perceptive commentaries on various subtexts in *BtVS* is an important example of what anthropologist Clifford Geertz describes as "deep play" (Geertz, 1973). Bacon-Smith uses Geertz' concept of "deep play" as a means to describe how fandoms confront and step beyond social structures:

> Deep play often represents those stresses and tensions inherent in the social institutions that cannot be expressed more directly without risking real damage to the social structure. It may vent the frustrations of members of the group, thus allowing the structures to continue without change. The most important point here is that deep play may lessen rather than increase the potential change in a culture, but cannot stop change from occurring outside the game [Bacon-Smith, 1992, p. 287].

As illustrated above in relation to Spike/Angel slash, the creative "deep play" of *BtVS* vidders,' in addition to their often thoughtful responses to this researcher's questions, provides a means to explore the social implications behind many of the characters on *BtVS*. The following will look at one such vidding example in relation to the character Buffy's psychological breakdown in season six, featuring unused dailies from the episode *Dead Things* (6.15). This vid is set to the song *Dig Ophelia* by American indie goth band Rasputina. This New York group came to the attention of *BtVS* fans when their song, *Transylvanian Concubine* (which linked vampirism with anorexia) provided the accompaniment for the insane vampire Drusilla's dance in the episode *Surprise* (2.13). Rasputina are three lady cellists who dress in corsetry and other nineteenth century attire — a look, as noted by Hodkinson,[21] associated with the current Goth subculture — and whose songs also often explore nineteenth century gothic themes.[22] When asked why she saw *Dig Ophelia* as appropriate for the character of Buffy, the vidder explained:

In the *Dig Ophelia* vid, Buffy is Ophelia. Like Ophelia, Buffy's gone 'round the bend a bit. Buffy is traumatized from her resurrection and driving herself mad by using Spike [for sex] when she knows it's wrong to do so. Buffy's digging herself in deep. By *Dead Things*, she's already dug in deep. The song also has a haunted quality that went well with how haunted Buffy was in *Dead Things*. Plus, it was pretty and I though it would look nice with the dailies scenes. I hadn't thought of this till now, but Buffy even drowned once. Like Ophelia did in the play (Vidder O, 28 July 2004).

The song *Dig Ophelia* lends a haunting quality to this vidder's work. The constant swirling cellos as Buffy tosses and turns in bed, inter-cut with the sex scenes from this episode and the dailies, captures Buffy's distress and the idea of her "drowning" in her relationship with Spike. The combination of this music with the carefully chosen visuals brings to mind Pre-Raphaelite, John Everett Millais' 1852 painting of Ophelia drowning—a victim of Hamlet's insane behavior—thus suggesting similarities between sixth season's "mad" Buffy and Spike's first lover—the mad, psychic vampire Drusilla. Both female characters are known for their "abnormal" sexual relationship with Spike (previously a nineteenth century gentleman called William). In the mid–nineteenth century it was believed "normal" women were "not very much troubled with sexual feeling of any kind" and that in the rare case of sexual desire in a woman the end result was insanity.[23] As Drawmer (2003, p. 21) notes, in Victorian times while "male sexual desire and activity [was seen as] natural and innate," female sexual desire was considered "pathologically deviant—the product of a diseased mind and body."[24] Whedon's observation concerning Buffy's "normal" relationship with previous boyfriend Riley: "A lot of people have been twitchy about the fact that Buffy got herself into a happy relationship, where she actually gets to have sex. That makes people nervous" (in Gross, 2000, p. 4), suggests, in terms of the popular media's presentation of sexuality, double-standards still exist.

A common figure in mid–nineteenth century art and literature was the *femme fatale*—the sexually aware woman who lures men to their destruction. The creation of the *femme fatale* resulted from "the transmutation of male anxieties about female sexuality into concepts of excessive, transgressive demoniac sexuality" (Drawmer, 2003, p. 21). This could be a description of the vampire Drusilla. When this researcher outlined these ideas to the vidder who made the *Dig Orphelia* vid, they responded by quoting passages from an article they had read on the social repression of women in nineteenth century society:

> While many middle class women were unpaid laborers in the home, working class women and girls were also actively employed in the public sphere. Far from exemplifying personal ability or ambition, a woman's paid employment suggested a loss of cast for both her and her husband.... The Victorian feminine ideal not only discouraged female action and emancipation, it defined these as inherently aberrant and amoral [in Vidder O, 2 August 2004].

This nineteenth century view would explain why talented women, like the author Jane Austen, had to hide their work for fear of being socially ostracized.[25] In *BtVS*, this Victorian female is represented in the young woman predestined to become Drusilla. The human Drusilla possessed psychic powers. Told by her mother her premonitions are sinful, and fearing eternal damnation, Drusilla, the dutiful Catholic daughter, went to confession. Unfortunately the "priest" to whom she revealed her secret was the sadistic vampire Angelus. Delighted at being able to play the part of priest confessor, Angelus informed Drusilla she was the spawn of Satan and beyond salvation. In order to fulfill his own predictions, he killed Drusilla's family, then drove her insane, after which he turned her into a vampire — the sadistic *femme fatale BtVS* fans know and love. In view of discussions with the vidder who made *Dig Orphelia,* one could interpret Angelus' actions as patriarchal punishment, carried out by an appointed "dead white male" against a woman who has stepped beyond her appointed social position. Do comparisons proposed by this vid between Buffy and Drusilla suggest that despite her prior role as an iconic figure of "girl power" in the late 1990s, the resurrected, psychologically damaged Buffy on the UPN network in 2001 was now a pale imitation of her original self—a victim of unacknowledged social double standards? The above illustrates not only how much thought can go into vid making but how vidding in general can contain subtexts the casual viewer or even the vid maker may not be consciously aware of. Such intertextual readings or "deep play" (Geertz, 1973) — the result of discussions with fan vidders about their selected music — may not be possible by studying the primary text alone. The following illustrates another example of what fans perceived as the character Buffy's departure in the last two seasons from the original premise of feminist empowerment.

Over the seven seasons of the show, Buffy remained an iconic figurehead but under the weight of her calling, she always had a tendency to suppress her feelings. To many fans, Buffy became an increasingly withdrawn and unsympathetic character. The following question was presented to vidders who have addressed this issue of Buffy's emotional evolution in their vids:

> I think it's wonderful how you use music to be "Buffy's voice" and express things she cannot. Who do you think Buffy is as a person? Academics and journalists talk about her as a feminist icon but I have problems with that. I am trying to work out where she is at.

Admittedly a specific response may have been suggested by stating the problematic nature of Buffy as a feminist icon, but all respondents had very strong views on the subject as illustrated in the following remarks by a twenty-year-old female vidder from Southern California:

> I do not think she's a feminist role model. True feminism is about choice, and she never had any choices. Apparently to Joss, feminism means strength — but women are already strong. Women don't need strength; they need the opportunity to fight, the opportunity to live the way they want. I disagree a lot with Joss's message, and I think he was so blinded by this message that he nearly assassinated his own creation. In too many cases, Buffy was stereotypically "male" and that's not what feminism is about [Vidder P, 11 July 2003].

This vidder's interpretation of Buffy as stereotypically "male" is illustrated in her vid to the song *Hurt* as interpreted in 2003 by Johnny Cash. Originally written by Trent Reznor of the Nine Inch Nails (and featured on the album *The Downward Spiral,* 1994), "Hurt's" gothic statement of self-loathing, desertion by loved ones and a painful need for love, could be Buffy's own admission that she has entered a destructive sexual relationship with the masochistic vampire, Spike, in order to dull the pain of self-denial and commitment that is the life of "The Slayer."[26] The lyric *Everyone I know goes away in the end* reflects how Buffy's sense of self-loathing originates from her belief that she has caused everyone she ever loved to leave her: her mother, her father, first boyfriend Angel, second boyfriend Riley, her Watcher, Giles. This is what the vidder had to say about how she saw the character of Buffy as represented by this song:

> The first time I heard *Hurt* I *knew* it was about Buffy. I don't think she's purposely a bitch or cold hearted. I don't think she's a bad person. I think she's a complicated person with complex emotions and motivations, and it's really hard to vid her. There's love in her, loyalty, friendship, and yet, there is pain, desperation, disgust, and hate. It's hard to find a song that reflects those complexities — you don't want to go too far in either direction [Vidder P, 11 July 2003].

Such emotional themes, recalling the gut wrenching intensity of Hank Williams, are suited to Cash's painfully honest delivery more than Reznor's dehumanized voice in the Goth original. Conceivably this song could have been performed by a female country singer. If so it would have been interesting to know if the vidder of *Hurt* would have preferred a female voice to Cash's. It should also be noted how much *Hurt* illustrates a potential crossover between contemporary Goth and traditional country music.

Buffy's psychological breakdown in season six is just one example of how, for many female fans, later seasons of *BtVS* fell short in terms of the original feminist text about empowerment. The following will look at one fan's attempt at textual poaching or reappropriating the primary text to create her own "cultural capital" (Bourdieu, 1984) i.e. personal subversive reading. The second most powerful female character on *BtVS* is her Jewish lesbian friend, Willow. By the end of season seven, Willow is an extremely powerful witch but previously, during season six, Willow is depicted as an addict with a habit, descending uncontrollably into "dark magicks." That Willow's discovery of her true power was reduced to a metaphor for drug abuse annoyed many fans because Whedon had already established magic as a sexual metaphor. In the episode, *A New Man* (4.12), Willow and her girlfriend Tara, join hands to levitate a rose, accompanied by heavy breathing and ecstatic facial expressions. This was Whedon's way of depicting the lesbian Wiccas' first sexual encounter.[27] Willow's descent into "dark magic, grief and madness" subsequent to Tara's death at the end of season six was interpreted by both fans and critics as reinforcing "the dead/evil lesbian cliché" — the stereotyped portrayal of lesbian relationships discussed in *The Celluloid Closet* by Vito Russo to reestablish patriarchal authority (see Greenman, 2002, para 4)—but as Ramlow argues, *BtVS*'s creator and scriptwriters did not make a conscious decision to:

> cast lesbianism as social pathology and physical addiction ... the Willow-Tara story arc in addiction and death only proves exactly how dominant ideologies (in this case homophobia and intolerance) function on the unconscious level) for readers as well as creators" [Ramlow, 2002, para. 4].

One vidder's (Vidder Q) response was to use the song *Misery Land* by Virginian independent rock duo Fisher[28] to create a commentary on female emancipation. She does this by creating an alternate reality vid that ignores the drug references presented in the primary text, concentrating instead on Willow's fight to establish her own identity separate from her mentor—The Watcher, Giles. Giles is Buffy's "Watcher" but he is also Willow's father figure, constantly warning her against experimenting with "dark magicks." The song *Misery Land* opens with a lyric that speaks of the singer "learning to fly," and refers to someone else who "shoot[s] them down." When asked to explain in what ways she mixed the primary text with an alternate reality story line, this vidder (Vidder Q, March 2005) replied:

> The song describes this relationship where one person can't bare [sic] to see the other person happy. I think that this song translated to Willow/Giles in my mind ... especially after the scene where they are in the kitchen and he calls her a "rank amateur" at magick. As Willow started getting more powerful with her powers, there was always this tension between Willow and Giles. He always disapproved of her overuse of magick. In the beginning of the song the line is "I learned to fly ... but you ran to find the gun'" In Willows' mind she was unstoppably powerful and had this sense of freedom. And I think that she might have felt that Giles was always trying to ruin her "fun" or trying to keep her at a level below himself.

Noting a possible feminist subtext, specifically the argument put forward by Nash that "girl-centered texts [including *BtVS*] offer their young female consumers implicit lessons [in] self-subordination to paternalistic authority" (Nash, 2006 p. 13),[29] this researcher (8 March, 2005) remarked:

> *Buffy* is about female empowerment and the constant fight against the old established patriarchy that is constantly trying to bring women back into line.... It's interesting that you don't depict anything negative about Willow's magic powers in your *Misery Land* vid other than Giles' negative reactions.

To which this vidder responded:

> Definitely! The tension between Willow and Giles is simply a reflection of the larger tension between empowered females and males. Although, commonsense tells us that obviously the magick was bad for Willow, that she should have heeded Giles warning. I wanted to do the vid from Willow's point of view, before she began to regret her use of magick. Obviously she didn't see that Giles was trying to pro-

tect her ... she say that Giles was scared of her surpassing him.... I didn't want to make a video showing the downfall of Willow through magick, I wanted to make a video showing the downfall of the Willow/Giles relationship [Vidder Q, 9 March 2005].

This vidder's response suggests she may not have considered the Willow/Giles relationship in feminist terms. As discussed by McRobbie (1991/2000), for many younger women today the word "feminist" has only negative connotations, but a feminist reading of this vid is possible. This vidder acknowledges her vid *Misery Land* contains a "shipper" element. Shippers are stories exploring romantic relationships outside the primary text. In her vid Giles is not only a father figure but is also depicted as the jilted lover unwilling to let Willow leave him. Nash notes the frequent pairing of daughters and fathers in media texts concerning rites of passage of adolescent girls (such as *Gidget, Patty Duke Show* and *BtVS*) "signals the broader fact of girls' significance to patriarchy writ large: her sexual maturation vexes her father because it also vexes the societal 'Father'"(Nash, 2006, p. 25). This vidder's use of a scene from Willow's dream in *Restless* (4.22) in which she moves into the dark red drapes — a metaphor within the context of this episode for her awakening lesbian sexuality and the deepening of her relationship with girlfriend Tara — is followed by a scene of Giles following disapprovingly behind her. The implication is a patriarchal figure disapproving of Willow discovering her mature feminine nature and sexual self. According to Burns and Torre (2004, p. 127), since 1997 the Bush administration has funded a 3000 percent increase in the teaching of abstinence programs over sex education in American school. This contrasts with the liberal sexual message communicated by *BtVS* on mainstream American television between 1997 and 2002. It is perhaps no coincidence that this vidder has recently moved away from home in order to attend university. This vid may be expressing her own first steps to find herself away from the patriarchal constraints of home.

This study has only hinted at the depth of analytic possibilities — the ethnographic "deep play" — contained within the opinions and creativity of the *Buffy the Vampire Slayer* fans known as vidders. In attempting to illustrate how the textual poaching of media fandom reflects and comments on established research in the fields of cultural studies, feminism, media studies and popular music, this article hopes to suggests possible avenues for further research.

Notes

1. Because the immeasurable ways such a text is explored by its fans has similarities with the processes of transmission seen in the primary orality of pre-literate cultures, Ong (1982, p. 136) describes the exploration of texts by the electronic media as secondary orality.

2. Matt Hills, referencing Eco (1995), uses the term "living textuality" to explain the same process: "the cult text exists beyond the legislation of an author, being a 'text or texts' which has no origin other than pure textuality" (Hills, 2002, p. 132).

3. The final episode of *BtVS*, "Chosen" (7.22), was transmitted in the United States on the 20 May 2002.

4. For primary literature on slash fanfics see Lamb and Veith (1986); Cicioni (1998); Green, Jenkins and Jenkins (1998); Penley (1992) and Russ (1985).

5. See Penley (1992, p. 494) for further discussion of intertextual meanings of fan pseudonyms in relation to *Star Trek*.

6. See Dunne (2001) for discussion of intertextuality in the popular media. For a study of intertextuality in the postmodernist television text, *The Simpsons*, see Irwin and Lombardo, 2001.

7. Lexias work on many levels. Wilcox (2005, p. 193) defines three different varieties: "extra-textuality (references to the 'real' world outside the text), intertextuality (reference to other texts), and intratextuality (reference to other elements within a long text such as the *BtVS* series)."

8. Sometimes fan vids can be perceived by fellow fans as better than the primary text itself. To quote English genre critic Keith Topping:

> The first time I saw ANY of "When She was Bad" [first episode of the second season of Buffy] was when a friend in LA sent me a tape which contained a scratch-video that someone in the States had done using clips of this episode with Oasis's "Live Forever" as its soundtrack. Looked MAGNIFICENT and, perhaps unwisely, I expected something towering and awesome from the episode and, when it turned up a couple of weeks later I was, frankly, disappointed [Topping, 6 September, 2004].

9. Hills (quoting Sconce, 1995, p. 375) in defining what forms the cultural capital of "trash cultures" may take, describes them as sites of "refuge and revenge" (2002, p. 58).

10. In response to Longworth's observation: "everyone assumes that the demos for your shows are thirteen to twenty-six, but what's the truth?," Whedon replies: "They charted it in our second year, and the median viewer age is twenty-six. There are young kids watching it, but I consider it as a college kind of show" (in Longworth, 2002, p. 215).

11. As Frith continues:

> ... from 1895 to 1925 song lyrics were "abandoned and unorthodox" and reflected the patriotism, proletarianism and hedonism of the rising American empire; from the 1920s to 1940s songs were "negativistic and rather morbid" and reflected the disillusion, the quiet despair of the Depression; in the 1950s pop reflected a new zeal, as "the mass mood" invested the post-war consumer boom with Cold War fervor [Frith, 1988, p. 107].

12. See Horton (1957); Carey (1969); Cole (1971) and Cooper (1986 and 1991).

13. For examples see Bradby (2005); Fish (1995) and McDonald (1987).

14. Such research has been used by the moral right in America to support the claim that music subgenres associated with juvenile delinquency, such as heavy metal, exercise a form of mind control over adolescents. To quote Christenson and Roberts (1998, p. 62): "[for adolescents] lyrics play a cognitive role. They are attended to as language — interpreted for meaning, processed, discussed, memorized, even acted on." This study of *BtVS* vidders hopes to reveal a far more critically interactive response to popular music culture than the Pavlovian response proposed by moral right-wing groups such as the Parents Music Research Centre (PMRC). For examples, see PMRC's founder Tipper Gore's book *Raising PG Kids in an X-Rated World* (1987).

15. Florida metal band Shinedown, to quote *Allmusic.com*: "[write] blustery lyricism about personal pain, relationship woes, and other "boy, is life sucky stuff" — essentially, the same set of issues that seemingly all of these aftermarket grunge rockers rant about" (Loftus, no.date). In other words, Shinedown represent the move by many post-grunge alternate bands into the genre called "Emo" or emotional rock, a current music genre popular with many *BtVS* vidders.

16. Major female performers, Joni Mitchell for example, were side-lined into other genres such as jazz, folk and country. This lacunae or the lack of the female voice in rock music in the early 1970s arguably led to the male appropriation of female roles in glam.

17. For example, in his DVD commentary to the 7th season episode "Lessons," Joss Whe-

don makes the following cryptic remark about avoiding referencing the gender of 7th season character, Robin Wood: "when I wrote the script I never used any pronouns because we didn't know if we wanted him to be a man or a woman. And that's why I gave him the name Robin. You never hear he or she, its always 'Principal Wood walks away'" (Whedon, 2004a). Wilcox (2005, p. 48) observes the name Robin Wood may be a homage to the film critic Robin Wood. It is perhaps no coincidence that in his critiques of the horror genre, Wood, like Whedon, often questions gender stereo-typing. For example in his essay "The American Nightmare: Horror in the '70s," Wood notes: "the whole edifice of clear-cut sexual differentiation [of] bourgeois-capitalist ideology [is erected] on the flimsy and dubious foundations of biological difference: the social definitions of manliness and womanliness" (Wood, 2003, p. 65).

18. As this vidder acknowledges in private correspondence (please note the following retains her faulty English):

> My writing muse just worships [Ani DiFranco's] music and I love her too.... One of her favorite pairings is Spike/Angel, one she got a unique writing style for, too bad your German is not that good. So I went through my Ani D. CD collection to search for THAT song, which would fit the slash pairing and my hold of it. With almost two hundred songs written and hundred on CD not that easy. On her album *Imperfectly* when I almost lost hope, I got strike by the lightning or really "Circle of Light." Here was the actually vidding done so much faster than the search for the right song.

It should also be noted the high quality of this vidder's work brought her to the attention of the music industry. In August 2003 the threat of legal prosecution for copyright infringements forced her to remove her vids from the Internet. The irony of this is that many *BtVS* fans, this researcher included, are also music fans, and may have been motivated after seeing this vid to seek out more of DiFranco's music.

19. Bacon-Smith defines "hurt-comfort" fan fiction as stories in which: "one of the heroes suffers while the other ... comforts him.... The source of the suffering may in some instances be illness, but more often inflicted injury causes the pain. Unlike sadomasochistic fantasy material, hurt-comfort places the source of the injury outside the dyad of sufferer and comforter. Alternatively, the story may originate the hurt within the relationship and move toward eradicating the hurtful behavior through better mutual understanding by the ending" (1992, p. 255).

20. At a fan convention in Melbourne in August 2004, this researcher witnessed a woman tell the American actor who portrays Spike, James Marsters, how much he has emotionally helped her and fellow members of a rape support group.

21. According to Hodkinson the "wearing of dark-colored corsets, bodices and lacy or velvet tops and dresses" (2002, p. 46) associated with the current gothic revival can be traced back not only to punk and late 1980s artists such as Patricia Morrison and Julianne Regan, but also to Hollywood adaptations of popular vampire fictions in the early 1990s such as Francis Ford Coppola's *Bram Stoker's Dracula* (American Zoetrope/Columbia Pictures/Osiris Films, 1992) and director Neil Jordan's adaptation of Anne Rice's novel *Interview with the Vampire* (Geffen Pictures/Warner Brothers, 1994).

22. For example, as well as "Transylvanian Concubine," Rasputina's 1996 album *Thanks for the Ether* includes a track "My Little Shirtwaist Fire"—a song about the death of a child sweat shop worker in the famous Triangle Shirtwaist factory fire in New York in 1911: "such a sweet face, trapped in the staircase, by the smell of her own burning hair."

23. As Drawmer (2003, p. 21) observes, quoting the following from Acton's 1857 *The Functions and Disorders of the Reproductive Organs*:

> I should say that the majority of women (happily for them) are not very much troubled with sexual feeling of any kind. What men are habitually, women are exceptionally. It is too true, I admit, as the divorce courts show, that there are some few women who have sexual desires so strong that they may surpass those of men [...] I admit, of course, the existence of sexual excitement terminating even in nymphomania, a form of insanity which those accustomed to visiting lunatic asylums must be fully conversant with.

24. Hence Freud's psychological premise that suppression of sexuality in women leads to hysteria or imagined physical illnesses

25. Joss Whedon has on various occasions expressed his admiration for Austen. Asked in an online interview by *BtVS* fan, Little Willow: "If you could have dinner with anyone, living or dead, who would it be and why?" Whedon replied: "Jane Austin, 'cause, apart from being brilliant, she'd probably have kick-ass table manners" (in Kimberley Hirsch/Kiba, no date).

26. This can be seen in Buffy's admission to Tara in DeKnight's script for the episode "Dead Things" (6.15). It should be noted that one could interpret Tara's response as showing the link between Buffy's dilemma and the sexual ambiguities often explored in slash vids:

> BUFFY: He's [Spike] everything I hate. Everything I'm supposed to be against. But the only time I feel anything is when we.... Don't tell anyone. Please.... The way they would look at me.... You don't know how hard it is. Lying to everyone you love about who you're sleeping with.
>
> TARA: Sweetie, I'm a fag. I've been there (DeKnight, 2002, Part 2, p. 15).

27. This scene was Whedon's response to censorship regulations imposed by the WB network on the presentation of homosexuality: "[The WB] have certain regulations, they mustn't kiss. Every regulation makes me more determined to be imaginative. Hence the spell casting scene, which I view as borderline pornography! But your young kids can watch and never have the slightest idea it has any meaning other than 'oh, this is a really hard spell'" (in Bassom, 2000, p. 8). According to Whedon the studio did not understand this metaphorical presentation of Willow and Tara's relationship: "We were playing it as a metaphor and it was like, 'Why don't they come out? They're not gay enough!' And eventually we did start to say, 'Well, maybe we're being a little coy' ... [but] of course, once you bring it out in the open, it's no longer a metaphor" (in Robinson, 2001, p. 7).

28. The initial success of West Virginian modern-rock duo Fisher was the result of heavy promotion of songs, including "Misery Land," in 1999 on the music download site *www.mp3.com*. This subsequently led to the release of their album *True North* on the "indie" label Interscope in 2000. Fisher are one of the many bands illustrating how the Internet is making it possible for *BtVS* vidders, along with other music fans, to discover music outside the mainstream market dominated by the major record companies

29. For further discussion on the submissive and/or subversive depiction of teenage girls by patriarchal forces within the media, see also essays in Gateward and Pomerance eds. *Sugar, Spice and Everything Nice: Cinemas of Girlhood* (2002).

Works Cited

Ali, Lorraine. "The Glorious Rise of Christian Pop: With Big Best Sellers, New Movies and Religious Rock, The $3 Billion Christian Entertainment Industry is Exploding. On Tour with Young Believers." *Newsweek* (16 July 2001): 38.

Arnett, Jeffrey Jensen. "Adolescence and Heavy Metal Music: From the Mouths of Metalheads." *Youth and Society*. 23.1 (1991): 76–98.

Bacon-Smith, Camille. *Enterprising Women: Television Fandom and the Creation of Popular Myth*. Philadelphia: University of Pennsylvania Press, 1992.

Barthes, Roland. *S/Z*. Trans. R. Miller. New York: Hill and Wang, 1974.

Bassom, David. "Meet the Maker" *Buffy the Vampire Slayer Magazine* 11 (October 2000): 6–8.

Botting, Fred. *Gothic*. London and New York: Routledge, 1996.

Bourdieu, P. *Distinction: A Social Critique of the Judgement of Taste*. London: Routledge, 1984.

Bradby, Barbara. "She Told Me What to Say: The Beatles and Girl-Group Discourse" *Popular Music and Society* 28.3 (July 2005): 359–390.

Burns, April, and María Elena Torre. "Shifting Desires: Discourses of Accountability in Abstinence-only Education in the United States." *All About the Girl: Culture, Power and Identity*. Ed. Anita Harris. New York and London: Routledge, 2004: 127–137.

Bury, Rhiannon. *Cyberspaces of Their Own: Female Fandoms Online*. Morehouse Publishing, 2005.

Carey, James.T. "Changing Courtship Patterns in the Popular Song." *American Journal of Sociology* 74.6 (May 1969): 720–731.

Christenson, Peter and Donald Roberts. *It's Not Only Rock 'n' Roll: Popular Music in the Lives of Adolescents*. Cresskill, NJ: Hampton Press, 1998.

Cicioni, Mirna. "Male Pair-Bonds and Female Desire in Fan Slash Writing." *Theorizing Fandom: Fans, Subculture and Identity* Ed. Cheryl Harris and Alison Alexander, Cresskill, NJ: Hampton Press, 1998. 153–177.

Clover, Carol J. *Men, Women and Chain Saws: Gender in the Modern Horror Film*. Princeton, NJ: Princeton University Press, 1992.

Cole, R.R. "Top Songs in the Sixties: a Content Analysis." *American Behavioral Scientist* 14 (1971): 389–400.

Cooper, B. Lee. *Popular Music Perspectives: Ideas, Themes, and Patterns in Contemporary Lyrics*. Bowling Green, Ohio: Bowling Green State University Popular Press, 1991.

_____. *A Resource Guide to Themes in Contemporary American Song Lyrics*. London: Greenwood, 1986.

Davis, Jonathan. "Interview." *The Queen of the Damned* DVD Warner Brothers, 2003.

De Certeau, Michel. *The Practice of Everyday Life*. Berkeley: University of California Press, 1984.

DeKnight, Steven S. "Dead Things" *Buffy the Vampire Slayer* Broadcast USA 5 February 2002. *<http://buffyscripts.net/scripts/buffy/season6/13b.htm>*.

Denisoff, R. Serge, and Mark H. Levine. "Brainwashing or Background Noise: The Popular Protest Song." *The Sounds of Social Change*. Ed. R. Serge Denisoff and Richard A. Peterson. Chicago: Rand McNally, 1972: 217–221.

Drawmer, Lois. "Sex, Death and Ecstasy: The Art of Transgression." *Vampires: Myths and Metaphors of Enduring Evil* Ed Carla T. Kungl. Conference Proceedings Budapest, Hungary May 22–24, 2003. Oxford, UK: Inter-Disciplinary Press, 2003: 21–26, volume 6 in the At the Interface Project. "Monsters & and Monstrous: Myths & Metaphors of Enduring Evil." Series Ed. Dr. Robert Fisher. *<http://www.inter-disciplinary.net/publishing/idp/eBooks/Vampires.pdf>* Available at *<www.inter-disciplinary.net/publishing/idp/eBooks/vmmeeindex.htm>*.

Dunne, Michael. *Intertextual Encounters in American Fiction, Film, and Popular Culture*. Bowling Green University Popular Press, 2001.

Eco, Umberto. "Casablanca: Cult Movies and Intertextual Collage." in *Travels in Hyperreality: Essays*. Trans. William Weaver. London: Picador, 1986. 197–211.

Ervin-Gore, Shawna. "Joss Whedon on Fray." *Dark Horse Online*. 1 June 2001 *<http://www.darkhorse.com/news/interviews.php?id=737>*.

Feigenbaum, Anna. "'Some Guy Designed This Room I'm Standing In': Marking Gender in Press Coverage of Ani DiFranco." *Popular Music* 24.1 (2005): 37–56.

Fish, Duane R. "Serving the Servants: An Analysis of the Music of Kurt Cobain" *Popular Music and Society* 19.10 (Summer 1995): 87–102.

Frayling, Christopher. *Vampyres: Lord Byron to Count Dracula*. London: Faber and Faber, 1991.

Frith, Simon. *Sound Effects: Youth, Leisure and the Politics of Rock 'n' Roll*. 1981. New York: Pantheon, 1983.

_____. "Why Do Songs Have Words." *Music for Pleasure: Essays in the Sociology of Pop*. Oxford: Polity Press and New York: Routledge, 1988. 105–128.

Fury, David. "Shadow" (5.08) Script *Buffy the Vampire Slayer* Broadcast 21 November 2000. 9 May 2003 *<http://buffyscripts.net/scripts/buffy/season5/08.htm>*.

Gantz, W., Gartenberg, H., Pearson, M., and Schiller, S. "Gratifications and expectations associated with popular music among adolescents." *Popular Music and Society* 6.1 (1978): 81–89.

Gateward, Frances, and Murray Pomerance, eds. *Sugar, Spike and Everything Nice: Cinemas of Girlhood*. Detroit: Wayne State University Press, 2002.

Gore, Tipper. *Raising PG Kids in an X-Rated World*. Nashville: Abingdon, 1987.

Green, Shoshanna, Cynthia Jenkins, and Henry Jenkins. "Normal Female Interest in Men Bonking: Selections from The Terra Nostra Underground and Strange Bedfellows." *Theorizing*

Fandom: Fans, Subculture and Identity. Ed. Cheryl Harris and Alison Alexander, Cresskill, New Jersey: Hampton Press, 1998. 9–38.

Greenman, Jennifer. "Witch Love Spells Death." *Sacramento News and Reviews* "Arts and Culture" (6 June 2002) *<http://www.newsreview.com/issues/sacto/2002-06-06/arts.asp>*.

Gross, Edward. "Vampire Creator": An Interview with the Creator of BUFFY and ANGEL Cinescape (23 May 2000) *<http://www.cinescape.com/0/Editorial.asp?aff_id=0&this_cat= Television&action=page&obj_id=21365#>*.

Hall, Stuart, and Tony Jefferson, eds. *Resistance Through Rituals: Youth Subcultures in Postwar Britain*. Originally pub. as *Working Papers in Cultural Studies 7/8*, 1975. London: Routledge, 2004.

Harris, Cheryl, and Alison Alexander, eds. *Theorizing Fandom: Fans, Subculture and Identity*. Cresskill, NJ: Hampton Press, 1998.

Hebdige, Dick. *Subculture: The Meaning of Style*. 1979. 11th Rpr. London and New York: Methuen, 1988.

Hellekson, Karen, and Kristina Busse, eds. *Fan Fiction and Fan Communities in the Age of the Internet*. Jefferson, NC: McFarland, 2006.

Hendershot, Heather. *Shaking the World for Jesus: Media and Conservative Evangelical Culture*. Chicago: University of Chicago Press, 2004.

Hills, Matt. *Fan Cultures*. Sussex Studies in Culture and Communication. London and New York: Routledge, 2002.

Horton, Donald. "The Dialogue of Courtship in Popular Song." *American Journal of Sociology*. 62.6 (May 1957): 569–578.

Irwin, William, and J.R. Lombardo. "The Simpsons and Allusion: 'Worst Essay Ever!'" *The Simpsons and Philosophy: The D'oh! of Homer*. Ed. William Irwin, Mark T. Conrad, and Aeon J. Skoble. Chicago: Open Court, 2001. 81–92.

Jenkins, Henry. "Digital Land Grab." *Technology Review* 103.2 (March 2000): 103.

_____. *Textual Poachers: Television Fans and Participatory Cultures*. New York: Routledge, 1992.

Kaufman, Gil. "Evanescence: Fallen To the Top. Amy Lee talks female lead singers, being a drama queen, and the business of singing about faith." *VH1.Com* (29 May 2003) 30 August 2006 *<http://www.vh1.com/artists/interview/1472058/05232003/evanescence.jhtml>*.

Kelly, Karen, and Evelyn McDonnell, eds. *Stars Don't Stand Still in the Sky: Music and Myth*. London: Routledge, 1999.

Kimberley Hirsch/Kiba, "Interview" Joss Is a Hottie dot com (no date) http://www.jossisahottie.com/ index.php?interview.

LaHaye, Tim F., and Jerry B. Jenkins. *Left Behind: A Novel of the Earth's Last Days*. Wheaton, IL: Tyndale House Publishers, 1996.

Lamb, Patricia F., and Diana Veith. "Romantic Myth, Transcendence, and Star Trek Zines." *Erotic Universe: Sexuality and Fantastic Literature* (Contributions to the Study of Science Fiction and Fantasy no. 18). Ed. Donald Palumbo. New York: Greenwood Press, 1986. 235–256.

Larbalestier, Justine. "Buffy's Mary Sue Is Jonathan: Buffy Acknowledges the Fans." *Fighting the Forces: What's at Stake in Buffy the Vampire Slayer*. Ed. Rhonda Wilcox and David Lavery. Rowman and Littlefield, 2002. 227–238.

Lazarsfeld, Paul, and Robert K. Merton. "Mass Communication, Popular Taste, and Organized Social Action," 1948 in Lyman Bryson, ed., *Communication of Ideas*. New York: Harper, 1964: pp. 78–115.

Loftus, Johnny. Album Review *Leave a Whisper* by Shinedown. *Allmusic.com* no date 21 January 2007 *<http://www.allmusic.com/cg/amg.dll?p=amg&sql=10:rfuw6j2371r0>*.

Longworth, James L., Jr. "Joss Whedon: Feminist." *TV Creators: Conversations with America's Top Producers of Television Drama*. 2. Syracuse: Syracuse University Press, 2002: 197–220.

Lord, B. Albert. *The Singer of Tales*. Cambridge, MA: Harvard University Press, 1960.

Lowe, Melanie. "Colliding Feminisms: Britney Spears, 'Tweens,' and the Politics of Reception." *Popular Music and Society* 26.2 (2003): 123–140.

McDonald, James R. "Suicidal Rage: An Analysis of Hardcore Punk Lyrics." *Popular Music and Society* 11.3 (Fall): 91–102.

McRobbie, Angela. "Sweet Smell of Success? New Ways of Being Young Women." *Feminism and Youth Culture*. Ed. Angela McRobbie. London: Macmillan, 1991; 2nd ed. (2000): 198–214.

Miller, Kevin A. "Rock's Real Rebels" *Christianity Today* 45.1 (8 January 2001): 90.

Mooney, H.F. "Song, Singers and Society, 1890–1954." *American Quarterly* 6.3 (Autumn 1954): 221–232.

Nash, Ilana. *American Sweethearts: Teenage Girls in Twentieth-Century Popular Culture*. Bloomington: Indiana University Press, 2006.

Nussbaum, Emily. "A DVD Face-Off: The Official vs. the Homemade." *The New York Times* 21 December 2003. Factiva *<http://opac.library.usyd.edu.au/search/tNew+York+times+%28Online%29/tnew+york+times+online/-2%2C-1%2C0%2CB/l856&FF=tnew+york+times+on+the+web+online&1%2C1%2C%2C1%2C0>*.

_____. "Must See Metaphysics." *New York Times* 22 September 2002. sec. 6: 56, column 1. Factiva 30 August 2006. *<http://opac.library.usyd.edu.au/search/tNew+York+times+%28Online%29/tnew+york+times+online/2%2C1%2C0%2CB/l856&FF=tnew+york+times+on+the+web+online&1%2C1%2C%2C1%2C0>*.

Ong, Walter J. *Orality and Literacy: The Technologizing of the Word*. London and New York: Routledge, 1982.

Peabody, Berkley. *The Winged Word: A Study in the Technique of Ancient Greek Oral Composition as Seen Principally through Hesiod's Works and Days*. Albany: State University of New York Press, 1975.

Penley, Constance. "Feminism, Psychoanalysis, and the Study of Popular Culture." *Cultural Studies*. Ed. Lawrence Grossberg, Cary Nelson and Paula A. Treichler. New York and London: Routledge, 1992.

Powell, Mark Allan. "Jesus climbs the charts: the business of contemporary Christian music." *The Christian Century* 119.26 (18 December 2002): 20–27.

Press, Joy. "The Axers of Evil." *Village Voice* (5–11 March, 2003) 11 March 2003 *<http://www.vilagevoice.com/issues/0310/press.php>*.

Prinsky, L., and J. Rosenbaum. "'Leer-ics' or Lyrics?: Teenage Impressions of Rock 'n' Roll." *Youth and Society* 18 (1987): 384–397.

Ramlow, Todd R. "Ceci n'est-ce pas une lesbianne." *PopMatters* "Television Review" (18 June 2002). *<http://www.popmatters.com/tv/reviews/b/buffy-the-vampire-slayer4.shtml>*.

Robinson, John P., and Paul M. Hirsh. "Teenage Responses to Rock and Roll Protest Songs." *The Sounds of Social Change: Studies in Popular Culture*. Eds. R. Serge Denisoff and Richard A. Peterson. Chicago: Rand McNally, 1972. 222–231.

Robinson, Tasha. Joss Whedon Interview with Tasha Robinson. *The Onion AV Club* 5 September 2001. 12 December 2005 *<http://avclub.com/content/node/24238>* and "Web Exclusive" *<http://avclub.com/content/node/24240>* Rpt. in *The Tenacity of the Cockroach: Conversations with Entertainment's Most Enduring Outsiders*. Ed. Stephen Thompson. New York: Three Rivers Press, 2002. 369–377.

Roe, K. "Swedish Youth and Music: Listening Patterns and Motivations." *Communication Research* 12(3) (1985): 353–362.

Rouner, D. "Rock Music Use as a Socializing Function." *Popular Music and Society* 14.1 (1990): 97–107.

Russ, Joanna. "Pornography by Women for Women, with Love." *Magic Mommas, Trembling Sisters, Puritans and Perverts: Feminist Essays* Trumansburg, NY: Crossing Press, 1985. 79–99.

Sandler, Lauren. "Holy Rock 'n' Rollers." *The Nation* 276.2 (13 January 2003): 23.

Sconce, J. "'Trashing' the Academy: Taste, Excess, and an Emerging Politics of Cinematic Style." *Screen* 36.4: 371–393.

Shaheen, Jack. *Reel Bad Arabs: How Hollywood Vilifies a People* Interlink, 2001.

Topping, Keith. "There was a little girl and she had a little curl: New Season, New P." *Buffy Watchers* (6 September 2004) 7 September 2004 at *<http://groups.yahoo.com/groups/BuffyWatchers/message/3235?unwrap+=1>*.

Whedon, Joss. 2002b. DVD commentary to "The Body." *Buffy: Season 5* DVD 20th Century–Fox, 2002.

_____. 2004a. DVD commentary to "Lessons" *Buffy: Season 7* DVD 20th Century–Fox, 2004.

_____. 2004b. DVD commentary to "Chosen" *Buffy: Season 7* DVD 20th Century–Fox, 2004.

Wilcox, Rhonda. "Song: Singing and Dancing and Burning and Dying." First presented as lecture titled "A Complex of Echoes: Once More, with Textual Feeling" at the Sonic Synergies: Creative Cultures conference at the University of South Australia, Adelaide, Australia, 17–20 July 2003. Rpt. in *Why Buffy Matters: The Art of Buffy the Vampire Slayer* London and New York: I.B. Tauris, 2005. 191–205.

Wood, Robin. 2003. "The American Nightmare: Horror in the '70s." in *Hollywood from Vietnam to Reagan ... and Beyond* 1986. New York: Columbia University Press, 2003. 63–84.

Glossary

Angel. May refer to Angel, the first vampire with a soul.

Angelite. A fan of the television series *Angel: The Series*.

Angelverse. The mythos and reality in which the series *Angel* was set.

AtS. Short form of *Angel: The Series*.

BtVS. Refers to the television series *Buffy the Vampire Slayer*.

Buffyite. A fan of the television series *Buffy the Vampire Slayer*.

Buffyverse. The mythos and the reality in which the two series, BtVS and AtS are set; sometimes used to refer only to the mythos and reality of BtVS.

CMC. Computer-Mediated Communication — communication effected through the Internet.

Fan Board/Fan Forum. An online chat room devoted to a particular fandom.

Fan Fic. Fan fiction is often referred to as "fan fic" or "fanfic" or "the fic." These are stories and novels that use characters from the series to re-tell the mythos of the series or to tell new stories using the same characters. Authorized fan fiction is that which is authorized by a TV series' creators and executive production companies. They own the series, and they authorize writers to produce "novelizations," for sale in bookstores and on the 'Net. Such works can produce a profit. Unauthorized fan fiction is the fan fiction produced by the fan for the enjoyment of oneself/other fans. Some creators, most notably J. K. Rowling and Anne Rice, deplore fan fiction and do whatever they can legally to prevent it. Others, like Joss Whedon, the creator of BtVS and AtS, encourage the fans to produce fan fiction. See Hellekson and Busse, in the Bibliography.

Fandom. A fan culture that develops around a specific entertainment phenomenon — in the case of this book, the television series *Buffy the Vampire Slayer* and *Angel: The Series*.

Fanvid. A fanvid is generally a three-to-six minute video made by a fan. Fans use DVDs, tapes, and screencaps to re-tell the mythos, or to create new stories involving the characters. Fanvids are usually accompanied by popular music, and resemble music videos.

Jossverse. The mythos and realities created by Joss Whedon, the creator of *Buffy the Vampire Slayer*, *Angel: The Series*, and *Firefly/Serenity*.

Online fans. Fans that communicate through the Internet are referred to as online fans.

Production of Culture. This term refers to creative works produced by fans: illustrations, sculptures, costumes, fan fiction, fan videos, etc. All such work must carry a legal disclaimer, since images and characters are copyrighted.

'Shippers. Fans who favor the sexual pairing of two particular characters in a television series. For example, "B/A 'shippers" refers to fans who believe that Buffy and Angel are perfect for each other. Such a fan is said to "'ship A/B" or to "'ship B/A." Occasionally 'shippers will also code the 'ship by combining syllables of each character's name into one name. For example, using the B/A 'ship, 'shippers might call themselves "Bangels." The most popular online 'ship in the 'verse is Spike/Buffy, which is then referred to as Spuffy.

'Shippers are one of the most divisive elements in any fandom, because 'shippers are emotionally invested in the relationships they 'ship. During the run of both series, there was internecine fighting among their many online fans as to which pairing — or 'ship — was better for Buffy and for Angel.

'Ships. This is an online fan term for "relationships" that are sexual in nature. When written, sexual relationships contain a slash "/" between the characters' names. For example: the relationships between Buffy and Angel are written: Angel/Buffy, or conversely, Buffy/Angel.

The 'verse. This is code for the Buffyverse or Angelverse or both 'verses, combined.

Selected Bibliography

Popular Culture

Bourdieu, Pierre. *Distinction: A Social Critique of the Judgement of Taste.* London: Routledge, 1984.

Chow, Rey. *Writing Diaspora: Tactics of Intervention in Contemporary Cultural Studies.* Bloomington: Indiana University Press, 1993.

Clifford, James, and George E. Marcus. *The Predicament of Culture: Twentieth-Century Ethnography, Literature, and Art.* Cambridge, MA.: Harvard University Press, 1986.

______, and ______, eds. *Writing Culture: The Poetics and Politics of Ethnography.* Berkeley: University of California Press, 1986.

Dines, Gail, and Jean M. McMahon Humez, eds. *Gender, Race, and Class in Media: A Text-Reader.* Belmont: Wadsworth, 1995.

Early, Frances H., and Kathleen Kennedy, eds. *Athena's Daughters: Television's New Women Warriors (The Television Series).* Syracuse: Syracuse University Press, 2003.

Hall, Stuart, and Tony Jefferson, eds. *Resistance Through Rituals: Youth Subcultures in Postwar Britain.* 2nd ed. London: Routledge, 2007. Originally published as *Working Papers in Cultural Studies,* 7/8, 8th printing, London: Harper/Collins Academic.

Heinecken, Dawn. *The Warrior Women of Television: A Feminist Cultural Analysis of the New Female Body in Popular Media.* New York: Peter Lang, 2003.

Jenkins, Henry. "Digital Land Grab." *Technology Review.* 103.2 (March 2000)103.

______. *Textual Poachers: Television Fans and Participatory Culture.* New York: Routledge, 1992.

Kellner, Douglas. *Media Culture: Cultural Studies, Identity and Politics Between the Modern and the Postmodern.* London: Routledge, 1995.

Metz, Cade. "Make Contact." *PC Magazine,* January 20, 2004, 131–134, 136, 138.

O'Neill, J. M. "Pop Culture Cracks College Curriculums." January 20 2004. 1 January 2004. Philadelphia, PA: Knight Ridder Tribune Information Services. <http://www.whedon.info/Pop-culture-cracks-college.html>.<http://www.freerepublic.com/focus/f-news/1047649/posts>

Pugh, Sheenagh. *The Democratic Genre: Fan Fiction in a Literary Context*. Bridgend: Seren/Poetry Wales Press, 2005.

Radway, Janice A. *Reading the Romance: Women, Patriarchy, and Popular Literature*. Chapel Hill: University of North Carolina Press, 1991.

_____. "Reception Study: Ethnography and the Problems of Dispersed Audiences and Nomadic Subjects." *Cultural Studies* 2 (1988): 359–376.

Rheingold, Howard. *The Virtual Community*. 1998. 12 December 2003. <http://www.rheingold.com/vc/book/>

Russ, Joanna. "Pornography by Women for Women, with Love." *Magic Mommas, Trembling Sisters, Puritans and Perverts: Feminist Essays*. Trumansburg: Crossing Press, 1985. 79–99.

Schultze, Quentin, and Roy M. Anker, eds. *Dancing in the Dark: Youth, Popular Culture, and the Electronic Media*. Belmont: Wadsworth. 2000.

Shuttleworth, Ian. "Bite Me Professor." *Financial Times*. *FT.com*, September 11 2003. 5 January 2004. <http://www.whedon.info/article.php3?id_article=1567&img=>

Traudt, Paul J. *Media, Audiences, Effects: An Introduction to the Study of Media Content and Audience Analysis*. Boston: Pearson/Allyn & Bacon, 2005.

Turkle, Sherry. *Life on the Screen: Identity in the Age of the Internet*. New York: Touchstone/Simon & Schuster, 1995.

Williamson, Milly. *The Lure of the Vampire: Gender, Fiction and Fandom from Bram Stoker to Buffy*. London: Wallflower Press, 2005.

Joss Whedon

Biography for Joss Whedon. *IMDb*. 22 June 2007 <http://imdb.com/name/nm0923736/bio>.

Angel: The Series and Buffy the Vampire Slayer

Abbott, Stacy, Ed. *Reading Angel: The TV Spin-off with a Soul*. London: Palgrave Macmillan, 2005.

Battis, Jes. *Blood Relations: Chosen Families in Buffy the Vampire Slayer and Angel*. Jefferson, NC: McFarland, 2005.

Beatrice, Allyson. *Will the Vampire People Please Leave the Lobby? True Adventures in Cult Fandom*. Naperville: Sourcebooks, Inc, 2007.

Connolly, Mark. *BuffyWorld.com*. 13 June 2007. <http://www.buffyworld.com>.

Burr, Viv. "Friends Are the Family We Choose for Ourselves': Young People and Families in the TV Series Buffy the Vampire Slayer," *Young*, Vol. 13, No. 4, 383–384, 2005.

_____. Scholar/'shippers and Spikeaholics: Academic and Fan Identities at the Slayage Conference on Buffy the Vampire Slayer, *European Journal of Cultural Studies*, 8 2005; vol. 8: 375–383 (2005).

Golden, Christopher, and Nancy Holder. *The Watcher's Guide*. Vol.1. New York: Pocket Books/Simon & Schuster, 1998.

Guzzetta, Marli. "When Trekkie Met Buffy." *Miami New Times*. December 25, 2003. 4 January 2004. <*http://www.miaminewtimes.com/2003-12-25/news/when-trekkie-met-buffy/*>

Holder, Nancy; Jeff Marriotte, and Maryelizabeth Hart. *Angel: The Casefiles*. Vol. 1. New York: Simon and Schuster, 2002.

_____, _____, and _____. *Buffy the Vampire Slayer: The Watcher's Guide*. Vol 2. New York: Simon Spotlight Entertainment, 2000.

Jowett, Lorna. *Sex and the Slayer: A Gender Studies Primer for the Buffy Fan*. Middletown: Wesleyan University Press, 2005.

Kaveney, Roz, Ed. *Reading the Vampire Slayer: An Unofficial Critical Companion to Buffy and Angel*. London: Tauris Parke, 2001, 2004.

Kirby-Diaz, Mary. "The Fandom Project: What Makes a Fandom Run—'Ships, Fanfiction, Plot Devices, Favorite Characters, and FanCons," in the *International Journal of the Humanities*, Volume 3, Issue 4, pp. 257–266.

"Kiss Me Jane. *It's Never Too Late to Become a Buffy Fan*. Ottawa: KMJ Productions, 2004.

Larbalestier, Justine. "Buffy's Mary Sue Is Jonathan: Buffy Acknowledges the Fans." *Fighting the Forces: What's at Stake in Buffy the Vampire Slayer*. Eds. Rhonda Wilcox and David Lavery. Lanham: Rowman and Littlefield, 2002. 227–238.

Lindlof, Thomas R., Kelly Coyle, and Debra Grodin. "Is There a Text in This Audience? Science Fiction and Interpretive Schism." *Theorizing Fandom: Fans, Subculture and Identity*. Ed. Cheryl Harris and Alison Alexander. Cresskill, NJ: Hampton Press, 1998. 2199–247.

Macnaughtan, Don. "A Bibliographic Map to the Buffyverse: The World of Buffy the Vampire Slayer and Angel." *Don Macnaughton, Lane Community College Library*. 2004. 1 July 2007 <http://www.lanecc.edu/library/don/bvs/buffy.htm>

Pateman, Matthew. *The Aesthetics of Culture in Buffy the Vampire Slayer*. Jefferson, NC: McFarland, 2006.

Pauwels, Luc. "Websites as Visual and Multimodal Cultural Expressions: Opportunities and Issues of Online Hybrid Media Research." *Media, Culture & Society*, 27: 4. 604–613.

Princess Twilight. "Fandom Sociology: The Mechanics Behind the Beast." *Octaves of the Heart*. 2003. 1 March 2003. <http://www.octavesoftheheart.com/octaves/fandom.htm>

Ruditis, Paul. *The Watcher's Guide*. Vol. 3. New York: Simon and Schuster, 2004.

_____, and Diana C. Gallagher. *Angel: The Casefiles*. Vol. 2. New York: Simon and Schuster, 2004.

Shuttleworth, Ian. "Bite Me, Professor," FT.com, September 11, 2003. December 15, 2003. <http://news.ft.com/ContentServer?pagename=FT.com/StoryFT/Full Story&c=Story>

South, James B., ed. *Buffy the Vampire Slayer and Philosophy: Fear and Trembling in Sunnydale*. Chicago, 2003.

Stafford, Nikki. *Bite Me! An Unofficial Guide to the World of Buffy the Vampire Slayer*. Toronto: ECW Press, 2002.

_____. *Once Bitten: an Unofficial Guide to the World of Angel*. Toronto: ECW Press, 2004.

Topping, Keith. *Hollywood Vampire: The Apocalypse: An Unofficial and Unauthorized Guide to the Final Season of Angel*. London: Virgin Books, 2005.

_____. *Hollywood Vampire: A Revised and Updated Unofficial and Unauthorized Guide to Angel*. London: Virgin Books, 2002, 2000.

_____. *Slayer: An Expanded and Updated and Unauthorized Guide to Buffy the Vampire Slayer*. London: Virgin Books, 2001.

_____. *Slayer: The Last Days of Sunnydale. An Unofficial and Unauthorised Guide to Season Six of Buffy the Vampire Slayer*. London: Virgin Books, 2004.

_____. *Slayer: The Next Generation. An Unofficial and Unauthorised Guide to the Final Season of Buffy the Vampire Slayer*. London: Virgin Books, 2003.

Wilcox, Rhonda. V. *Why Buffy Matters: The Art of Buffy the Vampire Slayer*. London: Palgrave Macmillan, 2005.

_____. and David Lavery, eds. *Fighting the Forces: What's at Stake in Buffy the Vampire Slayer*. Lanham: Rowman & Littlefield, 2002.

Yeffeth, Glenn. *Five Seasons of Angel: Science Fiction and Fantasy Writers Discuss Their Favorite Vampire*. Dallas: Benbella Books, 2004.

_____. *Seven Seasons of Buffy: Science Fiction and Fantasy Writers Discuss Their Favorite Television Show*. Dallas: Benbella Books, 2003.

Fandoms and Fandoms Other Than BtVS/AtS

Aden, Roger C. *Popular Stories and Promised Lands: Fan Cultures and Symbolic Pilgrimages*. Tuscaloosa: University of Alabama Press, 1999.

Ang, Ien. *Watching Dallas: Soap Opera and the Melodramatic Imagination*. London: Metheun, 1985.

Bacon-Smith, Camille. *Enterprising Women: Television Fandom and the Creation of Popular Myth*. Philadelphia: University of Pennsylvania Press, 1992.

Borsellino, Mary. "It's a Fan's World: How Devotees Blur the Boundaries." *Rocky Road/Inkstigmata*. May 2001. 20 March 2004. <http://fan.inkstigmata.net/rockyroad/culttv.html>

Bury, Rhiannon. *Cyberspaces of Their Own: Female Fandoms Online*. New York: Peter Lang Publishing, 2005.

Cartmell, Deborah, et al., eds. *Trash Aesthetics: Popular Culture and Its Audience*. London: Pluto Press, 1997.

Cicioni, Mirna. "Male Pair-Bonds and Female Desire in Fan Slash Writing." *Theorizing Fandom: Fans, Subculture and Identity*. Ed. Cheryl Harris and Alison Alexander. Cresskill, NJ: Hampton Press, 1998. 153–177.

Green, Shoshanna; Cynthia Jenkins, and Henry Jenkins. "Normal Female Interest in Men Bonking: Selections from the *Terra Nostra* Underground and Strange Bedfellows." *Theorizing Fandom: Fans, Subculture and Identity*. Ed. Cheryl Harris and Alison Alexander. Cresskill, NJ: Hampton Press, 1998. 9–38.

Harris, C., and Alexander, A., eds. *Theorizing Fandom: Fans, Subculture and Identity*. Cresskill, NJ: Hampton Press, 1998.

Hellekson, Karen, and Kristina Busse, eds. *Fan Fiction and Fan Communities in the Age of the Internet*. Jefferson, NC: McFarland, 2006.

Hills, Matt. *Fan Cultures*. London: Routledge, 2002.

Jenkins, Henry. *Convergence Culture: Where Old and New Media Collide.* New York: New York University Press, 2006a.

______. *Fans, Bloggers, and Gamers: Media Consumers in the Digital Age.* New York: New York University Press, 2006.

______. "'Strangers No More, We Sing': Filking and the Social Construction of the Science Fiction Fan Community." *The Adoring Audience: Fan Culture and Popular Media.* Ed. Lisa A. Lewis. New York: Routledge, 1992. 208–236.

______. *Textual Poachers: Television Fans and Participatory Culture.* New York: Routledge, 1992.

Lamb, Patricia Frazier and Diana L.Veith. "Romantic Myth, Transcendence, and Star Trek Zines." *Erotic Universe: Sexuality & Fantastic Literature.* Ed. Donald Palumbo. New York: Greenwood Press, 1986. 235–255.

Lewis, Lisa A., ed. *The Adoring Audience: Fan Culture and Popular Media.* London and New York: Routledge, 2001 (1992).

Pugh, S. (2005). *The Democratic Genre: Fan Fiction in a Literary Context.* Bridgend: Seren/Poetry Wales Press, 2005.

Anthropology, Sociology and Psychology

Anderson, Benedict. *Imagined Communities: Reflection on the Origin and Spread of Nationalism.* London: Verso, 1991.

Brehm, Sharon S. *Intimate Relationships.* 2nd ed. New York: McGraw-Hill, 1992.

Dillman, Don.A. *Mail and Internet Surveys: The Tailored Design Method.* 2nd ed. New York: John Wiley & Sons, 2002.

Emerson, Robert M., Rachel I. Fretz, and Linda L. Shaw. *Writing Ethnographic Fieldnotes.* Chicago: University of Chicago Press, 1995.

Fischer, Claude. *To Dwell Among Friends: Personal Networks in Town and City.* Chicago: University of Chicago Press, 1982.

Flanagan, Wiliam G. *Urban Sociology: Images and Structure.* 4th ed. Boston: Allyn & Bacon, 2002.

Hebdige, Dick. *Subculture: The Meaning of Style.* London: Methuen, 1998, 1979.

Sternberg, Robert. "Real and Ideal Others in Romantic Relationships: Is Four a Crowd?" *Journal of Personality and Social Psychology* 49 (1985): 1589–1596.

Tonnies, Ferdinand. *Community and Society: Gemeinschaft und Gesellschaft.* Trans. and ed., Charles P. Loomis. East Lansing: Michigan State University Press, 1957.

Wellman, Barry, and Barry Leighton. 1979. "Networks, Neighborhoods, and Communities: Approaches to the Study of the Community Question." *Urban Affairs Quarterly* 14: 363–390.

About the Contributors

Asim Ali founded and directs the Project on Religion, Culture, and Globalization at the University of Maryland, where he is a doctoral candidate in the Department of American Studies. His research interests include cyberculture, race and slavery, and religion in American culture. Asim has been a *Buffy* fan since the first episode, but it wasn't until the second season of the show that he became interested in the official fan site known as the Bronze. He chose to conduct ethnographic research on the Bronze because he was a *Buffy* fan, but was a complete stranger to online communities. At some point along the way — he's not quite sure when — Asim became a member of the Bronze community himself.

Rebecca Bley is a doctoral student in media and cultural studies, which is part of the Department of Communication Arts at the University of Wisconsin–Madison. She has been involved in fannish activities since elementary school, much to her mother's exasperation. From *The Cutting Edge*, through *seaQuest DSV*, *Highlander*, and *La Femme Nikita*, Rebecca is an unabashed fan. She is somewhat astonished to find that she can combine her life's passion with her life's occupation. Some days she still marvels that this is actually a "choice" in life: to study fandoms. Rebecca's previous scholarly works in fandom include a study of the bisexuality in the character of Faith on *BtVS*, and a study of the Browncoats (*Firefly/Serenity*) online fandom.

Kathryn Hill is a musicologist who taught the history of popular music for over a decade at the Sydney Conservatorium of Music, a part of the University of Sydney in Australia. She is currently completing a Ph.D. on popular music and *Buffy the Vampire Slayer*. She first discovered the world of fandom surrounding the *Buffyverse* in 2001. Not surprisingly, her favorite *Buffy* episode is "Once More with Feeling."

Mary Kirby-Diaz is a professor at Farmingdale State College, State University of New York, in Farmingdale. Since 1974 she has taught courses in family, marriage, popular culture and mass media, sociology in the movies, urban sociology, women men and social change, technology and social change, social problems, minorities in America, and introduction to sociology. Her research, writings, community work, consulting and grants focus on the problems of marginalization — perceived and/or real: outsiders and strangers, the perceptions of dental hygiene as a non-profession, curriculum development and pedagogical innovation, inter-ethnic marriage, community mediation, arbitration and divorce fees, and bereavement counselling. Mary's introduction to *BtVS* came as she watched early morning television while treadmilling. Going online to catch up with missed episodes, she realized that she was more fascinated by the fans than by the show — which remains a favorite.

David Kociemba currently serves as the union president of the Affiliated Faculty of Emerson College in Boston. He has taught at Emerson and at four other area colleges and universities for the past seven years. David's past courses include introductory media history classes and seminars devoted to exploring topics like American film censorship, the representation of physical disability, video art, and *Buffy the Vampire Slayer*. His writing focuses on the work of Todd Haynes, Joss Whedon, and Jane Espenson. David has previously written for *Slayage*, *Charming and Crafty* (forthcoming), and *At Sixes and Sevens: Buffy the Vampire Slayer in the UPN Years* (forthcoming). He won the 2007 Short Mr. Pointy Award for his article, "'Actually, it explains a lot': Reading the Opening Title Sequences of *BtVS*."

Elizabeth L. Rambo Ph.D., teaches medieval English literature, Chaucer, and other courses at Campbell University in Buies Creek, North Carolina. She and her husband own a cat named Xander. She has been reading (and re-reading) Dorothy Dunnett's historical novels since the mid–1970s. When she heard about the 1992 *Buffy the Vampire Slayer* movie, she immediately became a fan, because it is the Best. Title. Ever. She has been watching *Buffy* on TV since 1997. Elizabeth became involved with Buffyverse fandom in 2001, when she and Simon Hedges created the *SunnydaleU* YahooGroup, which led her to *All Things Philosophical on Buffy the Vampire Slayer* (http://www.atpobtvs.com/) and then to *Slayage: the Online International Journal of Buffy Studies*, and whedonesque.com. Vampires, beware!

Claudia Rebaza earned B.A.s in history and English, then earned a master's degree in library and information science (LIS), and is a practicing academic librarian. In 2003 she entered the LIS doctoral program at the University of Illinois, Urbana-Champaign. Her Ph.D thesis is still in progress. She began watching *Buffy the Vampire Slayer* and *Angel: The Series* in 1999. It wasn't until the summer of 2002 that she began going online for news about the show's future. In 2003 she began regularly visiting *Whedonesque* for news and searching out fanfic through online archives and award sites. In January 2004 she began a qualitative research project for a course that involved online communities. Claudia is interested in the segmentation of the Whedonverse fan community across different technological platforms and virtual spaces.

Index

www.ingramcontent.com/pod-product-compliance
Ingram Content Group UK Ltd.
Pitfield, Milton Keynes, MK11 3LW, UK
UKHW041355190726
13851UKWH00014B/116

9 780786 442058